YESTERDAY'S HOUSES OF TOMORROW

YESTERDAY'S HOUSES OF TOMORROW

Innovative

American

Homes

1850 to 1950

H. WARD JANDL

WITH ADDITIONAL

ESSAYS BY

JOHN A. BURNS, AIA,

AND

MICHAEL J. AUER

The Preservation Press National Trust for Historic Preservation

The Preservation Press
National Trust for
Historic Preservation
1785 Massachusetts Avenue, N.W.
Washington, D.C. 20036

The National Trust for Historic
Preservation is the only private,
nonprofit organization chartered
by Congress to encourage public
participation in the preservation
of sites, buildings, and objects
significant in American history
and culture. Support is provided
by membership dues, endowment
funds, contributions, and grants
from federal agencies, including
the U.S. Department of the
Interior, under provisions of the
National Historic Preservation
Act of 1966. The opinions expressed here do not necessarily reflect
the views or policies of the Interior
Department. For information about
membership in the National Trust,
write to the Membership Office at
the address above.

Printed in the United States of
America
95 94 93 92 91 5 4 3 2 1

Library of Congress Cataloging in
Publication Data
Jandl, H. Ward.
  Yesterday's houses of tomorrow:
  innovative American homes 1850
  to 1950 / H. Ward Jandl, John A.
  Burns, Michael J. Auer.
     p.   cm.
  Includes bibliographic references
  and index.
  ISBN 0-89133-186-7
  1. Architecture, Domestic—
United States. 2. Architecture,
Modern—19th century—United
States. 3. Architecture, Modern—
 20th century—United States. I.
Burns, John A., AIA. II. Auer,
Michael J. III. Title.

NA7207.J36 1991
728'.0973'09034—dc20   91-17487

Designed and typeset by Grafik Communications, Ltd,
Alexandria, Virginia.

Printed by the John D. Lucas Printing Company,
Baltimore, Maryland.

CONTENTS

ACKNOWLEDGMENTS

The preparation of this book would not have been possible without the invaluable assistance of many people. My sincere appreciation is extended to Diane Maddex, former director of The Preservation Press, and Margaret Byrne Heimbold, former vice president of the National Trust for Historic Preservation, for providing support and encouragement as I began the project. The current staff of The Preservation Press, especially Janet Walker, have been extremely cooperative and a pleasure to work with; their editing and production skills aided considerably in crafting the final product. Special appreciation goes to Terry Adams for his thoughtful editing.

I would like to thank Michael Auer and John Burns for their significant contributions to the book: in particular, Michael's chapter on the Dymaxion house and John's chapters on Usonian houses, General Houses, and John Earley's Polychrome Houses. I am grateful to the Horace M. Albright Fund of the National Park Service, which provided much-appreciated financial assistance to undertake additional research on the houses of George Fred Keck, William Ward, and Thomas Edison.

I am also indebted to the following: Joseph Rosa and Michael Schwarting for their insights into Albert Frey and the Aluminaire; Albert Frey for taking the time to answer my questions about his work with Le Corbusier and, later, Lawrence Kocher; John Ingram and Catherine Grosfils at Colonial Williamsburg for helping me obtain illustrations from the Kocher Collection; Barbara Hammond and the staff of the Museum of Cartoon Art, current occupants of Ward's Castle; William Keck, FAIA, for background information on the House of Tomorrow; Dori Partsch of Indiana Dunes National Lakeshore for arranging a tour of the Century of Progress houses now located in Beverly Shores; George D. Tselos, archivist at the Edison

National Historic Site, National Park Service, for facilitating research on Edison's concrete houses; Thomas Brennan for opening up his Edison poured-concrete house to me and sharing with me the products of his research; Arthur C. Holden, FAIA, former partner of Robert McLaughlin, for some important leads on American Houses, Inc.; Leon Barth of Princeton University's School of Architecture for helping me locate records of the Motohome; Meredith Knowlton for giving me permission to reproduce materials relating to her father, Robert McLaughlin; Vincent Kohler of the University of Pittsburgh at Bradford for his extraordinary generosity in sharing his research on Lustron houses and for reviewing the chapter on Lustron; Ray Luce of the Ohio Historical Society for sharing period photographs of the Lustron plant in Columbus, Ohio; Beverly Zell of the Stowe-Day Foundation in Hartford, Connecticut, for an illustration of Catharine Beecher; Mrs. Edith Lutyens Bel Geddes for permission to use an illustration of Norman Bel Geddes's House of Tomorrow; Charles A. Ruch, historian with the Westinghouse Electric Corporation, for tracking down illustrations of the Westinghouse Home of Tomorrow; April Dougal of the Ward M. Canaday Center at the University of Toledo for information on Tomorrow's Kitchen; Mike Houlihan at Hedrich-Blessing in Chicago for locating several of the photographs used in the book; Christine Schelshorn and Myrna Williamson at the State Historical Society of Wisconsin for making documents relating to George Fred Keck available to me; Jim Draeger, also of the State Historical Society of Wisconsin, for giving me leads on a Motohome in Madison;

Sally Sims Stokes and her staff at the University of Maryland's National Trust Library for assistance in gathering photographs for several chapters; the staff at the American Institute of Architects Library in Washington, D.C., for facilitating use of architectural magazines from the 1930s and 1940s; Lee H. Nelson, FAIA, my former supervisor at the National Park Service, for his knowledge of construction technology; David Given for his encouragement on this project; and to my father, Henry A. Jandl, FAIA, for instilling in me a love of architecture and for turning over to me his numerous files of clippings.

H. Ward Jandl

Knowing of my interest in modern houses and construction technologies, friends and colleagues have generously shared the fruits of their own research. Among those whose knowledge contributed to the Polychrome House chapter are Alison Blanton, Holly Chamberlain, Emily Eig, Catherine Lavoie, Howard Newlon, Jr., and Marian Schlefer. In Chicago, Deborah Slayton tracked down the General Houses model home moved from the 1934 Century of Progress Exposition to suburban River Forest. At home, Debbie, Emily, and Andrew endured many husbandless and fatherless weekends with patience and good humor.

John A. Burns, AIA

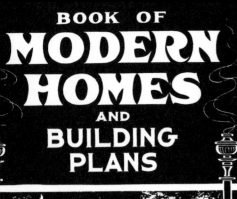

BOOK OF
MODERN
HOMES
AND
BUILDING
PLANS

SEARS, ROEBUCK & CO.
CHICAGO

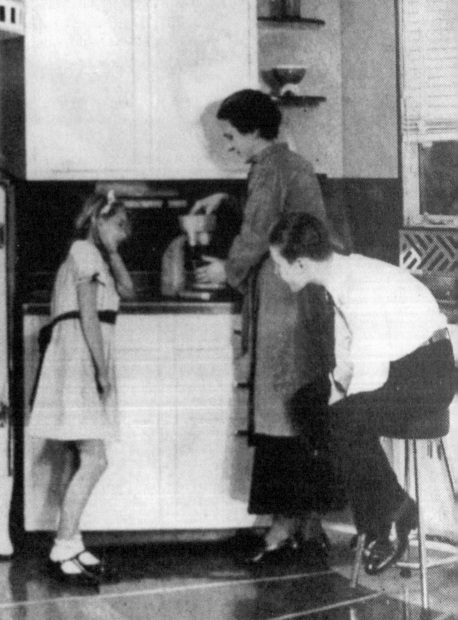

INTRODUCTION

Carefully designed to reflect the lifestyle of its owner, Jefferson's home, Monticello (1768–1809), was ahead of its time in many respects—from the self-opening double doors off the hall to the underground passages connecting the kitchen and servants' quarters with the main house. (Walter Smalling, Jr., Historic American Buildings Survey)

The freestanding single-family house has been at the center of our American dream ever since the first European settlers arrived on these shores to begin new lives. Throughout our history we have pursued this dream, seeking to improve the way we live and making use of new materials, technologies, and inventions to fashion comfortable, efficient, affordable dwellings for ourselves and our families.

The ability of architecture—and particularly residential architecture—to improve the social, moral, and economic fabric of our lives has been a long-held conviction. It is a recurring theme in numerous books, articles, and exhibitions from the mid-19th century to the present. The look, form, and function of the single-family house—and the search for the "ideal" home—continue to fascinate us, evidenced by the extraordinary popularity of today's "shelter" and home-improvement magazines.

The astonishing changes brought about by the industrial and political revolutions of the late 18th and early 19th centuries had a profound impact on how Americans lived. The country witnessed an unprecedented influx of immigrants needing homes. Great factories and new industries sprang up and, with them, an increased demand for decent housing. Cities and towns doubled and tripled in size in short periods of time. The invention of streetcars and the emerging promise of suburban living provided fresh housing alternatives for wealthier citizens. Newly introduced household technologies, from piped water to gas lighting, dramatically improved creature comforts. The evolution of balloon framing and the creation of new and improved building products, such as cut nails and portland cement, began to transform the way houses were conceived and constructed. It is no wonder that improving how Americans live—both in the present and in the future—became a major preoccupation of social reformers, political activists, theoreticians, and architects.

"The first thing to be done in planning a house, is to know the wants of the person who is to occupy it; the next to know the situation of the ground it is to cover; then to take into consideration the number, size, and height of the rooms wanted; also, proper convenient stairs, entries, passages &c.... The eye ought to see, at the same time, every part of the building, and be sure that no one part of it interferes with another; also, to see that the rooms are properly lighted, and at the same time, that there are a sufficient number of windows, and of a size suitable for the external part of the building.... Strength, convenience, and beauty, are the principal things to be attended to."

Asher Benjamin, *The American Builder's Companion,* 1827

For the past 150 years, the idea of home has been subjected to scrutiny and discussion on moral, socioeconomic, and aesthetic grounds. Thanks to the proliferation of books and periodicals on domestic architecture and family life, the popularity of fairs and exhibitions promoting model houses, and interest by the federal government in providing shelter for its citizens, the American public has long been inundated with proposals for ideal dwellings. And what an eager and hungry audience it has been!

Immigrants arriving in this country brought with them, of course, their own distinctive architectural traditions and their own ideas of what constituted comfortable and practical houses. In early 19th-century America new housing ideas were disseminated principally through "builders' guides," books that typically included sketches, floor plans, elevations, or drawings of special architectural components. Although these guides tended to be published in small quantities, they nonetheless had a significant effect on the way American houses looked and were constructed. Individuals who bought the builders' guides

took their selected designs to local "carpenter-builders" who drew up actual working plans and specifications. While the resulting houses were not exact replicas of each other, they had in common certain architectural details and construction techniques. Among the most important early guides were those by Asher Benjamin, whose influence can still be discerned in houses throughout New England.

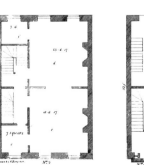
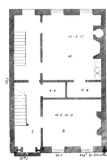

While not particularly innovative, Asher Benjamin's designs, such as this plan and elevation for a town house taken from his book, The American Builder's Companion *(1827), set the standard for early 19th-century architecture in New England.*

Pattern books began appearing in the 1830s and, thanks to improvements in printing and distribution, reached a broad audience. These books differed from their predecessors in that they provided renderings and full floor plans aimed at the homeowner rather than the builder. Often they included long treatises on what constituted appropriate architecture and on the physical and moral benefits of a well-designed house.

Perhaps the most popular author of pattern books was the landscape architect Andrew Jackson Downing, whose designs captured the public's fancy and whose ideas inspired many American families. His publications, the first of which appeared in 1841, dealt not only with the house itself but with its setting and surrounding landscape.

Downing's pattern books featured essays on social and moral issues and presented models of "smiling lawns and tasteful cottages." His designs were not particularly original, but they provided the American public with examples of solid, well-planned residences to suit all budgets and social positions. As such, they were frequently copied. In Downing's footsteps followed George and Charles Palliser, George Barber, William Tuthill, Calvert Vaux, and a host of others.

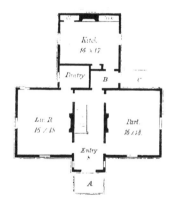

Andrew Jackson Downing's designs reflected the taste of the times and, although not technologically advanced, were widely copied in the mid-19th century. Illustrated here is a plan and elevation of a cottage from Downing's The Architecture of Country Houses *(1850).*

Although Catharine Beecher and Orson Fowler did not produce pattern books per se, they were among the most influential of these early crusaders, promoting what might today be considered "houses of the future"—dwellings that dazzled the public by introducing new inventions, creative floor plans, innovative construction materials, and original technologies (see Chapters 1 and 2). Beecher's and Fowler's books went through numerous printings, reaching a large number of Americans who read their ideas with interest and adapted the designs, or portions thereof, for their own homes.

In the 19th century, popular magazines began increasingly to focus on residential architecture, bombarding their readers with designs and ideas and predicting how Americans would live in the future. The periodical *Godey's Lady's Book* promoted an "Own Your Own Home" movement in 1846 and over the next 50 years published at least 450 different cottage and villa styles. Starting in 1885, the influential *Ladies' Home Journal* offered advice to homemakers on architectural styles and furnishings. Among the model houses published by the magazine in 1901 were several designed by Frank Lloyd Wright. In the 1930s, designer Norman Bel Geddes contributed to the magazine vivid images and glowing descriptions of a "house of tomorrow." With an audience of nearly a million readers, the *Ladies' Home Journal* was a significant tastemaker in the early 20th century. Indeed, *Godey's Lady's Book* and *Ladies' Home Journal* showed how effectively the popular press could promote reform and renewal in house design. In both cases, the targeted audience was the woman of the house, aptly dubbed "Mrs. Consumer" in 1929 by home economist Christine Frederick. By the 20th century, coverage in the popular press was needed to ensure the success of any housing prototype.

"There is a tide of wealth and prosperity setting in to our country unparalleled in extent and power, and many Christian men and women will be drawn into a current of worldliness and self-indulgence from which they now would shrink with dismay. Let those who are planning for future life take thought in good time. Shall your future homes become the abodes of an industry, thrift, and benevolent economy that shall provide means to bless the community all around, by a wise example and an outpouring of beneficence? Or shall they be the proud residences of the indolent, the self-indulgent, the exclusive, and the worldly?"
Catharine Beecher, *Harper's New Monthly Magazine,* May 1866

Norman Bel Geddes, one of the 20th century's most versatile and influential designers, was asked by *Ladies' Home Journal* in 1931 to predict what technology held in store for the end of the decade. Here are some of his predictions:

"Ten years from now... all the following prophecies will be old-fashioned: • Synthetic materials will replace the products of Nature in buildings. • Every roof will be a garden. • Exterior walls of buildings will be of thinner material to effect economy of space. • Houses, in all climates, will have flat roofs. • Every floor will have one or more terraces. • The garage will be part of the house and will be placed on the street front. • Service quarters will be at the front of the house; living rooms at the back. • Houses, in the main, will tend to be smaller, but the fewer rooms they will contain will be larger. • Windows, while admitting violet rays, will not open. • The home will become so mechanized that handwork will be reduced to a minimum. • Mechanical devices, controlled by the photo-electric cell, will open doors, serve meals, and remove dirty dishes and clothes to the appropriate departments of the building."

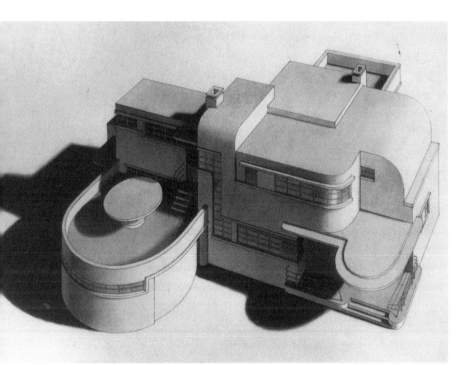

The house of tomorrow as designed by Norman Bel Geddes, known for his streamlined products. He speculated in a 1931 issue of Ladies' Home Journal *that by the end of the decade houses would be ventilated by artificial means, eliminating the need for operable windows; neon would replace incandescent lighting; electro-mechanical gadgetry would simplify the homemaker's life; and that the automobile would gain sufficient importance to warrant garages at the front of the house rather than at the rear. (Humanities Research Center, University of Texas. Reproduced with permission of Edith Lutyens Bel Geddes)*

Professional magazines aimed at architects, such as *Architectural Record*, *Architectural Forum*, *House and Home*, *Better Homes and Gardens*, and *Arts and Architecture*, were also influential in promoting prototype residences. Magazines as diverse as Scientific American, Popular Mechanics, Life, and Business Week also got into the act. Depending on the magazine, articles focused on the creators of the houses, the innovative nature of the designs, the utilization of new construction technologies and building products, or the public's reaction to the new concepts.

Expositions and fairs became another popular means of introducing new inventions and products, including model or demonstration houses. Although this form of promotion had antecedents in London as early as 1851, when the Prince Albert Model Cottages were constructed as part of the Great Exhibition, it was not until the 1930s that model houses became a prominent feature of American expositions. The Century of Progress exhibition, held in Chicago in 1933–34, was one of the first to include demonstration houses open to the public. It was this exhibition that introduced Americans to George Fred Keck's House of Tomorrow (see Chapter 8) and Howard T. Fisher's General Houses (see

Chapter 10). Department stores, quick to recognize the potential, began around this time to sponsor model homes as a means of attracting media attention, drawing shoppers, and promoting merchandise. Macy's in New York City, Marshall Field in Chicago, Woodward and Lothrop in Washington, D.C., and Wanamaker's in Philadelphia all undertook to market model homes. Robert McLaughlin's Motohome (see Chapter 9) and Buckminster Fuller's Dymaxion Dwelling Machine (see Chapter 5) were introduced to the public in this manner.

The movies became another medium through which Americans were exposed to futuristic images of the home, although with mixed results. Donald Albrecht notes in his 1986 study *Designing Dreams*, "While modern architects sought to reform the design of the house and progressive reformers worked to make women's lives easier with more efficient and humane settings for their labors, the cinema's response to domestic issues was a highly conservative one, reflecting popular anxieties about the status of women."[1] Nonetheless, images of futuristic kitchens, bathrooms, and bedrooms appeared in such films as *The Easiest Way* (1931), *The Women* (1939), and, most spectacularly perhaps, *The Fountainhead* (1949).

Many of the new or improved building materials developed in the 1920s and 1930s were marketed for use in houses and promoted as products "of the future." Traditional materials—brick, stone, and wood for the exterior, plaster and wood for the interior—had served Americans well, yet they were being upstaged by a bewildering array of synthetics and other materials not previously used in residential architecture: Carrara, Vitrolite, and Thermopane glass; aluminum and Duralumin; asbestos concrete; Vinylite flooring; Lumarith, Formica, Textolite, Micarta, and Homosote for wall surfaces; plywood; enameled metal panels; asphalt shingles; and glass block. Manufacturers and architects extolled these products' presumed virtues of low maintenance, durability, and beauty and eagerly endorsed their use. Some of the new synthetic materials performed poorly, however, and were in time replaced with more traditional materials.

Two major advances in construction technology were also reflected in the houses of the 1930s: the widespread availability of materials in large sheets (some as large as four by eight feet) and the growing acceptance of a standard four-foot construction module. Like the invention of the balloon frame, which revolutionized American house construction early in the 19th century, the perfection and promotion of other technologies between 1850 and 1950 opened up new building and design possibilities: Orson Fowler's gravel-wall construction; Buckminster Fuller's mast construction, in which floors, walls, and roofs were suspended on cables from a central core or mast; and all-glass-and-steel construction, exemplified in George Fred Keck's two houses for the Century of Progress exhibition in 1933–34. Panel wall construction using steel studs was championed by Robert McLaughlin and Howard Fisher in their prefabricated houses of the 1930s.

The introduction of modern utilities in the 19th century—water, electricity, gas, telephone, and sewers—had a dramatic and positive impact on the lives of Americans. These advances in household technology, coupled with the advent of central heating and cooling systems, transformed the activities that occurred within the house. Many of the innovations, such as indoor plumbing lines, required changes in floor plans. Catharine

Beecher and Orson Fowler were among the earliest supporters of these modern features and gave them prominent attention in their published house designs. The introduction of electric refrigerators, electric and gas ranges, and, to a lesser extent, dishwashers, washing machines and dryers, radically altered food preparation and housekeeping chores in the American house; these and other pieces of labor-saving equipment were quickly incorporated into model houses. What had once been luxuries soon came to be seen as necessities.

The collapse of the stock market in 1929 was followed by a renewal of interest in the potential of prefabrication to create affordable housing. Prefabrication—the mass production of interchangeable building parts—was not a new phenomenon in the American building industry; indeed, portable, demountable houses had been shipped to California to provide temporary shelter for gold prospectors as early as 1849. Although there were numerous experiments in the field throughout the 19th century (most of them using wood and cast iron as building materials), prefabrication had remained outside the mainstream of the burgeoning housing industry. Early prefabricated or "sectional" houses were considered suitable only for military installations, campgrounds, farms, and rustic resorts.

"Within a lifetime, American homes have evolved from LABOR-PLACES to EASE-ABODES! The twenty-year-old bride cannot even imagine the home inconveniences which her grandmother was forced to accept. It is difficult for one in the meridian of life either to realize, or visualize, the sharp contrast between the living conditions today and those of yesterday. The chief difference between the homes of today and those of our forebears is that our mothers and grandmothers 'served' their homes; whereas, the homes of us moderns 'serve' us! That differentiation marks a somersault turn in living conditions which has a tangible value. The Machine Age has liberated the world from the slavery of drudgery. The 'efficient contrast' in the old and in the new Home produces a startling change. Then the housewives were old, bent, and wrinkled at forty; now, modern wives are just maturing into the most glamorous stage of womanhood at that age.... Thanks to man's inventive genius, young Mrs. 1934 touches the button of an electric thermostat, and the temperature of her house quickly rises to a desired '70' degrees or drops to '60' degrees.... Her kitchen is a scientist's laboratory. She cleans it by turning the hose on it!... Everything has been arranged to enable her to move swiftly and efficiently through the morning's work—to the tempo of the radio if she chooses! Like the automobile, the modern home is a product of the laboratory. But this Machine Age has not robbed the '1934 Model' of its individuality, its soul, or its charm. The new note in Homemaking has come to stay. It is based on Economy, Efficiency, and Beauty."

Dorothy Raley, *Home and Furnishings: A Century of Progress,* 1934

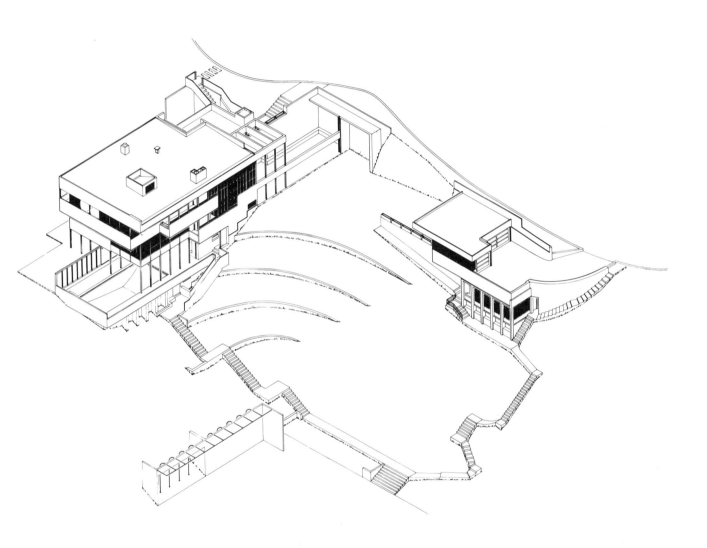

Richard Neutra's Lovell House (also called the Health House because of its health-preserving features) received tremendous publicity in architectural journals when it was constructed in Los Angeles in 1929. With a welded steel frame, an exterior finish of stucco on metal lath, and ribbon windows, the house gave the appearance of being machine-made. Throughout his career Neutra experimented with prefabrication as a means of producing affordable housing. (Jeffrey B. Lentz, Historic American Buildings Survey)

"A great epoch has begun.

There exists a new spirit.

Industry, overwhelming us like a flood which rolls on towards its destined end, has furnished us with new tools adapted to this new epoch, animated by the new spirit. Economic law unavoidably governs our acts and our thoughts.

The problem of the house is a problem of the epoch. The equilibrium of society today depends upon it. Architecture has for its first duty, in this period of renewal, that of bringing about a revision of values, a revision of the constituent elements of the house."

Le Corbusier, *Towards a New Architecture,* 1927

In the first three decades of the 20th century, Sears, Roebuck was the leading American company to design, market, and, in some cases, construct "pre-cut" wood-frame houses. Although by no means "houses of the future," Sears's Modern Homes program offered American consumers a wide range of buildings at reasonable cost.

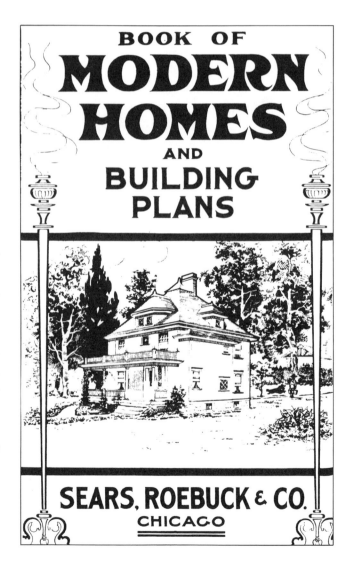

In 1934 Westinghouse Electric designed and constructed a house "that forecasts the home of tomorrow." Erected in Mansfield, Ohio, where it still is located, this rather stolid-looking structure boasted hundreds of specially developed mechanical and electrical devices, including central air conditioning, indirect lighting, an intercom system, and an electric garage-door opener. (Westinghouse Electric Corporation)

Mail-order "ready-cut" or "precut" houses helped change American attitudes toward prefabrication. Marketed by such companies as Sears Roebuck, Montgomery Ward, Alladin, and Hodgson in the early decades of the 20th century, these structures consisted of standardized pieces that were assembled and packaged in a central location and then shipped by truck or rail to the building site.

The houses came in sizes, shapes, and styles to suit almost every taste. Although technically not prefabricated—"ready-cut" houses were constructed at the site using traditional methods—they offered high quality at affordable prices. And they showed that mass-production methods could be used to advantage in the housing industry.

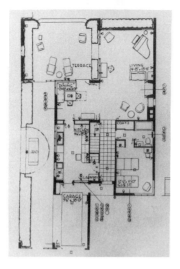

The winning entry in the Home Electric Competition could be characterized as streamlined Moderne, with a flat roof and large windows.

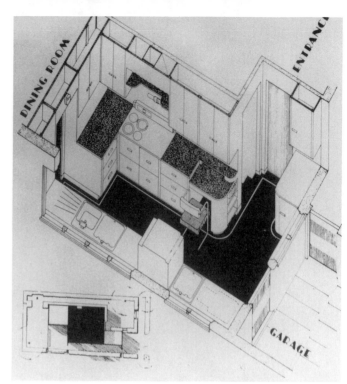

Despite the success of "ready-cut" houses, experts recognized that these and other traditionally built houses, which tended to cost $5,000 or more, were available only to a small segment of the population. Eager to tap new markets, private corporations—among them U.S. Steel, Republic Steel, the Homosote Company, General Electric, and Westinghouse—developed an increased interest in housing as a means of establishing new

markets for their products. In 1934, for example, Westinghouse teamed up with *Good Housekeeping* magazine to build an experimental house with every state-of-the-art appliance then known to man. Also in 1934 General Electric and *Architectural Forum* magazine sponsored a competition to design a home for a prototypical American family ("the Bliss family"); the competition attracted more than 2,000 entries from around the country.

Some of these companies looked to the success of Ford and General Motors, which just a decade earlier had révolutionized the growing automobile industry by adopting mass-production techniques. Idealistic designers and engineers were hired, research was undertaken, and experimental houses were

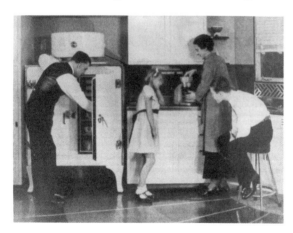

In 1935 the General Electric Company sponsored the Home Electric Competition for an ideal—but fictitious—American family: Mr. and Mrs. Bliss and their two children. The winning entry, by the architectural firm of Hays and Simpson of Cleveland, incorporated 32 different electical appliances made by General Electric. In this photograph, the Bliss family is shown in their all-electric kitchen.

erected— with "Houses like Fords" an often-used slogan and the hoped-for goal. Findings, be they new products or simply new ideas, were incorporated into the companies' advertisements and promotional pieces. Frequently these promotional campaigns were directed at the homemaker, who was optimistically promised freedom from the drudgery of cooking and cleaning. The Libbey-Owens-Ford Glass Company, for example, designed a "glassical kitchen" that was promoted through *National Geographic* and *Better Homes and Gardens*, whose readers were assured that "tomorrow's kitchens won't wear you out with the work of living."

This futuristic kitchen and dining area was designed by H. Creston Dohner for Libbey-Owens-Ford Glass Company in 1943 to demonstrate new uses for glass. Kitchen counters permitted food preparation while seated; glass cabinet doors were easy to keep clean; and the dining room table could be pushed up against the wall when not in use (as shown here), its legs doubling as a picture frame. (Hedrich-Blessing)

"It was sadly too true that women's time wasn't worth saving because there was nothing worth doing with one's leisure, or no way of turning it into cash. Today the consumer has countless interests and ways of employing her freedom from household responsibilities. This then is the second strong appeal which the seller must always keep in mind when offering household equipment: does this tool, device, or appliance give Mrs. Consumer more leisure? . . . Any woman who washes the dishes or clothes by hand, sweeps a rug, or stokes a furnace, etc., is doing work that an electrical utility can do for three cents an hour—any workman who does by hand any task that electricity can do is working for a few cents a day."

Christine Frederick, *Selling Mrs. Consumer*, 1929

This 1942 brochure from American Houses, Inc., was intended to promote the use of prefabricated units and materials among architects. Although the house designs were traditional, the construction technology was not. Prefabrication was welcomed by many architects as a major cost-cutter.

Several companies built demonstration houses in the Washington, D.C., area and invited federal officials to inspect them. Here visitors tour a home being built with Berloy steel frames, made by a subsidiary of Republic Steel Corporation.

Of perhaps greater significance, the 1930s saw the rise of entirely new companies to develop and market forward-looking processes and products for the American home. These companies included Howard Fisher's General Houses, Inc., which operated out of Chicago and was consciously modeled after General Motors, and American Houses, Inc., founded by Robert McLaughlin and his partners in New York. Scores of demonstration houses were built in this period to serve as testing laboratories for new techniques and technologies; the models also tested public interest— and stimulated sales.

Extensive noncommercial research and experimentation was undertaken during this period as well. Privately endowed organiza-

*Martin Wagner's "igloo" house of 1941
was designed to be assembled quickly.
Constructed of prefabricated steel
components, each unit featured two
folding beds, a small lavatory and
stall shower, and a built-in kitchen.
Units could be combined, as shown
here, to form a larger structure.
(Architectural Forum)*

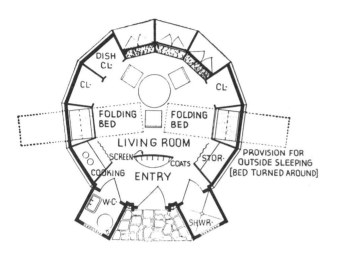

"Prefabrication is all things to all men, and a source of confusion to many. To Foster Gunnison, pioneer prefabricator of New Albany, Indiana, it is the way to turn a scattered, handicraft industry into centralized Big Business, by mass production of panel houses for a national market. To Roland Wank, chief architect of the TVA [Tennessee Valley Authority], it is a way to build houses in two or three boxlike parts small enough to truck on the highway. ... To Buckminster Fuller, famed inventor of a bathroom stamped from sheet metal, it offers an overnight route to a technological millennium when every house will come equipped with a color television set, an automatic laundry that returns ironed shirts in three minutes, and a wonderful contraption that emits a soapy mist in which you can bathe from head to foot while standing in a dishpan on the living room rug.... It is said to offer the possibility of revolutionary changes in land development and house financing, through separation of house and site.... It is obscured by a fog of claims and counter-claims, and yet manages to rise above this fog as one of the few widely recognized objectives of a rudderless industry. Its basis is not so much a logical theory as a cult. And as a cult it has won ardent and persuasive adherents, united by a belief in a better house, for less money, through more efficient methods of house production."

Bruce and Sandbank, *A History of Prefabrication*, 1944

tions, notable among them the Albert Farwell Bemis Foundation of Boston and the John B. Pierce Foundation of New York, were established with the primary purpose of sponsoring research projects involving housing prefabrication. These two particular organizations were founded by businessmen committed to harnessing new technologies to create affordable housing.

A Tennessee Valley Authority home in two pieces.

At the federal level, agencies such as the Bureau of Standards, the Farm Security Administration, the Forest Products Laboratory, and the Tennessee Valley Authority took an equally serious look at America's housing problem. The Forest Products Laboratory, for example, conducted tests to improve and promote the structural uses of wood in prefabricated houses; it pioneered the use of plywood in residential architecture. The Farm Security Administration sponsored the development of entire communities of low-cost houses. The Tennessee Valley Authority, which was involved in similar projects, funded the design of a factory-built house that could be towed to a site. (In 1936 the Airstream Trailer Company introduced its aerodynamic, aluminum-clad Clipper, which took mobility in housing to its logical extreme.)

Organizations such as the National Association of Housing Officials, Better Homes in America, and the National Housing Committee also contributed to the cause of higher-quality low-cost housing, largely through educational campaigns. Ironically, many prefabricated houses of this period, while technically innovative, were stylistically conservative; the basic Cape Cod design, perennially popular with homeowners, was adapted by many a prefabricator.

For a Wisconsin homes show in 1935 seven men erected one of the U.S. Forest Products Laboratory's experimental plywood-panel houses (below) in just 21 hours. Perhaps anticipating public reaction to the house's industrial appearance, the house was richly landscaped.

World War II gave a tremendous impetus to mass-produced housing and stimulated further experimentation with prefabrication. Federal agencies alone purchased, over a two-year period, almost 75,000 units for housing war workers, single-handedly

"After the second house beyond the polystyrene you'll come to a two-story phenol-formaldehyde. That's it."

Alan Dunn's cartoons poking fun at contemporary design and construction appeared in
Architectural Record for many years. (The Last Lath, 1947. Reprinted with permission)

In January 1936, Wally Byam's Airstream Trailer Company introduced the Clipper, a
revolutionary aluminum mobile home that slept four. With windows that could be fully
opened, pressurized water, electric lights, and a steel frame, the Airstream Clipper boasted
"the most advanced heat insulation and ventilating system of the day." Priced at $1,200,
the Clipper was seen by many as a house of the future. The company is still active today.
(Archives of Airstream, Inc.)

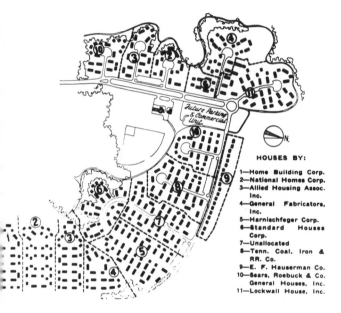

HOUSES BY:

1—Home Building Corp.
2—National Homes Corp.
3—Allied Housing Assoc. Inc.
4—General Fabricators, Inc.
5—Harnischfeger Corp.
6—Standard Houses Corp.
7—Unallocated
8—Tenn. Coal, Iron & RR. Co.
9—E. F. Hauserman Co.
10—Sears, Roebuck & Co. General Houses, Inc.
11—Lockwall House, Inc.

causing a boom in the prefabrication industry. During this time the home-building industry acquired a vast reservoir of experience in advanced methods of construction, which would have an enormous effect on postwar production. Shortages of critical materials during the war, however, ended housing experiments that made use of steel and other metals and forced the prefabrication boom to focus on wood construction.

In 1941 the U.S. government sponsored at Indian Head, Maryland, a development of prefabricated houses from different manufacturers. Four of the entries are shown here. Most of the models incorporated plywood or an insulating board such as Homosote on a wood frame with plasterboard on the interior.

Not surprisingly, when veterans returned home at war's end, they faced a tremendous housing shortage. Federal agencies such as the Federal Housing Authority and the Veterans Administration stepped in to facilitate homeownership by these individuals and their families, primarily in suburban areas; to speed the transformation from a wartime to a peacetime economy, the government pumped money into companies that promised to mass-produce houses quickly and efficiently. Factories that had once mass-produced airplanes turned their attention to the mass production of housing. Washington established programs that enabled veterans to purchase houses with little money down and low monthly payments. It was in this economic climate that the

Lustron house, promising a "new standard of living," came into being (see Chapter 12).

The years immediately following World War II also saw the rise of the so-called merchant builders, including William J. Levitt on the East Coast and Joseph Eichler on the West Coast, who specialized in building entire communities of identical, detached single-family houses. Levittowns sprouted in New York, Pennsylvania, and New Jersey.

"Using industrial techniques in other fields as a basis, we think tomorrow's house will be built in pieces in factories and assembled at the site. It may be full of all sorts of queer curves, strange slanting walls, and odd materials that absorb sound but can be cleaned off with a hose. Its windows will not be single sheets of glass but insulated sandwiches with two or even three panes in a single frame, whose surfaces may be treated, as photographic lenses are now treated, so that reflections are entirely eliminated. . . . Tomorrow's house will be highly mechanized. Its present supply of fractional horsepower motors will be multiplied by two or three, and all sorts of things will happen at the push of a button instead of the heave of a back."
George Nelson and Henry Wright, *Tomorrow's House,* 1945

"Now the obvious economic solution to [the production of workingmen's homes] lies in the standardization, not necessarily of the general plan, but of its various component units and structural elements. Carried to its logical conclusion this principle would result in a system of standard dwelling manufacture, in a ready-made system, if you please—of wholesale fabrication like that which has already given the worker his cheap shoes and his ready-made suit of clothes."
Grosvenor Atterbury, *Charities,* October 1906 (reprinted in *The Economic Production of Workingmen's Homes,* 1930)

The years between 1850 and 1950 saw many radical, startling, and bizarre ideas for "houses of tomorrow." In some cases, these houses reflected the social and economic theories of their designer-promoters; in other cases, specific inventions or technical breakthroughs. Frequently, the houses mirrored the personal idiosyncrasies of their promoters, who tended to make extravagant promises to a public eager for new ideas. Ease of construction, reasonable cost, freedom from maintenance, improved health for the occupants, enhanced efficiency, and timeless good looks were just a few of the guarantees offered.

While the houses often delivered less than promised, the ideas they embodied had a tremendous impact on American domestic architecture as a whole. The outlandishness of some of the designs, the inventiveness of the technology, and the lavishness of the claims and marketing hyperbole served an important purpose: to focus attention on how to improve the way we live. Many of these "houses of tomorrow" contributed, in one way or another, ideas that have since been put into actual practice in a modified— usually more conservative—form.

Designers of the "houses of tomorrow" recognized that all human habitation must, at the very minimum, provide shelter from the elements as well as facilities for sleep, food preparation, dining, entertaining, and hygiene. Once these basic needs are met, other factors—how a house looks, how well it works, or how economical it is—come into play. "Houses of tomorrow" commonly promised:

- to promote health and a sense of general well-being;

- to be inexpensive to build;

- to be inexpensive to maintain;

- to be safe against fire;

- to be environmentally compatible (a relatively recent theme);

- to be durable;

- to permit all domestic activities to be performed efficiently;

- to provide a refuge from the bustle of daily life;

- to be attractive or possesses a distinctive appearance.

This eight-family row house was constructed of hollow-cored, precast concrete elements, including walls, floors, roofs, dormers, and chimneys. Designed by Grosvenor Atterbury, a New York architect, several hundred such houses were built between 1910 and 1918 in Forest Hills Gardens, Long Island.

Few, if any, of the houses in this book meet all of these goals. What sets "houses of tomorrow" apart from their more ordinary siblings is that they deliberately approach one or more of these goals in an innovative way: they are designed to be *more* durable, *more* efficient, *more* inexpensive, or *more* distinctive than their predecessors.

This book focuses on 12 houses built between 1850 and 1950 that were consciously designed and promoted as prototypes. The houses sparked debate and generated consid-

erable publicity at the time of their respective debuts. Several of the houses are of interest primarily as aesthetic objects; others represent technological advancements; still others are significant for their impact on family organization and interaction. Yet each in its own way was intended as a glimpse of the future. By seizing the public imagination, these houses and others like them helped to inspire homeowners and architects alike.

The houses selected for inclusion in this book were, with a few notable exceptions, not designed by architects who are well known today. Indeed several of the houses—such as the poured-concrete houses of Thomas A. Edison—were not designed by architects at all but by inventors and promoters. Some of the houses are traditional in appearance; others are consciously modern. Although some of the houses are mentioned in such pioneering studies as Siegfried Giedion's *Mechanization Takes Command*, Reyner Banham's *The Architecture of the Well-Tempered Environment*, James Marston Fitch's *American Building 1: The Historical Forces That Shaped It*, and Gwendolyn

Wright's *Building the Dream: A Social History of Housing in America*, most have been largely ignored in the body of literature on American architecture.

This book is intended not as a comprehensive look at American "houses of tomorrow," but, rather, as an introduction to the subject. The difficulty of choosing just 12 houses was enormous; literally hundreds of advanced, forward-looking houses were conceived and constructed in cities and towns across America between 1850 and 1950. While the houses that appear in this book tend to be the personal favorites of the authors, an effort was made to provide a fair sampling that balanced those "houses of tomorrow" that were technologically advanced with those that reflected new attitudes toward the family and social relations.

There are omissions that will be obvious to many students of American architecture. It could be argued that the first balloon-frame house was truly a "house of tomorrow," since it revolutionized American residential construction technology. (Invented in 1832, the balloon frame is a structural system made up of single studs, or supports, extending the full

In the early 1940s, Walter Gropius and Konrad Wachsman devised a system of prefabrication based on a cubical module. Standardized panel units could be used in a variety of positions, as wall or ceiling, without structural change. The innovative system permitted great flexibility in design. This particular house was designed by Dahong Wang, one of Gropius's architecture students at Harvard. A company formed to market the product, General Panel Corporation, ran into problems similar to those of Lustron (see Chapter 12) and was liquidated in the early 1950s. (New Pencil Points)

height of the structure. Lumber for this framework is sawed into boards of standard size, permitting unskilled workers to erect houses quickly and soundly.) Another omission is the General Panel House designed in the 1940s by Walter Gropius and Konrad Wachsmann, which has been analyzed at some length in Gilbert Herbert's *The Dream of the Factory-Made House*. The numerous research and model houses designed by Richard Neutra are not discussed in detail in this book, partly because much has already been written about Neutra's groundbreaking work in experimental housing (see, for example, Thomas S. Hines's *Richard Neutra and The Search for Modern Architecture*). The houses of architects Rudolf Schindler and Philip Johnson—while well known, highly influential, and often imitated—were never promoted as prototypical residences.

Other houses, such as Carl Koch's innovative Techbuilt House, which was marketed in the 1950s and 1960s, fall outside the period covered by the book yet are clearly worthy of future study. Mobile homes—the Airstream Clipper and its successors—have not been included, although they, too, were technologically advanced and revolutionized how many

Americans lived. Examples of forward-looking multifamily housing, from tenements to apartment buildings, have also been omitted; arguably the most realistic solution for housing future generations, multifamily housing is a subject unto itself. The focus here is on the enduring American dream: the detached single-family dwelling.

A chapter is devoted to each house: how it came about; the social, aesthetic, and technical innovations it promised; its physical appearance and how it was constructed; the men and women responsible for promoting the design; public and professional reaction to the house; and how the house fared architecturally, functionally, and financially. In cases where the houses are still standing, their long-term preservation needs are discussed.

Yesterday's Houses of Tomorrow introduces readers to some very special houses: houses that dared to be different and, in so doing, captured the interest, however transitory, of the American public. The impact of many of these houses can be felt in our houses of today. ⏹

Ground-plan.

a, Porch.
b, Parlor, 15 by 16
  feet.
c, Dining-room,
  15 by 16 feet.
d, d, Small Bed-
  rooms.
e, Stairs.
f, f, f, Closets.
g, Pantry.
h, Store-closet.
i, i, i, Fireplaces.

One   CATHARINE BEECHER AND THE AMERICAN WOMAN'S HOME

There is no point of domestic economy, which more seriously involves the health and daily comfort of American women, than the proper construction of houses.

Catharine Beecher, *A Treatise on Domestic Economy*, 1841

Catharine Beecher, c. 1870, about the time The American Woman's Home *was published. (Stowe-Day Foundation)*

At the height of her career in the mid-19th century, Catharine Esther Beecher was one of the best-known and most widely admired women in the United States. An extraordinary teacher and educator, Beecher tirelessly championed the cause of education for women and over the course of three decades founded academies for women in Hartford, Connecticut, Cincinnati, Ohio, and Milwaukee, Wisconsin. In her spare time she wrote more than two dozen books on such diverse topics as religion, ethics, arithmetic, suffrage, physical education, and abolition. Despite poor health, she lectured frequently, traveled extensively, and kept up spirited correspondence with family members and friends. When Beecher turned her considerable literary energies to domestic science, she produced two bestsellers, books that introduced architectural innovations for promoting the health and well-being of the American family and, not coincidentally, for saving the housewife time, labor, and expense. How did this remarkable woman, who never established a permanent residence, become such an authority on the design and construction of houses? What impact did her forward-looking ideas have on American domestic architecture?

Catharine Beecher was born in East Hampton, Long Island, in 1800, the first child of Roxana Foote and Lyman Beecher, an ambitious, conservative clergyman. Catharine was eventually joined by eight siblings—two sisters and six brothers—but she remained her father's favorite, accompanying him on his rounds and enjoying lively debates with him at home. Although she grew up in a society that tended to view females as creatures of limited abilities, Beecher absorbed much of her father's intellectual curiosity, independence, and ambition. After her family moved to Litchfield, Connecticut, in 1810, she enrolled in Sarah Pierce's Female Academy—a finishing school for young women—to learn "those rules of delicacy and propriety" appropriate to the town's "singularly good" society.[1]

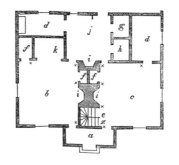

Elevation and plan of small house from A Treatise on Domestic Economy.

With her mother's untimely death in 1816, Beecher was cast in the role of housekeeper for her father and surrogate mother to her younger siblings. This job ended a year later when her father remarried and she headed off to New London, Connecticut, to teach— one of the few respectable professions open to women.

During her years in New London, Beecher met and became engaged to Alexander Metcalf Fisher, a professor of science at Yale University. Shortly after the engagement was announced, Fisher departed for England by ship and drowned in a heavy storm off the coast of Ireland. The distraught Catharine moved to Hartford to be closer to her family. The tragedy of Fisher's death, however, did not delay her pursuit of a career in education; indeed, it seemed to steel her resolve. Perceiving the need for an educational institution for local women and eager to assert her independence, Beecher, at age 23, founded her first school atop a Hartford harness shop in May 1823. Within five years, thanks to her hard work, persistence, and good family connections, the Hartford Female Seminary boasted eight teachers (one of whom was Beecher's younger sister Harriet), a board of trustees culled from Hartford's finest families, and a grand new building. Beecher wrote several textbooks for the school, including books on arithmetic, ethics, and physiology. The seminary was considered by many to be a "milestone in the history of women's education."[2] By instituting a strong academic curriculum and attempting to establish a permanent endowment, Beecher succeeded in creating an educational alternative to finishing schools for young women, an alternative that was both challenging and intellectually rigorous.

Beecher tried to repeat her Hartford success in Cincinnati, where she moved in 1832 to be with her father; she recruited teachers from the East and founded the Western Female Institute. Beecher's considerable energies and growing reputation, however, were not sufficient to overcome weak local support; a lack of funds forced the school to close in 1837.

Her disappointing experience in Cincinnati did not deter Beecher from establishing a third institution, the Milwaukee Female College, in 1850. This time she encountered a community willing and eager to follow her recommendations. She even helped design a

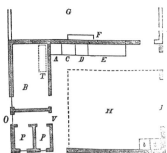

Plan for a kitchen yard from A Treatise on Domestic Economy.

Gothic Revival structure to house the college, which, when completed, accommodated 120 students and a staff of four teachers. Beecher's association with the institution ended in 1856 over a disagreement about a personal residence for herself, but the college remained in business until it merged with the University of Wisconsin in the mid-20th century.

Although Beecher was a strong proponent of improved education for women, she saw this training as serving a definite purpose—to make women better housekeepers. Beecher drew a clear distinction between the two sexes when it came to work: the appropriate place for women was in the home, while men pursued careers outside the home, in business or in politics. In Beecher's opinion, the profession of housekeeper was not accorded its rightful respect as the most influential and vital of all jobs. This disregard was due in large part, she argued, to American women's lack of the tools and training necessary to carry out their "peculiar responsibilities."

Beecher wrote her first bestseller, *A Treatise on Domestic Economy*, in 1843, "because she herself [Beecher] suffered from want of such knowledge, in early life; because others, under her care, suffered from her ignorance."

In the opening chapters of *A Treatise on Domestic Economy*, Beecher challenged her readers:

"... are not the most responsible of all duties committed to the care of woman? Is not her profession to take care of mind, body and soul? And that, too, at the most critical of all periods of existence? And is it not as much a matter of public concern, that she should be properly qualified for her duties, as that ministers, lawyers, and physicians, should be prepared for theirs? And is it not as important to endow institutions that shall make a superior education accessible to all classes, for females, as much as for the other sex? And is it not equally important, that institutions for females be under the supervision of intelligent and responsible trustees, whose duty it shall be to secure a uniform and appropriate education for one sex as much as for the other?"

A Treatise on Domestic Economy was encyclopedic in scope. Its 37 chapters included practical discussions of cleanliness, healthful food and drink, the benefits of exercise and early rising, the care of children, sensible clothing, proper deportment, mental health, gardening, and the importance of preserving a "good temper" in a housekeeper. In short, the book covered all aspects of the housekeeper's work, guiding her footsteps from sunrise to bedtime, from the Monday washing to the Saturday baking. It has rightfully been called "the first modern book treating the household in a large way."[3] Not unexpectedly, Beecher accorded considerable attention in the book to the design and construction of houses.

Until Beecher's book was published, architecture was a profession dominated by men. Women had little, if any, say in the design of their own houses. Decisions concerning room configuration and size, building materials and finishes, kitchen arrangement and the placement of gardens were made by men. Beecher, recognizing the importance of the physical workplace itself, set out to educate women about architecture by devoting an entire chapter to house construction and by including other chapters on such related matters as the proper ventilation of the home and the proper care of the kitchen.

There were five principles that governed Beecher's common-sense approach to house design, gleaned from years of visiting homes of friends and family: economy of labor, economy of money, economy of health, economy of comfort, and, last and least, good taste. Beecher contended that houses should be functional,

planned around a woman's needs and capabilities. In deciding upon the size and style of a house, a family should allow the health and capacity of the housekeeper, along with the probability of obtaining servants, to be the determining factors. "Double the size of a house," she wrote, "and you double the labor of taking care of it." Beecher was one of the first to realize that as the prosperity of the country increased, the pool of reliable domestic servants would decrease and the woman of the house would be forced to handle the majority of housekeeping chores herself.

Like her contemporary and family friend Orson Fowler, Beecher understood that houses with long wings and detached kitchens were expensive to construct and inefficient to operate. Accordingly, she advocated plans that were square in shape, with less surface area exposed to the cold. She was critical of houses with grand piazzas and porticos; such features were in her opinion too costly. Money could be better spent on an additional room.

Beecher also had little regard for architectural ornament; the most beautiful and agreeable houses were those that were plainly detailed. She warned against spending money on "handsome parlors and chambers" and against scrimping on the kitchen. "Cramping the conveniences and comfort of a family, in order to secure elegant rooms, to show to company, is a weakness and folly," she admonished.

Five house designs were included in Beecher's *A Treatise on Domestic Economy*, each of them illustrated with annotated floor plans and elevation drawings. While each is distinct in its own way, the five designs share certain features unusual for the period that reflect Beecher's sensibilities:

- Kitchens are well lit, generously scaled, and centrally located—the heart, physically and spiritually, of the house. Pantries and storage facilities are readily accessible.

- Built-in closets abound, especially in bedrooms. Beecher recognized that closets reduced clutter and eliminated the need for specially made pieces of furniture. Shelves and pegs, carefully located, provide additional storage.

- Multipurpose rooms—precursors of today's ubiquitous family rooms—are a means of maximizing space. Bedrooms can be converted into "genteel parlors" in the day by using folding doors to screen off bed alcoves.

- The house's heating source, be it a fireplace or furnace, is centrally located to conserve fuel and improve efficiency.

Beecher saved her greatest praise for a modest Gothic cottage "which secures the most economy of labor and expense, with the greatest amount of convenience and comfort, which the writer has ever seen." As depicted in *A Treatise on Domestic Economy*, the house was symmetrical in its external appearance, with pointed arch windows and with porches at the front and rear. While its exterior seemed modest and unexceptional, the interior plan reflected many new ideas. The interior was dominated by twin parlors separated by folding doors that could be "thrown open in Summer, thus making a large saloon, through the house, from one piazza to the other." The bedrooms, guest room, children's playroom, kitchen, library, and storerooms all opened off the parlors, eliminating the need for long corridors. Although the house lacked indoor plumbing, Beecher provided a schematic drawing showing the proper placement, behind the kitchen, of the boiler, furnace, pump, reservoir, sink, bathing tub, and privies.

Woodcut rendering of "A Christian House"
from The American Woman's Home.

A *Treatise on Domestic Economy* quickly became an indispensable reference tool for homemakers and was reprinted again and again. In 1869 the book was substantially revised and retitled *The American Woman's Home*. This time Beecher shared authorship with her famous younger sister, Harriet Beecher Stowe, whose *Uncle Tom's Cabin* had become a runaway success a decade earlier. Like its predecessor, *The American Woman's Home* was encyclopedic in scope: 38 chapters covered "all the employments that sustain the many difficult and sacred duties of the family state."

In the second chapter the authors presented the "Christian house," which exhibited "modes of economizing labor, time, and expenses, so as to secure health, thrift, and domestic happiness to persons of limited means, in a measure rarely attained even by those who possess wealth." While it owed a great deal to the designs in the earlier edition of Beecher's book, the Christian house was considerably more sophisticated and forward-looking than its predecessors. Most scholars agree that it was Catharine, rather than Harriet, who crafted this portion of the book. Indeed, Beecher's innovative principles of domestic economy are reflected in virtually every aspect of the design.

The Christian house was intended to be located in the country or in a suburban, rather than urban, setting, with the assumption that "the family state demands some outdoor labor for all." For Beecher, time, labor, and money were saved by "the close packing of conveniences"; the overall dimensions of the house

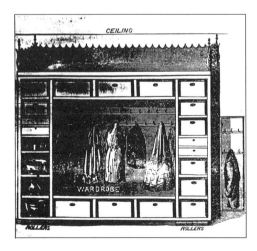

Woodcut of a wardrobe from
The American Woman's Home.

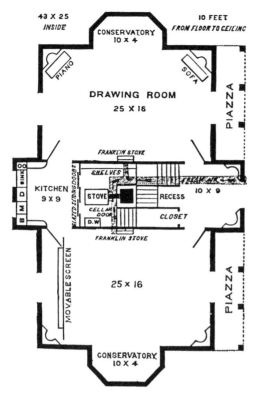

The figure shows:

43 X 25 INSIDE · 10 FEET FROM FLOOR TO CEILING

CONSERVATORY 10 X 4

PIANO · SOFA

DRAWING ROOM 25 X 16

PIAZZA

FRANKLIN STOVE

SHELVES · GLAZED SLIDING DOORS · STOVE · CELLAR DOOR · D.W. · RECESS · CLOSET · FRESH AIR · 10 X 9

KITCHEN 9 X 9 · SINK · B M D

FRANKLIN STOVE

MOVABLE SCREEN

25 X 16

PIAZZA

CONSERVATORY 10 X 4

First-floor plan showing a drawing room, a kitchen, and a large room from The American Woman's Home.

were only 43 by 25 feet, excluding conservatories and rear projections. Beecher assured readers that, with few changes, the plan could be adapted to a warm or cold climate and that, if more space were needed, an additional story could be added.

Unlike Beecher's earlier house plans, the plans for the Christian house included details on appropriate furniture and its placement, not to mention the art work on the walls! The description of the first floor betrayed Beecher's passion for organization:

The entry has arched recesses behind the front door, furnished with hooks for over-clothes in both—a box for over-shoes in one, and a stand for umbrellas in the other. The roof of the recess is for statuettes, busts, or flowers. The stairs turn twice with broad steps, making a recess at the lower landing, where a table is set with a vase of flowers….

The large room on the left can be made to serve the purpose of several rooms by means of a movable screen. By shifting this rolling screen from one part of the room to another, two apartments are always available, of any desired size within the limits of the left room. One side of the screen…what may be used as the parlor or sitting-room; the other side is arranged for bedroom conveniences.

At first glance, Beecher's floor plan is deceptively simple: two large rooms, each of them 25 by 16 feet, are flanked by an entryway, stairway, and kitchen. It is only through close examination of the drawings that Beecher's innovative concepts are revealed. The "rolling screen" is, in fact, far more than a room divider: it holds a full wardrobe, with hooks and "shelf boxes" for various articles of clothing. The couches, one conveniently fitting under the other, double as beds at night. An ottoman on casters serves

Floor plan of Beecher's carefully designed kitchen from The American Woman's Home.

as both a seat and a storage unit. All these items, noted Beecher, could be made by the man of the house. By having rooms and pieces of furniture serve more than one purpose, an efficiency of space could thus be maximized.

The Christian house also incorporated a rudimentary form of central heating, making use of Franklin stoves in the two large rooms and a large iron stove in the so-called "stove-room." Flues stacked behind the stairs carried warm air to the bedrooms on the second floor, and a duct connected to the various stoves pulled in fresh air from the out-of-doors.

It was in the kitchen, however, that Beecher's sense of order found its fullest expression. Here Beecher provided an enlarged plan showing a kitchen nine by nine feet and the adjacent nine-by-seven foot stove room. Her construction advice was explicit and detailed:

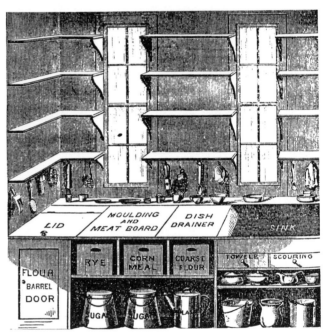

Woodcut drawing of a kitchen interior from The American Woman's Home.

Between the two rooms glazed sliding-doors, passing each other, serve to shut out heat and smells from the kitchen. The sides of the stove-room must be lined with shelves; those on the side by the cellar stairs, to be one foot wide, and eighteen inches apart; on the other side, shelves may be narrower, eight inches wide and nine inches apart. Boxes with lids, to receive stove utensils, must be placed near the stove.

On these shelves, and in the closet and boxes, can be placed every material used for cooking, all the table and cooking utensils, and all the articles used in house work, and yet much spare room will be left. The cook's galley in a steamship has every article and utensil used in cooking for two hundred persons, in a space not larger than this stove-room, and so arranged that with one or two steps the cook can reach all he uses.

Reconstructed kitchen in the Harriet Beecher Stowe House. (Stowe-Day Foundation)

By analyzing the various chores that took place in the kitchen and identifying specific storage needs for food and utensils, Beecher came up with a design that was both functional and efficient. Water was brought indoors by means of two pumps, one for well water and the other for rainwater. Gone were the center kitchen table and isolated storage bins. An illustration of the workspace clearly showed a continuous work surface, at waist height, well lit and ventilated by two windows, and storage space organized according to function. Beecher described her kitchen design:

The flour-barrel just fills the closet, which has a door for admission, and a lid to raise when used. Beside it, is the form for cooking, with moulding-board laid on it; one side used for preparing vegetables and meat, and the other for moulding bread. The sink has two pumps, for well and for rain-water—one having a forcing power to throw water into the reservoir in the garret, which supplies the water-closet and bath-room. On the other side of the sink is the dish-drainer, with a ledge on the edge next to the sink, to hold the dishes, and grooves cut to let the water drain into the sink. It has hinges, so that it can either rest on the cook-form or be turned over and cover the sink. Under the sink are shelf-boxes placed on two shelves run into grooves, with

other grooves above and below, so that one may move the shelves and increase or diminish the spaces between. The shelf-boxes can be used for scouring-materials, dish-towels, and dish-cloths; also to hold bowls for bits of butter, fats, etc. Under these two shelves is room for two pails, and a jar for soap-grease.

The logic of her design is inescapable: ingredients used to make bread are grouped together; utensils for cleaning dishes are conveniently beneath the sink, and a grooved dish drainer is adjacent to the sink, permitting water to drain unimpeded. Every item is consciously placed to increase efficiency within the kitchen. There is virtually no wasted space.

The second floor of Beecher's Christian house was set under the eaves and was identified as the "attic story." It contained two large bedrooms, each with its own balcony to the outdoors, and two smaller rooms, one of which presumably served as a bathroom. Both bedrooms contained large walk-in closets, as well as built-in corner dressing tables that "save much space for use, and give a handsome form and finish to the room."

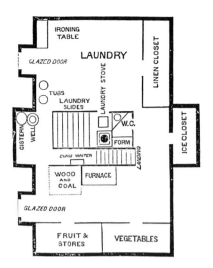

IRONING TABLE

LAUNDRY

GLAZED DOOR

LINEN CLOSET

TUBS
LAUNDRY SLIDES

LAUNDRY STOVE

CISTERN

WELL

W.C.

ICE CLOSET

FORM

DUMB WAITER

LANDING

WOOD AND COAL

FURNACE

GLAZED DOOR

FRUIT & STORES

VEGETABLES

Basement floor plan showing a laundry from The American Woman's Home.

Beecher advocated the use of indoor water closets, but cautioned that they "must have the latest improvements for safe discharge." Aware that indoor plumbing was still viewed with skepticism by most of the population, she argued that water closets "cost no more than an out-door building, and save from the most disagreeable house-labor." A reservoir for water was located in the garret, supplied by a forcing pump in the cellar.

Beecher also offered a detailed plan for the basement; it was to be well lit, with glazed doors and plaster walls. In addition to providing compartmentalized storage space for fruits, vegetables, and ice, the basement contained complete laundry facilities, including tubs, an ironing table, a linen closet, and a laundry stove. Beecher advocated drying clothes indoors to save "health as well as time and money" and made the point that locating laundry facilities within the house, rather than in a separate outbuilding, would save the housewife needless steps.

Like her earlier *A Treatise on Domestic Economy, The American Woman's Home* was an immediate success, selling out several printings and providing a new and welcome source of income. By the time the book was published, Beecher was an old woman and semiretired; despite her many ailments, she retained an inquisitive mind and never hesitated to speak out for her causes. She continued to write and to lecture between visits to the homes of various siblings. In 1877 Beecher relocated to Elmira, New York, to be with her brother Thomas and his wife and to partake of a nearby "water cure." It was there, a year later, that she suffered a stroke and died. Ironically, Beecher never got to live in a house of her own design.

It is true that Beecher wrote for an audience of white middle-class women and that her advice had little impact on the poor who worked in factories 12 and 15 hours a day and who came home to a cold tenement flat at night. It is also true that her exhortations for women to stay at home are today neither practical nor desirable for the majority of American women. Nevertheless, her architectural advice, offered during a period when little thought had been given to how houses

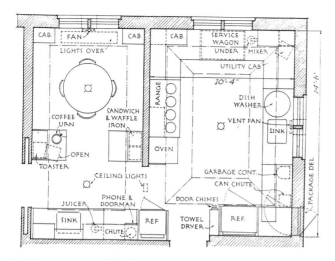

Photograph and floor plan of a kitchen from Westinghouse's Home of Tomorrow erected in Mansfield, Ohio, in 1934. This "all-electric" kitchen and pantry were designed for a household without servants. Beecher's spirit of innovation and sense of organization are reflected in the design. Every kitchen task has been accounted for by Westinghouse engineers. Labor-saving devices include an electrically heated serving wagon that fits under a kitchen work surface; a self-cleaning garbage disposal device, and automatically opening double doors between the pantry and the dining room. (Westinghouse Electric Corporation)

were organized and used, was remarkably innovative and sound.

Beecher's house designs are now recognized for what they were: precursors of the houses we live and work in today. Summarizing Beecher's achievements in *American Building: The Historical Forces That Shaped It*, James Marston Fitch said:

…her floor plans reflect quite accurately the new relationship of family to society, house to urban environment. Two qualities stamp them as essentially modern: the way in which all her enclosed volumes are designed to facilitate specific housekeeping tasks; and the masterly way in which she exploits the new urban services and absorbs them into the very fabric of her plans.

One has only to look at the 20th century's "kitchens of tomorrow" to recognize the abiding relevance of Beecher's designs. Beecher's principles of domestic efficiency, economy, and comfort have been almost universally accepted; her ideas, given architectural expression in her books of 1841 and 1869, are reflected in virtually every split-level, ranch, and colonial built in the United States in the 20th century. No small achievement for a woman who devoutly believed that a woman's place was in the home! ♦

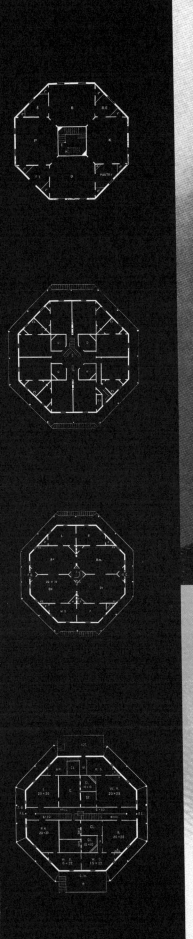

To cheapen and improve human hom
and especially to bring comfortable
ings within the reach of the poorer
is the object of this volume—an obje
the highest practical utility to man.
lineates a new mode of [e]nclosing

Two THE OCTAGON: A HOME FOR ALL

To cheapen and improve human homes, and especially to bring comfortable dwellings within the reach of the poorer classes, is the object of this volume—an object of the highest practical utility to man. It delineates a new mode of [e]nclosing public edifices and private residences, far better, every way, and several hundred per cent cheaper, than any other; and will enable the poor but ingenious man to erect a comfortable dwelling at a trifling cost, and almost without the aid or cost, as now, of mechanics.

Orson Squire Fowler, *A Home for All*, 1848

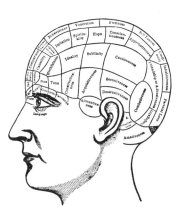

Various emotions and human qualities were assigned to specific portions of the head, as demonstrated by this phrenological head. (O. S. Fowler)

Engraving of Fowler at age 67.

With these opening words of his manual *A Home for All*, Orson Fowler introduced the American public to the mid-19th century's most unusual architectural fad: the octagon house. Fowler's book became an immediate bestseller, with at least seven editions published between 1848 and 1857, inspiring hundreds of families to build octagonal structures from Maine to Oregon. Within 10 years the fad had run its course, a victim of a severe economic panic in which scores of banks closed and a victim, too, of fickle popular taste.

What makes the octagon fad so astonishing is that its promoter was neither a trained architect nor a builder. Orson Fowler was born in 1809 in Cohocton, New York, a small farming community in the western part of the state. He planned to become a minister and enrolled at Amherst College; there he was introduced to the teachings of Johann Kaspar Spurzheim, a Viennese doctor who claimed that character could be analyzed by careful examination of the conformation of the skull. This new "science," dubbed phrenology, captured Fowler's full attention and energies after his graduation from Amherst. Statesmen and criminals, artists and community leaders came under his professional scrutiny. The results of his findings appeared in numerous pamphlets and manuals as well as in the *American Phrenological Journal and Miscellany*, a magazine that Fowler himself published.

Designed by Thomas Jefferson in the first decade of the 19th century, Poplar Forest, near Lynchburg, Virginia, is one of the best-known octagonal structures. (Corporation for Jefferson's Poplar Forest)

By the 1840s Fowler had become a nationally recognized authority on a variety of subjects, including mental well-being, marriage counseling, sex education, and health. It is not surprising that his attentions eventually turned to improving the way his fellow men lived. Fowler, writing in the third person, described his interest quite candidly in *A Home for All*: "Till past forty, his profession engrossed too much of his time and means to allow him to procure a comfortable home; yet for ten years he has been making observations, in all his professional peregrinations, and cogitating by months, upon the best mode of building the home of his future years." Fowler did not hesitate to point out that phrenology remained his primary interest and that he had "turned aside only to build…a good home." He also was quick to point out that he was not a builder by profession and that his manual "may lack occasional details and specifications."

And what did Fowler's observations, peregrinations, and cogitations lead him to discover? The revealing title of his first revised edition, *A Home for All, or The Gravel Wall and Octagon Mode of Building New, Cheap, Convenient, Superior and Adapted to Rich and Poor*, proclaimed his

two primary findings: (1) functionally and stylistically, eight-sided structures were more efficient than those with exterior walls at right angles; and (2) a mixture of readily available materials—coarse sand, gravel, lime, and water—could produce solid, inexpensive, and permanent walls.

Fowler claimed in his preface that "the [octagonal] form, as applied to domestic residences, is WHOLLY ORIGINAL with the author, and the [gravel wall] greatly improved upon…the other principles and suggestions the author has arrived [at] while planning and studying out his own house." In reality, both claims were overstated. While Fowler may have been one of the first to advocate eight-sided structures as dwellings, polygonal buildings were not uncommon in the United States in the early 19th century. Long before Fowler made his architectural pronouncements, numerous barns, garden houses, and churches had been built with six, eight, and even twelve sides. None other than Thomas Jefferson designed octagonal buildings, including Poplar Forest, a Virginia country estate constructed in the first decades of the 19th century. (It should be noted that one of America's most distinguished residences, the Octagon House, designed by William Thornton and built in 1800 in Washington, D.C., is *not* an octagon but a hexagon!)

It is not known where Fowler drew his inspiration for octagonal houses; in his writings he is silent on the subject. What we do know is that, as a lecturer in great demand, Fowler was well traveled and had occasion to see and inspect many buildings; he may have been inspired by the octagonal tollhouses along the National Turnpike in Pennsylvania and Maryland, or by the polygonal schoolhouses in the mid-Atlantic states. Fowler was also well read and may have been familiar with accounts of polygonal structures in ancient Greece and Rome.

The inspiration for gravel-wall construction is more clear-cut. This building technique, perfected by the ancient Romans, had been utilized in a remarkable building in a small Wisconsin town in 1844—nine years before it was written about, with great fanfare, in *A Home for All*. No structure made a greater impression on Fowler than Milton House, built by the entrepreneur Joseph Goodrich to serve as a hostelry for travelers. Milton House was a three-story hexagonal structure, with a two-story attached wing, constructed entirely of concrete. Fowler wrote: "In 1850, near Jaynesville, Wisconsin, I saw houses built wholly of lime, mixed with that coarse gravel and sand found in banks on the western prairies, and underlying all prairie soil. I visited Milton, to examine the house put up by Mr. Goodrich…and found his walls as hard as stone itself, and harder than brick walls." Goodrich was so confident of the superiority of his walls that he permitted Fowler to strike the walls with a sledgehammer as hard as he could "for six cents per blow, which he said would repair all damages."

In *A Home for All* Fowler credited Goodrich as "the original discoverer of this mode of building" and stated emphatically that "he certainly deserves to be immortalized, for the superiority of this plan must certainly revolutionize building, and especially enable poor men to build their own homes."

Fowler's manual was evangelical in tone, yet not without sincerity, humor, and warmth. That the book sold briskly is not surprising: it was full of new ideas, common sense, and good advice. A natural-born promoter and salesman, Fowler truly believed his ideas would revolutionize American domestic architecture and would bring homeownership within reach of all his fellow men. His enthusiasm was contagious—even to readers who did not build their own octagons.

For Fowler the octagon was superior to other shapes because it emulated what was found in nature.

Nature's forms are mostly SPHERICAL. *She makes ten thousand curvilineal to one square figure. Then why not apply her forms to houses? Fruits, eggs, tubers, nuts, grains, seeds, trees, etc., are made spherical, in order to [e]nclose the most material in the least compass. Since, as already shown, a circle incloses more space for its surface, than any other form, of course the nearer spherical our houses, the more inside room for the outside wall, besides being more comfortable.*

Entire pages of *A Home for All* were filled with mathematical calculations intended to prove the superiority of the octagon; one set of calculations was designed to show that the octagon "contains one-fifth more room for its wall."

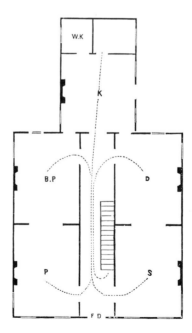

This floor plan of a "Large Double Mansion" from A Home for All *shows the inefficiencies of traditional room configuration.*

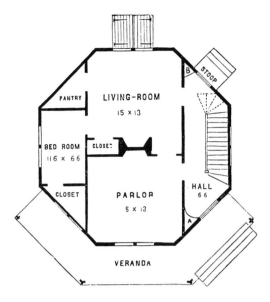

Floor plan of the Brown house from A Home for All.

*e residence of John J.
own, Williamsburgh,
w York, an octagon
use illustrated in
Home for All, was
ical of many built
cording to Fowler's
nciples of design.*

Fowler recognized from the outset that the octagon plan represented a radical departure from traditional practice and, consequently, throughout his text he made frequent comparisons with rectilinear floor plans of the "square, winged and cottage styles." As might be expected, the octagon came out the winner time after time!

In addition to saving construction materials—a fact that would please the head of the household—the octagon had several advantages to please the practical housekeeper. For one, the "superb arrangement of its rooms" made distances dramatically shorter, as Fowler was quick to verify in a series of formulas. The advantage, he asserted, "especially to a weakly woman," is "very great—MORE THAN DOUBLE—in the square, compared with the octagon house." Fowler facetiously commented that he would leave it to housekeepers "to say whether they could not do TWICE THE WORK with the same ease in the octagon."

Another advantage of the octagon, Fowler noted, was the improved ventilation that it provided, "for every human being requires a copious and constant supply of this commodity, so indispensable, not merely to human comfort, but even existence." In reality, most of the rooms in the octagons illustrating *A Home for All* had only one exposure and required access to an adjacent room for cross-ventilation. The construction of a cupola over a central staircase would, according to Fowler, completely "ventilate every large room in every story." To facilitate the delivery of fresh air, Fowler advocated ventilators in every room, both at the ceiling and at the floor; to control the intake of air, he recommended that registers be installed.

The Milton House and Joseph Goodrich

Innkeeper Joseph Goodrich was a practical man. It is said that he selected the site of his establishment by drawing a line on a map connecting Chicago and Madison and another connecting Fort Atkinson and the bend of the Rock River at which Jaynesville was being established. At the intersection of these lines he bought a considerable quantity of land, anticipating—correctly—that it would become a major stopping and transfer place. When Goodrich outgrew his first inn, a one-and-one-half story log cabin erected in 1838, he built a second, much larger structure. The design and construction of the Milton House were purely functional: the six-sided building enabled Goodrich to watch for hostile Indians from all directions. If an attack did occur, the concrete walls protected the building's inhabitants from fire—a frequent form of Indian attack. As late as the 1870s more than 25 stagecoaches made daily stops at the Milton House. In the 1850s the inn served as a haven for escaped slaves on their way from the South to freedom in Canada. The property was placed in the National Register of Historic Places in 1972 and today serves as headquarters for the Milton Historical Society.

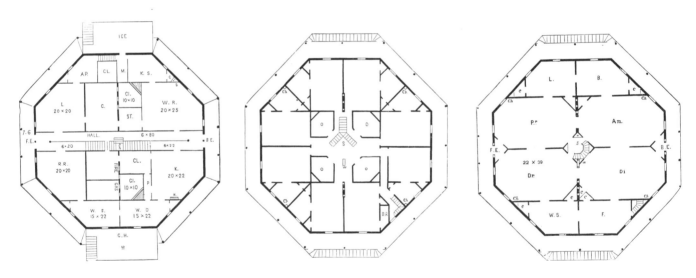

Fowler also asserted that octagonal plans had fewer right-angle corners, a decided advantage over traditional plans because "the corners of a square room are of little account . . . useless for furniture, and rarely occupied for any purpose." Again, Fowler's claim is suspect. A quick review of the octagonal plans shown in *A Home for All* reveals as many oddly shaped corners as in a rectilinear plan, if not more! It is testimony to Fowler's powers of persuasion that a liability is turned into a virtue—complete with mathematical calculations to support his argument.

The odd spaces created by the octagon could, according to Fowler, be made into closets. American houses typically were constructed without closets of any kind; chests of drawers and wardrobes supplied most of the needed storage space. Fowler was one of the first to advocate built-in closets, stating that "no room is really tenantable without one,

Milton House, Jaynesville, Wisconsin, a six-sided structure, utilized "gravel-wall" construction and was much admired by Orson Fowler. (H. Ward Jandl)

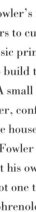

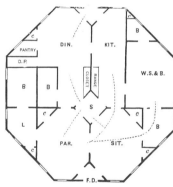

Floor plans of the basement, a parlor story, and upper stories in Fowler's own house from A Home for All, *as well as "The Best Plan Yet" (above).*

Floor plan of a 27-foot octagon from A Home for All.

because you must have very few things at hand, or else they must be under foot, or tossed from chair to chair, and mantlepiece, in one Babel of confusion."

A Home for All contained a variety of octagonal floor plans, from modest workers' houses to the author's own 60-room mansion. Unlike builders' guides of the period, from which builders were expected to copy the published plans exactly, Fowler's manual seemed to encourage readers to customize their designs, keeping basic principles in mind. Readers were told to build the largest house they could afford. "A small house and few rooms must be all clutter, confusion, and helter-skelter; but in a large house things once located can remain." Fowler noted, almost parenthetically, that his own house contained 60 rooms "but not one too many." Each family member, the phrenologist advised, should have his own room. "How much better every body can study, think, do business, any thing, in their *own place*, than in a place not theirs." In addition, Fowler recommended that readers reserve a "greater number of spare rooms for company than is [currently] found," because "hospitality is a heavenly virtue." Also desirable in every good house were a playroom for children, a gymnasium for females, and a dancing room, because "mankind are dying off like diseased sheep, in consequence of pure *ennui*...they want ACTION."

A Home for All contained a remarkable number of ideas that were innovative for the mid-19th century. One of these ideas was central heating; Fowler considered a furnace "by far a better plan for warming a house than separate fireplaces...it is much more effectual, and every way more convenient, less expensive, and easily tended." Not surprisingly, by Fowler's calculation the same amount of heat would go much further in an octagon than in a square.

Because the kitchen is "the stomach of the house," Fowler advocated positioning it in a central location, so that the lady of the house would be "only a step removed from the rest of the family." In a period when the kitchen was generally constructed in a separate building behind the main house, Fowler's suggestion must have seemed radical. In Fowler's own residence, the kitchen was located in the basement, near the washroom and storerooms.

Another of Fowler's requisites for a comfortable and efficient house was an indoor toilet. *A Home for All* was one of the first American manuals to advocate such a convenience. Anticipating some resistance to the idea, Fowler argued that it "need be used only in cases of *special* need," when the reader had an infirm, elderly, or feeble guest or during a cold, rainy night. The recommended location for this convenience was under the stairs.

Fowler also recommended indoor plumbing: "To have plenty of hot and cold water all through the house is a luxury too great to be wanting." Because municipal-supplied water was practically unheard of in small towns, Fowler suggested constructing a cistern at the top of the house, connected by a pipe to the furnace. Detailed instructions on constructing and installing filters were provided in the manual.

Because Fowler believed the most economical house was at least two stories tall, with a full basement, an efficient way of moving through the house vertically was required. The different octagon plans displayed in *A Home for All* show stairs in various parts of the house, but it seems clear that Fowler preferred them to be located at the center of the octagon, where they were equally accessible from all parts of the house and where the stairwell could be used to improve ventilation.

Another means of facilitating vertical movement through the house was the installation of a dumbwaiter, an uncommon feature in houses at the time. Fowler decreed that every two-story house should have one—preferably at the entry. Yet another convenience advocated by Fowler for multistory houses was the speaking tube; this invention, a precursor to the intercom, permitted conversations from floor to floor without having to ascend or descend stairs.

While Fowler had little patience for architectural ornamentation or styles—for him, nature provided the only patterns of true ornament—there were certain architectural features that he believed a comfortable house should possess. One such feature was the cupola already discussed. Another was the veranda, which on moonlit summer evenings was perfect for "either promenading or conversation." Having piazzas all around the house was the ideal, permitting the homeowner to choose sun or shade, breeze or shelter, as comfort dictated.

Just as considerable detail was given to the design and layout of rooms, so was equal attention accorded to the building materials utilized and the methods of construction. Although stacked-board construction was advocated in the first edition of *A Home for All*, concrete later became Fowler's building material of choice. In addition to being inexpensive and readily available, it was permanent in a way that wood (susceptible to fire) and brick (labor-intensive to install and damp in wet weather) were not. Fowler wacknowledged that gravel-wall construction was new and unproven in the United States; he readily admitted that the materials used to construct his own house were too coarse but expressed confidence that his readers would profit from his mistakes. Specifications on mixing gravel, sand, lime, and water were provided, along with locations where the best-quality materials might be found.

More astonishing in a sense than Fowler's recommendation for gravel-wall construction was his suggestion of glass as a roofing and floor material. Clearly Fowler was familiar with the success of Paxton's glass-and-steel Crystal Palace constructed in London in 1851. "Impervious to water, unaffected by extremes of weather, indestructible by time, and exactly adapted to light the house from the roof, why is it not as well adapted to roofing as to windows?" And if glass could be substituted for sheet-metal roofing, perhaps it could also be used for the walls of houses, replacing lath and plaster? So new was the technology of which Fowler wrote that answers to these questions could not be given in the manual; rather, Fowler anticipated that "some ingenious man" would use his suggestions to obtain some practical results "worth a fortune to him and the world."

When the first revised edition of *A Home for All* was published in 1853, Fowler had nearly completed work on his own octagon overlooking the Hudson River, near Fishkill, New York. Fowler himself had supervised the construction, and with the aid of a few assistants had built the necessary scaffolding, hauled in the materials, and poured the gravel walls. Five stories high (including a raised basement and cupola tower), the house contained 60 rooms and became an immediate curiosity in the neighborhood. The basement had a milk room, a laundry, cold cellars, and a kitchen. The main floor included a parlor, a dining room, a library, and a room for the display of minerals, not to mention what Fowler called "amusement rooms." The phrenologist not so modestly noted that "the appearance of [the central] stairway is really magnificent—

Residence of O. S. Fowler from A Home for All.

lighted from a glass dome, 70 feet straight up, cupola included, octagonal in form." The upper floors contained bedrooms and dressing rooms as well as four inner rooms lighted only by glass transoms over the doors. A continuous piazza circled the perimeter of the house at each story. Other innovations were found throughout the house: central heating that kept occupants warm in winter, a ventilating chimney for the summer months, piped gas for interior lighting, hot and cold water provided by a roof tank, a sand-and-charcoal water filter, speaking tubes, and an indoor water closet.

Given Fowler's national reputation as a phrenologist and the radical nature of the design, the Fishkill mansion attracted considerable attention. Visitors to Fowler's home included the journalists Horace Greeley and Charles A. Dana and women's rights activists Amelia Bloomer and Lucretia Mott. *Holden's Dollar Magazine* gave the house a favorable review in its May 1848 edition. *Godey's Lady's Book*, one of the most widely read magazines of the period, offered its readers a glowing account of the massive octagon:

The appearance is noble, massive, grand, and imposing, especially as seen from a distance. Its position, on an eminence in the basin of the Hudson formed by the Highlands, renders it 'the observed of all observers,' from all the regions round about. Its scenery as viewed from the top of the cupola, is surpassingly grand, far-reaching, and picturesque. It has piazzas all around at each story, which make delightful promenades.

It is said that imitation is the sincerest form of flattery. In the years immediately following publication of *A Home for All*, dozens of carpenters' and builders' guides provided plans for octagons. Particularly notable was Samuel Sloan's *The Model Architect*, first published in 1852. Sloan's design for an octagonal "Oriental villa" surmounted by an onion dome became the model for Longwood, commissioned in 1860, one of the grandest of the Mississippi plantation houses.

But perhaps the most flattering proof of Fowler's popularity was that octagonal houses began popping up in towns across the country. Most of them were constructed in New England and in Illinois, Indiana, Michigan, New York, and Wisconsin. In Ohio more than 30 octagonal houses are known to have been constructed. A deaf-mute couple built an elaborate octagon in Geneva, New York, in 1852. A three-story brick octagon was built by John Richards in 1854 in Watertown, Wisconsin. With its central staircase and octagonal cupola, the Watertown house drew direct inspiration from *A Home for All* (and, in turn, inspired Fred Keck's House of Tomorrow, constructed some 75 years later; see Chapter 8). In Yonkers, New York, a man built an octagon so that his crippled wife might get around more easily without the bother of passageways between rooms. Few, if any, of these houses incorporated all the suggestions made by Fowler, but their mere presence indicated both a dissatisfaction with the status quo and a desire to seek alternatives to the conventional American house.

Ironically, Orson Fowler lived in his monumental octagon only a few years. In 1855 Fowler sold his publishing business to his brother-in-law in order to devote additional time to writing. An economic panic in 1857, which led to a series of bank failures, substantially reduced Fowler's financial resources. In September 1857 Fowler moved to Massachusetts and rented his octagonal home, with its 130 acres, to a New York real estate magnate. The house, converted into a boarding house, witnessed a typhoid outbreak shortly thereafter. In 1859 Fowler sold the octagon to his daughter Orsena, who in turn placed it on the market. For a short time during the Civil War the house became a "Cuban Institute and Military Academy"; it subsequently reverted back to being a boarding house. By 1880 Fowler's octagon stood empty and was deteriorating. In 1897 it was condemned by the town of Fishkill as a "public hazard" and was dynamited.

Fowler's interest in octagons diminished in later years, and when he built another house for himself, in Manchester, Massachusetts, in 1877, it was entirely conventional in appearance and construction. On August 18, 1887, Fowler died in Sharon, Connecticut, the victim of spinal trouble induced by a heavy cold. His obituary in the *New York Times* noted that Fowler lectured for years on phrenology and physiology and was "probably the pioneer of American phrenologists." No mention was made of his unique contributions to American architecture. ⚓

Built in 1860, the Armor-Stiner House in Irvington, New York, a spectacular octagon, has recently undergone an extensive renovation. (Thom Loughman, Historic American Buildings Survey)

Richards House,
Watertown, Wisconsin.
(H. Ward Jandl)

Elevation of the Richards House.(Hugo Logemann, E. F. Bernhard, A. F. Keymar,
and W. H. Mitterhausen, Historic American Buildings Survey)

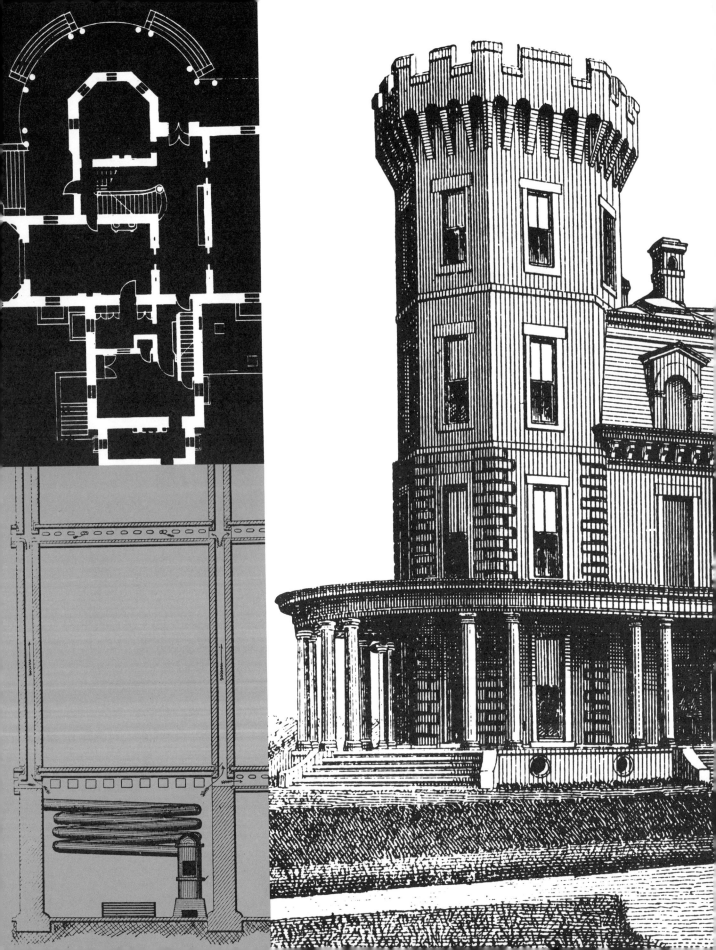

Three WILLIAM WARD'S CONCRETE CASTLE

It is needless to say that Mr. Ward is an enthusiast on Portland cement, but he is one of those whose enthusiasm is guided by sound reasoning and practical science. He has therefore not been led into the vagaries which so often beset those who, having but one idea, neglect important collateral matters while putting it into practice. Any one who visits this house expecting to find a vault-like structure, wherein the one idea of a house made in a solid block is predominant, will be disappointed.

American Architect and Building News, August 18, 1877

Contemporary view of Ward's Castle, which now houses the Museum of Cartoon Art. (H. Ward Jandl)

Woodcut of exterior of Ward's Castle as it appeared in the journal of the American Society of Mechanical Engineers.

In 1871 manufacturer William Evans Ward began planning for what would turn out to be one of the country's most remarkable houses. It was not its architectural style that distinguished Ward's house; the house was designed in the traditional French Second Empire mode by New York architect Robert Mook. It was also not the house's location: a picturesque piece of land in Port Chester, New York, overlooking the Byram River. Rather, what was original and astonishing was the building's method of construction: from basement to attic, from column base to chimney cap, the house was built entirely out of reinforced concrete.

The use of concrete as a building material did not originate with Ward; one of the greatest monuments of classical Rome—the Pantheon—had its walls and dome constructed of concrete in the second century A.D. Ward's concrete house and its method of construction were unique, nonetheless, in several respects. While concrete technology had advanced tremendously in the preceding hundred years in Europe, Ward took this technology one step further by combining concrete and reinforcing iron rods to create a dynamic new building material—one that is today in common use throughout the world. Ward also designed ingenious heating and plumbing systems as integral components of his house. While some of his contemporaries viewed Ward's concrete castle as a folly, its innovations were to have a profound impact on architectural construction.

Ward was born in frontier Indiana in 1821 to parents who were members of the Society of Friends. After moving east with his family at an early age, Ward trained in Philadelphia as a machinist, then moved to New York in 1844. While working in New York City, Ward met Ellwood Burdsall and Isaac Russell. Pooling their resources, the three men formed the Union Screw Company and set up headquarters at a small factory located on the Byram River at Pemberwick, Connecticut. The factory produced wood screws, which were made with machines that Ward designed and built. When another firm obtained a patent preventing Ward's machine from being used further, Ward and his partners began to manufacture and market threaded stove bolts and rods, again employing machinery designed and built by Ward.

Ward's inventions soon made the business profitable and the company's product line was expanded to include bolts for plows, carriages, and various machines. By 1858 Russell, Burdsall, and Ward, as the company was then known, employed almost 100 men.

As the business prospered, Ward began to buy land in the vicinity of his factory, from the Byram River in Connecticut to King Street in New York's Westchester County. Like many manufacturers of the period, Ward chose to reside close to his business; for many years he

lived in a small wood-frame house in Pemberwick, a few hundred feet from the factory.

What prompted Ward's decision to build a larger house for his wife and two children is not certain, but in the circumstances it seems reasonable to speculate that the decision may well have related to his growing interest in fire-resistant construction and a desire to experiment with the unique combustion-proof properties of concrete.

Concrete gates, which no longer exist, announced the entrance to the castle and appeared in a 1909 issue of Architectural Record.

Although active in the management of his company, Ward was nonetheless able to devote considerable time to study and research. He was active in the formation of the American Society of Mechanical Engineers and was one of its charter members; he was also a member of the American Society for the Advancement of Science.

In 1883, writing in *Transactions of the American Society of Mechanical Engineers* about his experiments with concrete, Ward noted that "while other departments of industry have received the benefits of improvement, the continuous and persistent use of combustible material for exposed portions of buildings has limited the intrinsic elements of the art of building construction, and confined improvements only to matters of design." Ward recognized that wood-frame construction had predominated in America because, as a building material, wood was in plentiful supply, was easily worked, and was inexpensive. But he was convinced that if a substitute for wood-frame construction could be developed, one that was cost-effective and fireproof, the public would favor the substi-

tute. Accordingly, in 1871 and 1872 Ward set out to "make some experiments in a new and special direction, for the purpose of ascertaining whether a practically fire-proof building could be designed and constructed at a comparatively moderate cost."

The use of concrete as a building material had been described in numerous architectural and scientific journals and books dating as far back as the Renaissance, yet its very real limitations made it an impractical alternative for ordinary construction. Concrete by itself can work only in compression, and it was rightfully considered unacceptable for structural members subject to high bending, such as beams and floor slabs. Because it required on-the-job mixing, concrete was seen as a utilitarian material at best—inaccurate and gross and ill-suited to residential use. And as long as traditional, less expensive building materials were still plentiful, concrete was not seriously considered as a viable alternative.

A number of significant improvements to the manufacture of concrete in the first half of the 19th century rekindled interest in the material. The first processes for making artificial hydraulic cement are generally attributed to James Frost of England and to L. J. Vicat of France. Frost was issued a

Types of Concrete

Unreinforced concrete is a composite material containing aggregates (sand, gravel, crushed shell, or rock) held together by a cement combined with water to form a paste, and gets its name from the fact that it does not have any iron or steel reinforcing bars. It was the earliest form of concrete. The ingredients become a plastic mass that hardens as the concrete hydrates, or "cures." Unreinforced concrete is relatively weak, however, and since the turn of the century has largely been replaced by reinforced concrete.

Reinforced concrete is concrete strengthened by the inclusion of metal bars, which increase the tensile strength of concrete. Both unreinforced and reinforced concrete can be either cast in place or precast.

Cast-in-place concrete is poured on-site into a previously erected formwork that is removed after the concrete has set.

Precast concrete is molded off-site into building components.

More recent developments in concrete technology include *post-tensioned concrete* and *pre-stressed concrete*, which feature greater strength and reduced cracking in reinforced structural elements.

William B. Coney, *Preservation of Historic Concrete: Problems and General Approaches*, 1987

patent for "British cement" and for a construction method for fireproof floors made of concrete arches between iron beams. In 1824 Joseph Aspdin of Leeds, England, patented his "Portland Cement," which was noticeably harder and stronger than other cements; Aspdin's patent identified the material as a stucco for exterior application, to be modeled and tooled to imitate limestone construction. It was not until 1871, however, with the opening of a mill in Coplay, Pennsylvania, that the artificial cement industry was established in the United States. Despite this event, most portland cement in the U.S., including that used for Ward's Castle, was imported from England until the turn of the century.

With his interest in concrete as a building material, Ward may well have been aware of early American examples of concrete construction, including a poured-in-place concrete building erected in Manhattan in 1835 and a Gothic Revival house in Staten Island built of concrete blocks in 1837. Ward, who read

widely, must also have known of European advances in concrete technology, particularly of experiments by Wilkinson, Gillmore, Coignet, Monier, Hyatt, and others with iron-reinforcing members. Nonetheless, in Ward's account of his own experiments in Port Chester no direct mention is made of his predecessors' work. Instead, Ward wrote: "The incident which led the writer to the invention of iron with beton [concrete] occurred in England in 1867, when his attention was called to the difficulties of some laborers on a quay trying to remove cement from their tools. The adhesion of the cement to the iron was so firm that the cleavage generally appeared in the cement rather than between the cement and the iron."

Ward's early experiments in 1871 and 1872 focused exclusively on working up the reciprocal value of beton, in combination with iron, in the construction of beams designed to support floors and roofs made of the same material. He rightfully concluded that the utility of both iron and beton could be greatly increased through a properly adjusted combination of their special physical qualities, rather than the exclusive use of either material separately.

Satisfied that concrete reinforced with iron was the best material for a fireproof residence, in 1873 Ward hired New York architect Robert Mook to draw up plans for a large, comfortable, and stylish home. Mook, born in New York City in 1830, had received his training in the architectural firm of Thomas and Son, and had begun his own practice in 1856. He designed many buildings in the New York area between 1860 and 1880, including "Marble Row," an imposing series of houses along Fifth Avenue, and the Aetna Life Insurance Building in Hartford, Connecticut. Mook favored the Italianate and French Second Empire styles and was considered a fashionable, although not particularly imaginative, architect.

According to a detailed account of the house published in the May 1909 issue of *Architectural Record*, William Ward instructed Mook to design the building "with walls such as would be required if they were of brick with a hollow space, and floors of the usual thickness required for construction with timber. In other words, Ward commissioned a conventional structure, one that by its design did not reflect or exploit the unique properties of concrete. Although some architectural elements were simplified to permit them to be poured in place, Mook's finished design borrowed heavily from styles popular during the period. Mook apparently designed the interior details as well.

The castle's music and dining rooms, as pictured in Architectural Record *in 1909, both included coffered ceilings.*

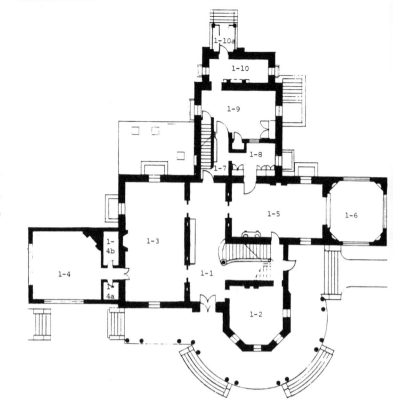

The first-floor plan shows the sweeping semicircular veranda. Later additions, constructed in the 1920s, greatly expanded the living area. (The Ehrenkrantz Group, with permission from the Museum of Cartoon Art)

On a hill, set back from the road, Ward's Castle is approached through an imposing concrete gate. The exterior of the house is dominated by a four-story octagonal tower with parapet and machicolations on the southeast corner. A large veranda supported by Doric columns extends around the base of this tower. A smaller, three-story square tower, housing water storage tanks, is attached to the north elevation. The main block of the house is capped with a mansard roof with classically inspired dormers and a modillion cornice. Walls are punctuated by numerous large windows, simply framed; corners of the exterior walls are distinguished by heavy quoins. A two-story service wing is attached on the north elevation between the main house and the square tower.

On the interior, the original first floor comprises a large central hall, a drawing room, a reception room, and a dining room (a breakfast room and sun room were added in the 20th century). The second story has three bedrooms, a large central hall, and an Elizabethan library with elaborate period woodwork. The third story, under the mansard roof, contains three more bedrooms, a central hall, and storage rooms.

With Mook's finished drawings in hand, Ward began construction in 1875, utilizing his own unskilled employees and the services of

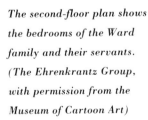

The second-floor plan shows the bedrooms of the Ward family and their servants. (The Ehrenkrantz Group, with permission from the Museum of Cartoon Art)

The third-floor plan includes an octagonal observation tower. From this room is a sweeping view of the countryside. (The Ehrenkrantz Group, with permission from the Museum of Cartoon Art)

the village carpenter. Ward supervised all aspects of the project, serving as his own general contractor and construction supervisor. Before the house was completed two years later, 4,000 barrels of English portland cement; 8,000 barrels of sand found on the property; 12,000 barrels of crushed, hard blue limestone; and an equal amount of white beach pebbles were consumed in construction.

William Ward appears to have been a cautious man; all aspects of the construction were thoroughly tested in advance, from the ingredients of the concrete to the size and placement of the iron-reinforcing beams. Ward's attention to detail is evident in his account of the house's construction, presented before the American Society of Mechanical Engineers in 1883, in which he described how he tested the strength and reliability of I-beams embedded in concrete. Through his experimentation, Ward determined that the iron members in the beams and floors should be near the bottom so as to act in tension to resist loads, while the upper portions of solid concrete would act in compression. In one test, Ward placed a load of 26 to 30 tons over the floor beams and left it there all winter to determine the deflection; it turned out to be negligible.

All foundation walls and heavy structural walls were poured in place into wooden forms, which were designed by Ward and built by his employees. The foundations were approximately 32 inches thick and the load-bearing walls 24 inches thick (interior partition walls were thinner). The concrete was poured in courses, or lifts, about two feet high, carefully tamped down, and allowed to set before the forms were raised another two feet for the next course. Vertical flues were molded in the walls as part of Ward's unique heating system. The position of the water and gas pipes was also planned in advance, permitting the equipment to be built into the concrete.

When the walls reached the appropriate height, beams to support the next floor were poured in place using plank molds. For the parlor, for example, a seven-inch-deep I-beam spanning 19 feet was placed on a one-inch cover of concrete. The rest of the mold was then slowly and carefully filled and tamped down, until the iron beam was buried within the concrete. The ends of the beam were supported on notched sills cast in the side walls. When the beams were strong enough to accept floor slabs, heavy plank centerings were placed in position between the beams and walls, with each plank's upper surface flush with the beam's upper surface. The flat planks acted as the bottom formwork for the

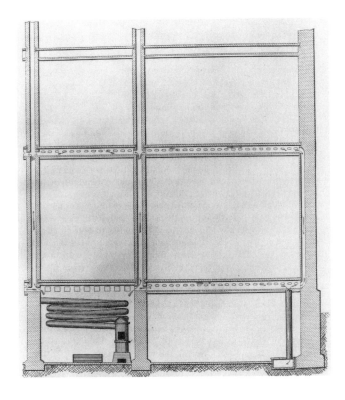

floor. Concrete was then poured over both planks and beams to a depth of about one inch. A course of ⅜-inch iron rods was laid on this concrete, and another inch of concrete was poured, deep enough to embed the rods. Upon this layer of concrete a second course of iron rods was then laid, crossing those in the first course. Another layer of concrete was poured. In this way a floor was constructed. When all the concrete had hardened, the planks were removed.

A second floor was built above the first utilizing the identical technique. The spaces left between the two floors served as heating flues; they connected with the hollow spaces in the walls and with the furnace.

In the cellar Ward constructed a heating chamber with a cast-iron furnace. Openings approximately a foot apart were made all around the top of the chamber walls; these openings led outward to the spaces between the cellar ceiling and the first floor and also up through the flues within the interior walls. Heat from the furnace rose through these spaces to warm the house—all 55,000 cubic feet of it. Ward reported that "with ordinary care, a temperature of sixty-eight degrees can be uniformly maintained on the first floor,

and from sixty to sixty-two degrees on the second floor, with a consumption of about three hundred and twenty-five pounds of anthracite coal per day in the furnace."

Another unique feature of the castle was the water supply. Roof water ran down to the basement through cast-iron pipes embedded in the walls and was then sent up again through a pipe into a holding tank in the house's square rear tower. The tank's capacity was 5,000 gallons. Ward also installed a system for spring water. This water, pumped by windmill into a 3,000-gallon holding tank in the rear tower, was piped into the bathrooms and kitchen.

Once the entire concrete structure was in place, it was finished with traditional materials according to the style of the day. Ornamental plaster was applied directly to the concrete walls and ceilings, wood doors and trim were installed, and the stairway was adorned with a newel post of Mexican onyx and other marbles. All rooms were carpeted, using nails that were pounded into brass sockets set in the concrete floors.

The completed house garnered considerable publicity in the fledgling American architec-

Parlor ceiling and chandelier.
(National Register of Historic Places,
National Park Service)

tural press. Articles appeared in *American Architect and Building News* in 1876 and 1877. The first article reported that the building had "several interesting features; among them a balcony weighing nearly four tons, and projecting four feet from the face of the building." The second article contained a much longer description praising all aspects of the house's design and construction:

Any one who visits this house…will see floors resembling single sheets of rubbed sandstone, hard-finished white walls, flat panelled ceilings moulded and enriched with moderation, and plaster cornices of good section and very tasteful ornamentation, while all the woodwork he sees or can find in the whole house is the necessary door and window finish in superb hard wood, of workmanship that would put to shame some of our best mechanics….

Considered as a whole, the house is a scientific success and should be an object of interest and study with every architect. As such it will well repay any one who goes out of his way to see it; and your correspondent feels that though it is a private residence, any member of the profession who takes an interest in fire-proof construction will be… cordially received….

The most extensive description of the house was provided by William Ward himself in his address to his fellow members of the American Society of Mechanical Engineers in 1883. Although the house allegedly cost Ward $100,000 to build—an enormous sum in those days—he championed the use of concrete as a cost-effective, fireproof building material:

The bulk of the material required for the work abounds in inexhaustible quantities, and is always obtainable at moderate cost. The essential skill required consists in a simple knowledge of the right proportions of the material, and of its proper manipulation, both of which can be acquired in a half-day's practice. The most inexperienced laborers can do all the work of the most elaborate beton construction, excepting only the surface finishing, and this, with all the other work, can be superintended by one competent, experienced builder.

Ward recognized that reinforced concrete houses were not going to sprout over the landscape as a result of his experiments. "Such radical departures from conservative ideas of building," he wrote, "must necessarily find a slow recognition and reach public favor like any other innovation—through small and gradual beginnings—and wait until their merits grow to be regarded as a public necessity." Indeed, reinforced concrete was slow in achieving widespread acceptance as a building material, particularly for houses. Not until the invention of a horizontal rotary kiln at the turn of the century was it actually possible to produce a cheap, reliable concrete. Grosvenor Atterbury, Thomas Edison, and others who experimented with construction technologies that utilized reinforced concrete (see Chapter 4) garnered favorable media attention yet produced few houses. Today reinforced concrete is widely used in construction in the United States, but it is limited primarily to commercial, rather than residential, structures.

Although not widely imitated, Ward's Castle was innovative in a number of respects. It proved that reinforced concrete could be a suitable building material for residential buildings, without the sacrifice of traditional architectural forms and details; it also stressed the importance of fireproofconstruction and radiant heating.

Deteriorated concrete under porch. (H. Ward Jandl)

After William E. Ward's death in 1900, his son William moved into the castle. The younger Ward, a New York politician of some note, made several changes to the house, including the addition of a breakfast room and a sun room. William E. Ward's granddaughters, Winifred and Dorothy, occupied the house until 1972, and for the following two years a family servant remained in the house. Between 1974 and 1977 the building was vacant. During this time deterioration of the exterior cement stucco and of the wooden window frames progressed unimpeded. The plumbing system developed leaks that damaged the interior plasterwork. Some vandalism also occurred.

In August 1977 the Museum of Cartoon Art bought Ward's Castle for use as its headquarters. Under the museum's direction, much of the damage that the building sustained during the three-year period of neglect was repaired, and some interior restoration was undertaken. The museum hired consultants to prepare an in-depth report on the history and current condition of the structure. This report, completed in 1981, remains the single best source of information about the castle.

Although the building's use has changed dramatically—pictures of Beetle Bailey, Bugs Bunny, and Batman now hang in the bedrooms—the integrity of the structure remains intact. In 1976 Ward's Castle was listed in the National Register of Historic Places. The American Society of Civil Engineers and the American Concrete Institute designated the structure a National Historic Civil and Concrete Engineering Landmark in 1978. While the current owners are respectful of the castle's unique place in the history of construction technology, the building's future is clouded; early in 1991 the Museum of Cartoon Art placed Ward's Castle on the market. ⬓

Four THOMAS EDISON'S POURED-CONCRETE HOUSES

Even though Thomas Edison has left his mark upon more different developments of the world's progress than perhaps any other living scientist, and is now past the age at which the majority are most productive, he is now giving most of his time to an invention which he himself considers the greatest thing he has ever done.... The ultimate object of the present invention is no less than the provision of a means whereby individual workingmen's homes—artistic, comfortable, sanitary, and not monotonously uniform—may be turned out in such quantity and so cheaply that their rent, including car fare to and from the tenant's work, will not exceed, say, nine dollars a month. Mr. Edison hopes thereby to depopulate the swarming tenements of congested cities, and provide their occupants with surroundings morally, mentally, and physically more healthful.

Scientific American, **August 28, 1909**

Thomas Edison, inventor.
(Edison Archives,
National Park Service)

By 1900 Thomas Alva Edison was America's best-known inventor, with a score of discoveries already to his credit, including such diverse products as the incandescent electric light bulb, the phonograph, gummed paper tape, the 110-volt electric motor, paraffin paper, the microphone, the electric railway, the motion picture camera, and the fluoroscope. Not satisfied to rest on such distinguished laurels, Edison continued to seek out new projects and to undertake new ventures. His decision to go into the business of cement houses surprised no one who knew him. It stemmed in part from an intense philanthropic desire to improve the housing conditions of his fellow men, but it also grew from an equally strong faith in new technologies to solve societal problems. His product—a poured-concrete house that could be constructed quickly and sold cheaply—turned out to be an engineering tour de force that attracted national and international attention.

After 80 years of experimentation, portland cement was by the turn of the century beginning to be accepted as a legitimate building material. The growing scarcity of wood, the increasing cost of masonry, and ever-present concerns about fire safety combined to make cement an attractive construction alternative. Edison had been a vocal supporter of concrete for many years, concluding that "wood will rot, stone will chip and crumble, bricks disintegrate, but a cement and iron structure is apparently indestructible."[1] Part of Edison's interest was personal: he had encountered difficulty obtaining fire insurance for some of his wooden factories in West Orange, New Jersey. Fireproof cement construction could mean lower insurance rates.

Before Edison entered the cement business, the American output of cement was placed at approximately 21,000,000 barrels per year, valued at more than $17,000,000. The inventor recognized that breaking into an already well-established industry would be an uphill battle; but as he had done in the past when beginning new ventures, Edison immersed himself in existing literature on cement manufacture. He quickly discovered that the basic processes for making cement—crushing, drying, mixing, roasting, and grinding raw materials—had been perfected and that, to be successful, his efforts might best be directed toward improving the equipment used in manufacturing cement.

Leaving the financial arrangements up to a colleague named Mallory, Edison took on the task of designing his own cement factory. This prodigious feat, reported to have been completed in one day, is described in some detail in an early biography:

Edison…invited Mr. Mallory to go with him to one of the draughting rooms on an upper floor of the laboratory. Here he placed a large sheet of paper on a draughting-table, and immediately began to draw out a plan of the proposed works, continuing all day and away into the evening, when he finished; thus completing within the twenty-four hours the full lay-out of the entire plant as it was subsequently installed, and as it has substantially remained in practical use to this time…. In that one day's planning every part was considered and provided for, from the crusher to the packing-house. From one end to the other, the distance over which the plant stretches in length is about half a mile, and through the various buildings spread over this space there passes, automatically, in course of treatment, a vast quantity of material resulting in the production of upward of two and a quarter million pounds of finished cement every twenty-four hours, seven days a week.[2]

Edison's West Orange Laboratory

Thomas Alva Edison began the fullest phase of his career when, at the age of 40, he moved his headquarters from Menlo Park to a laboratory in West Orange, New Jersey. The new building, constructed in 1887, was three stories high and 250 feet long; it housed machine shops, an engine room, glass-blowing and pumping rooms, chemical and photographic departments, rooms for electrical testing, stockrooms, and a library with 10,000 volumes. Four one-story laboratories were set at right angles to the main building. The West Orange facility became the site of Edison's experiments with poured-concrete construction. Remaining in operation until Edison's death in 1931, the laboratory is considered a prototype for today's private research and development laboratories that link business and technology. It is the centerpiece of the Edison National Historic Site, managed by the National Park Service.

By 1902 Edison's plant was operational, with specially engineered kilns 150 feet long and 9 feet wide, instead of the normal 60 by 6. Edison-designed equipment installed in the plant produced a cement more finely ground than the contemporaneous standard. The plant's high-quality cement found a willing market, and by 1907 the new company had grown to be the country's fifth largest producer. In that same five-year period, American production of cement had increased by more than 100 percent to 49 million barrels annually.

Eager to expand the market for concrete, Edison decided to take on the housing industry. Americans had by this time accepted the use of concrete in industrial and commercial buildings, but more traditional materials continued to be preferred in domestic architecture. Edison's interest in promoting concrete for residential purposes went beyond personal financial reward. Like many in the country, he was aware of the horrors of tenement living—families crowded into "two or three small rooms with poor light, poor air, poor sanitation, accompanied with appalling fire risks and generally unattractive and demoralizing surroundings."[3] Edison calculated that a decent concrete house of six rooms would cost only $300.

Edison's concept for a concrete house was deceptively simple: each individual house was to be created from interlocking cast-iron molds that could be used time and time again. Unlike concrete-block houses that utilized traditional, labor-intensive construction techniques or concrete houses created with a series of throwaway wooden molds, one of Edison's houses could be produced in just four days. Concrete would be poured into a set of interlocking molds fastened together from top to bottom; when the concrete had hardened sufficiently, the molds would be removed, revealing a structurally sound, fully detailed residence. Reusable molds would have the added advantage of conserving natural resources and preventing the depletion of the country's forest reserves, a concern then beginning to be discussed by naturalists.

Word of Edison's proposal for poured-concrete houses hit the popular press in early 1906. The promise of an inexpensive, mass-produced house, combined with the magic of the Edison name, led to literally hundreds of feature articles in such newspapers as the *Houston Chronicle*, the *Los Angeles Record*, and the *New York Times*. Most accounts were enthusiastic, marveling at the technology involved and praising Edison's altruistic spirit. Some, however, contained a healthy dose of skepticism. The *Boston Globe*, in its August 4, 1906, edition, noted, "Mr. Edison says that he is going to make it possible to build a $25,000 house for $500 by simply forcing concrete into molds. Many people hope, however, that he will give us that $500 automobile first."

To respond to the thousands of inquiries from across the United States and abroad

Edison's first design for a poured-concrete house appeared in Scientific American *in 1907.*

that flooded the Edison laboratories, a circular was printed in 1907 that described the basic advantages of the concrete house. In this circular Edison proclaimed: "I think the age of concrete has started and I believe I can prove that the most beautiful houses that our architects can conceive, can be cast in one operation in iron forms at a cost, by which comparison with present methods, will be surprising. Then even the poorest man among us will be enabled to own a home of his own—a home that will last for centuries with no cost for insurance or repairs, and be as exchangeable for other property as a United States Bond."

Edison's proposal was given its most serious scrutiny in the November 16, 1907, issue of *Scientific American*. When asked by a reporter what was innovative about his proposal, Edison admitted that "there is nothing particularly novel about my plan; it amounts to the same thing as making a very complicated casting in iron, except that the medium is not so fluid…. Someone was bound to do it, and I thought that I might as well be the man, that's all." In reality, there were others experimenting with mass-produced concrete houses at the same time. The architect William Ransome devised his own version of a poured-concrete house; another architect, Grosvenor Atterbury, developed a system of precast concrete panels that could be assembled on-site. It was Edison's scheme, however, that commanded the greatest attention.

Lauding Edison's system as opening "tremendous additional possibilities for the use of concrete," the *Scientific American* article provided the following description of the house:

The method consists in the use of molds, costing $25,000 the set, made of ¾-inch cast iron, planed, nickel-plated, and polished. The different pieces vary in size, some of the interior parts being but two feet square. When in position, the units are held in place by trusses and dowel pins. Into the top of these molds concrete is pumped continuously by compressed air, using two cylinders. The concrete itself acts as a piston, and the two cylinders are alternately filled and emptied. The delivery of the mixture must be continuous, for wherever it is stopped a line appears. To secure this rapid and continuous flow, at the rate of 175 cubic yards per day, a very efficient mixer is required. It has not yet been decided whether a Ransome or a specially designed machine will be used. No rubbing up is necessary, although a few flaws may be present, owing to the difficulty of expelling all air. The escape of air is permitted by the special design of the house, or, when necessary, by a temporary pipe, which may be removed later.

The concrete used is mixed according to the ordinary proportions of one part of cement high in lime, three parts of sand, and five parts of crushed stone. The cement is so finely ground that it readily takes up the requisite quantity of water to make it flow. Another result of the fine grinding, to which the possibility of reproducing minute details is due, is the absolute watertightness of this material, since there are none of the intergranular openings that are present when coarse ingredients are used. Great strength is assured at the points of stress by wire reinforcements set in the body of material.

Bath-tubs and similar fixtures will be cast in place. Pipes for the steam heat, conduits for the electric wiring, and the iron tubing through which the lead pipes for the plumbing are to be afterward drawn, are all set in the molds before the cement is run in. The only wood present will be the doors, window sashes, and perhaps a few strips to which to attach carpets.

Edison was eager to dispel the public perception of concrete as a coarse and unattractive material. To sell his idea, Edison's model house had to be more than a concrete box with holes punched in it for windows and doors. The inventor turned to the New York architectural firm of Horace B. Mann and Perry R. MacNeille to develop the house design. Mann and MacNeille produced a set of drawings for an elegant two-and-a-half-story residence in the French Renaissance Revival style. The traditional appearance of the house belied its radical construction, but that seems to have been Edison's intent. An extremely contemporary design might have put off potential customers.

Hardly a basic workingman's house, the structure was intended for two families and contained nine spacious rooms and a full basement. The house's exterior was dominated by a rounded bay with a conical top; walls were covered with relief ornamentation in the Francis I style. Elaborate chimneys and an imitation tile roof completed the design. Although no illustrations of the interior were provided, the *Scientific American* article promised that "the interior will be handsomely ornamented, making no further decoration work necessary after the molds are removed." Also noted was the energy-efficient nature of a poured concrete house; owing to the "perfect insulation" of a 12-inch-thick wall on the first floor and an eight-inch wall on the second, it was estimated that heating costs could be cut by as much as 75 percent. Floors and interior walls were to be four inches thick.

From the outset Edison recognized that his proposed system would not be cost-effective unless his houses could be mass-produced

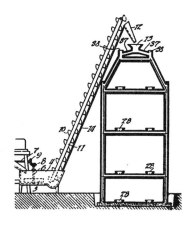

Patent drawing for Edison's proposed method of cast-in-place construction. (Bruce and Sandbank, A History of Prefabrication)

and constructed near each other. The high initial cost of the molds, combined with the necessity of special cranes to erect the molds, and the requirement of concrete mixers on-site to ensure a uniform mixture, made single-house construction impractical.

It was not until more than a year later, on December 22, 1908, that a patent (No. 1,123,361) was granted for the Edison poured-concrete house. By this time the inventor had worked out the logistics for erecting the cast-iron molds and pouring the concrete; he had also modified his original designs in response to further experimen-tation. Although the popular press had generally been kind to Edison's invention, *Scientific American*, which followed the inventor's progress closely, noted in its August 28, 1909, issue that "rumors...have been in the air for some time, and have been received with more or less incredulity or derision by the technical press."

The cast-iron molds, which were estimated to weigh between 250,000 and 450,000 pounds, presented a considerable challenge. It was suggested that the molds be moved "by railroad or team" to the building site. To assemble and disassemble the molds on-site, Edison proposed the use of four small,

"The Result of the Last Test Made by Thomas A. Edison to determine the flow of concrete in the forms for his proposed concrete house" from Scientific American *in 1908.*

electrically driven derricks. To maintain a continuous supply of concrete, plans called for installing at the site three or four large mechanical mixers arranged to discharge into a storage hopper, from which the concrete could be conveyed by bucket elevator to the distributing hopper at the top of the house. A specific-gravity device attached to the storage hopper was to make certain that the consistency of the concrete remained uniform. A system of power-driven plungers located at the top of the molds would keep the concrete agitated to prevent the segregation of materials, to expel excess air, to "secure a perfectly uniform face," and to assist in forcing the concrete throughout the horizontal molds.

Reinforcing rods for the floors and roof were to be placed inside the molds before the concrete was poured; the rods would be held in place by wires or spacers. Pipes for gas and all plumbing, as well as ductwork for electrical wiring, were to be inserted at the same time. (Edison later decided to put most of the pipes on the exterior of the house.)

At Edison's West Orange laboratories, experiments were undertaken to determine the flow of concrete within the molds. Of concern to the inventor was whether the concrete could flow down vertical molds, across horizontally, and then up vertically on the opposite side. Edison devised a special additive for his concrete—a gluelike colloidal substance—to facilitate a uniform flow. These tests proved successful and were duly noted in *Scientific American.*

Edison also experimented with coating products to apply to the concrete; one such product was a specially prepared paint that would "penetrate and mechanically combine with the concrete."[4] As an alternative, Edison suggested tinting the concrete to provide variation in color from house to house.

The original design for the poured-concrete house was a casualty of the 1908 experimentation. Indeed, *Scientific American* had noted in one of its early accounts—April 18, 1908—that the Mann and MacNeille design "seems poorly adapted to concrete construction, owing to the irregularity of outline and amount of detail attempted." The article went on to suggest, however, that "this is a matter of judgment and taste, and, of course, could be modified at will." Edison apparently agreed, and he asked draftsmen and mechanics on his own staff to help draw up new plans.

In place of the grandiose two-family house, a more compact, two-story structure was conceived, clearly intended for a single working-class family. Boxy in shape, the house featured a wide porch across the front and was capped with a hipped roof. The most distinctive element of the exterior was the oversized, paired brackets that flared out under the eaves. The basic floor plan was 25 by 30 feet, with a spacious living room and kitchen on the first floor and two bedrooms and a bathroom on the second floor. A large attic accommodated two additional rooms, and a full basement housed the boiler, laundry tubs, and coal bins. As in the earlier design, interior walls needed no plaster finish thanks to the fineness of the concrete.

Second model of an Edison-designed concrete house, c. 1912. (Edison Archives, National Park Service)

At Edison's direction, the system of molds was modified to permit endless variations in the basic plan. In its August 28, 1909, issue *Scientific American* noted this flexibility:

The completed "form" for a single house may require as many as five hundred different sectional molds of cast iron bolted together, but the latter are so designed that a dozen houses in a row may be built on the same cellar plan, the first floor molds being disposable in several different ways, and the second floor molds likewise, so that no two houses of the dozen need to be alike, thus avoiding monotonous uniformity of appearance.

Edison estimated that molds could be assembled in four days, with only six hours needed to pour the concrete. Another six days were required for setting, and removing the molds would take a construction team four

Model of an Edison-designed concrete house, 1911. (Edison Archives, National Park Service)

days. A complete set of molds would, therefore, be occupied for 14 days in the building of one house. Edison projected that with six complete sets of molds, up to 144 houses could be produced annually. Increased production would help amortize the initial expense of the molds and lower the cost of individual houses to $1,200—a figure four times higher than his initial calculations.

Given Edison's varied interests, it is not surprising that he was frequently sidetracked from his work on the poured-concrete houses and that serious project delays ensued. In a letter in 1912 Edison wrote:

It was my intention to have gotten this enterprise started some time ago, and I had a corps of engineers, draftsmen and mechanics at work for over two years preparing the drawings, patterns and molds for this first type of house. As the work was approaching completion, other important matters arose in connection with my phonograph, storage battery and motion picture enterprises. These being active enterprises, which must be kept going, and the poured house not yet having reached its commercial stage, the choice naturally lay in favor of my active interests.[5]

Two men who had worked on the project, Heinrich Johann Harms and George E. Small, left Edison's employ under mysterious circumstances and subsequently turned up in Holland, where they claimed that they were the inventors of a system of poured-concrete houses. Unbeknownst to Edison, the two men succeeded in obtaining patents in Holland and France for the system, and, with the Dutch architect H. P. Berlage, they proceeded in May 1911 to build a "molded" house in Sandpoort, Holland. The project received wide attention in the European press.

Steps were taken by the Edison laboratory to stop Harms and Small and to have their European patents declared invalid. "These men," wrote one of Edison's attorneys, "were engaged merely as draftsmen to work under Mr. Edison's instructions... [They] had nothing to do with inventing any part of the system, and were merely employees acting under Mr. Edison's directions entirely.... After a while Mr. Edison became convinced that there were some irregularities in their behavior, and he discharged them."[6] The threat of legal action seems to have been successful in deterring the "two unprincipled men who have appropriated [Edison's] invention and claimed it as their own." Still, this episode shows the intensity of interest in Edison's invention.

Since his initial announcement in 1906 that poured-concrete houses would soon be a reality, Edison had received letters from all over the world inquiring when plans would be available. Edison would read these letters and scrawl on them instructions to his secretaries: "Send

The Lambie Concrete House Corporation built this poured-concrete house in Montclair, New Jersey. (H. Ward Jandl)

[1907] booklet. Say not ready yet to talk biz." Meanwhile work on designing and constructing the molds continued at a snail's pace. Experimental pourings into a few of the molds were made in the yards adjacent to the Edison

factories, and the inventor reported that "the results have been highly satisfactory and promise well for the ultimate production of complete structures in accordance with my ideas."[7]

It was not until 1912 that the first houses utilizing at least some of Edison's ideas were erected in the United States. These houses were built by Frank D. Lambie, a neighbor of Edison's who for five years had been closely following the inventor's experiments. Apparently with Edison's blessing, Lambie's Steel Form Company, based in New York City, erected two structures in Montclair, New Jersey, pouring the houses not in a single mold, as specified by Edison, but one complete story at a time using steel molds. Both houses were substantial in size and appearance. Although both houses survive, one of them has been greatly altered. The intact house is two stories in height, with a decorative cornice and a parapet hiding a pitched roof; a projecting center porch and corner pilasters relieve the flatness of the facade. Interior rooms are spacious, with a large living room, a dining room, and a kitchen on the first floor, and four bedrooms and a bathroom on the second.

The success of these houses prompted Lambie to expand his base of operations. Plans were filed in 1914 in Springfield, Massachusetts, to construct 50 poured-concrete cottages with mansard roofs; it is uncertain, however, whether these houses were actually constructed. In 1916 Lambie reported constructing houses "one complete story at one cast" for the American Steel and Wire Company in Donora, Pennsylvania. General Motors and a housing company in Bridgeport, Connecticut, also approached Lambie about potential projects.

This monolithic concrete housing development was built by the Lambie Concrete House Corporation for American Steel and Wire Company in Donora, Pennsylvania. (Edison Archives, National Park Service)

Other enterprising businessmen adapted the poured-concrete-and-reusable-steel-mold technology, using Edison-built molds but devising their own designs. A May 5, 1914, article in the *Hartford Post* announced that Austin C. Dunham, president of the Hartford Electric Light Company, would be constructing concrete houses on his farm in Newington for "thrifty families that are anxious to get property of their own by saving and steady work." The article referred to a project involving 500 "all concrete workmen's houses near Pittsburgh for the Crucible Steel Company" and 300 houses "for a steel company at Gary, Ind." It also noted that "Henry Ford, the automobile builder, wants 3,000." It is not known how many of these houses were actually constructed.

In 1917 Lambie joined forces with Charles Ingersoll (whose company had developed the technology to manufacture wristwatches for a dollar apiece) to construct 40 poured-concrete houses in Union, New Jersey. Unlike his previous houses, which were cast in two pieces, the Union houses were to utilize Edison's single-mold technology. With this in mind, Lambie wrote a letter to one of Edison's assistants "to see if we could not possibly get Mr. Edison's consent to lend his name or become a director or something."[8] The response was terse:

Ingersoll Terrace under construction in Union, New Jersey, c.1917, using Edison's single-mold technology. (Edison Archives, National Park Service)

Four of the 11 houses in Ingersoll Terrace. All were constructed using Edison's poured-concrete methods, but, as evident here, most have been modified over time. (H. Ward Jandl)

One of the least-altered houses in Ingersoll Terrace today. (H. Ward Jandl)

[Edison] wants me to say to you that it is very interesting, and he is glad that you are making such progress, but he cannot violate the policy which he had laid out for himself, namely, that he is resolved to keep out of everything except his own enterprises.[9]

Despite the lack of official endorsement from Edison, Ingersoll and Lambie proceeded with their plans. But in the end, whether due to financial or technical difficulties, only 11 of the houses were constructed. Utilizing Edison's special cement formula and Lambie-built reusable steel forms, the houses were boxlike, two stories tall, with flat roofs. The only ornamentation consisted of brackets under projecting eaves and a canopy over the front door supported by wooden brackets. All 11 houses survive today, although most have been resurfaced with aluminum or vinyl siding, stucco, veneer brick, or Permastone. The actual cost of construction is not known, but records indicate that Ingersoll sold the houses for $1,200 apiece, in keeping with his intent to provide quality housing for working-class families of limited means.

Interest in Edison's construction theories eventually spread to the West Coast, which was undergoing a population boom. In 1922

Cartoon making fun of Edison's concrete furniture. (Edison Archives, National Park Service)

the Edison Pyramid Builders, Inc., acquired the exclusive rights to Edison's system in seven states west of the Rocky Mountains and announced plans for constructing houses in the $2,000 to $5,000 range. A Los Angeles newspaper noted that "thousands of these houses have already been built by this process in the East and abroad" and that "patent rights have been granted in all the principal foreign countries."[10] The positive tone of the article notwithstanding, the success of Edison Pyramid Builders in drumming up contracts seems to have been mild at best. This article remains one of the last in the news media describing Edison's poured-concrete houses.

Edison continued trying to find new uses for concrete after his housing experiments of 1905–12. One of the more intriguing projects was his effort to manufacture and market cast-concrete furniture. Like his earlier

Edison designed these concrete phonograph cabinets to imitate wood. (Edison Archives, National Park Service)

experiments, this one attracted considerable attention in the press. The first piece of furniture he cast was an elaborate phonograph cabinet. Using a special additive, Edison was able to obtain an exceptionally smooth concrete finish that could be either painted or stained to resemble wood. The florid scrollwork favored by Edison followed line for line the wooden models, and the completed pieces were indistinguishable from their wooden counterparts, except for their weight. The cost to produce the phonograph cabinet was $10, but with demand and markup, the selling price would probably have been somewhat higher. Prototype tables and chairs were also manufactured.

To test the durability of his new furniture, Edison had a concrete cabinet shipped by rail from New Jersey to Chicago. Several weeks later, it was returned to the Edison laboratory in perfect condition. Wary of the public's reaction to concrete, Edison never attempted to market his furniture; he did, however, make the technology available to others. Several of the remaining original pieces are on display at the Edison National Historic Site.

The poured-concrete house was clearly a commercial venture, but the spirit in which it was conceived reflected a sincere desire to improve the dismal living conditions of America's factory workers and laborers. From the outset Edison declared that it was not his intention to benefit financially from the project but, rather, to provide the technology for creating low-cost, efficient, and sanitary housing. Edison never intended to become a housing mogul; he knew that if poured-concrete houses were to become popular, they would need to be manufactured by someone other than himself.

There is no question that Edison's endorsement of this revolutionary construction method helped win broader acceptance of concrete as a suitable building material for houses. In evaluating Edison's contributions to the field, recognition must be given to his consistent use of reinforcement, the ability to pour in a single operation, and the use of adjustable, interchangeable, and reusable forms. Of equal significance was Edison's ability to apply industrial concepts to housing; he understood that the efficiencies and economies inherent in mass production could benefit working-class families, not only in the United States but around the world. ♠

Five THE DYMAXION DWELLING MACHINE

Its function is to aid living.

Theodore Morrison, *House Beautiful*, September 1929

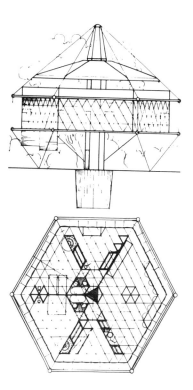

*Dymaxion house elevation
and floor plan, 1927. (©1960
The Estate of Buckminster
Fuller. Courtesy Buckminster
Fuller Institute, Los Angeles)*

*(top left)
R. Buckminster Fuller with the first
model of the Dymaxion house, 1927.
(© 1960 The Estate of Buckminster
Fuller. Courtesy Buckminster Fuller
Institute, Los Angeles)*

In 1929 the Marshall Field department store in Chicago imported a collection of daringly modern furniture from France. To attract attention to the furniture show, the store's promotion manager asked an engineer named Richard Buckminster Fuller, Jr., to set up and demonstrate a model of a house he had recently designed. Fuller, presumably, was to be the "conversation piece" in the display. Whether Fuller's demonstrations sold furniture is not known, but his house caused a sensation: "For three weeks, Fuller gave five talks a day to capacity audiences largely composed of artists, architects and engineers, plus a few simple citizens who could believe neither their eyes nor their ears."[1]

The hexagonal house hung suspended from a central "mast," a full story off the ground. Anchored by cables, it could survive hurricane-force winds. Electricity was provided by the house's own power source: a diesel engine supplied with oil from a tank beneath the mast. Another buried compartment contained the septic tank. The windows could not be opened, nor was it necessary to open them, since the environment was perfectly controlled at all times. The house was entered by an elevator in the central mast. The walls were an early example of Thermopane construction, consisting of hollow, triangular pieces of casein, a material made from vegetable waste. Walls functioned not just as partitions between rooms, but also as containers for kitchen appliances and as closets filled with "ovolving" shelves—shelves that revolved vertically until the desired item was within easy reach of an opening in the wall. The house came complete with a living-dining room, two bedrooms, two bathrooms, a kitchen, a study, and a covered rooftop deck. The entire house weighed a mere three tons; the accepted weight of a brick house of the same size was 150 tons. Fuller estimated that the house would cost 50 cents a pound, or $3,000. No wonder audiences gaped.

The house was so new it required a new word. Fuller's own name for it—"4-D," for the fourth dimension—lacked the needed catchiness, so the promotion manager called on Waldo Warren to come up with a more marketable name. Warren had already achieved linguistic immortality by coining the word *radio*. "Warren spent two days listening to Fuller talk, jotting down such typical Fuller jargon as 'maximize,' …'earthian,' 'dynamic,' and 'teleologic.'" He combined syllables at random until he formed a new word that clicked: "Dymaxion."[2] Fuller loved it.

If Fuller adopted someone else's name for his house, the rest of it was purely his own, and he "pitched" the house with the fervor of a used-car salesman. The flavor of his talk was captured by *Architectural Forum*, which offered the following "brief but illuminating" description of the house "taken largely from an address by Mr. Fuller":

This house is 40 feet high, 50 feet in diameter, proof against earthquake, flood, tornado, electrical storms, marauders, etc. It contains two bedrooms, each with its bath; foolproof wormgear elevator; laundry unit in which each piece of soiled clothing is individually deposited, and completely finished and ready to use in 3 minutes; cooking grills which are like a piano and have nothing to do with a servant; refrigerator; dish closets in which the shelves come around to one instead of one's going around for them!; incinerator pocket in which one shells the peas, etc., without ducking down under pipes; pneumatic, soundproof floors and doors on which the children cannot hurt themselves; library in which the bookshelves come around to one, completely equipped with maps, globes, atlases, drawing board, typewriter, mimeograph, calculating machines, television unit, radio loud speaker and microphone; individual power plant providing both light and heat; sewage disposal; compressed air cleaner; pneumatic beds; built-in furniture; semicircular hanging coat closets with capacity of 32 overcoats or 50 dresses; hangar in which the transport unit, an amphibian airplane-automobile, is found as part of the equipment of the house; a 50-foot diameter play deck on top of the house sheltered from storms but where sun baths may always be had; windows that cannot be broken and are never opened, as the air is brought in mechanically without losing any of its fresh, spring smell, but freed of all dust and combined with the proper amount of humidity—air never too wet nor too dry— and of the proper temperature, blown in through the rooms so that at the North Pole or at the equator no bed clothes need ever be used as the air is always perfect; where any amount of light or coloring of the light may be had in any room from completely indirect, translucent lighting of ceilings or partitions; rooms that are all soundproof so that when anyone rests he may rest in perfect peace.

Fuller's tireless promotion of the Dymaxion house was a reflection of his zeal to make the world better for all mankind. Born in 1895 to a prominent New England family, Fuller had entered Harvard (the fifth generation of his family to do so) in 1913 but, putting other pursuits ahead of school, was twice expelled. After a brief period at the U.S. Naval Academy in 1917, Fuller worked for an importer of cotton-mill machinery and at Armour and Company; during World War I he was an ensign in the navy. From 1922 to 1927 he worked out of Chicago for a company marketing a building material invented by his father-in-law, but that effort failed and Fuller again found himself out of work. Battling his sense of personal failure, the depressed Fuller considered suicide and made a decision that changed his life. "I made a bargain with myself that I'd discover the principles operative in the universe and turn them over to my fellow men."[3]

Fuller's Dymaxion house of 1929 was written up in hundreds of newspaper and magazine articles. Although some of the comments were critical, many were friendly, yet all were fascinated. The "house on a pole" received a great deal of attention on its own merits, but Fuller's flair for publicity helped things along considerably. Some of his attention-getting devices were as transparent as they were harmless. In the model of the Dymaxion house, for instance, he placed a tiny nude doll on a bed for headline-catching purposes. The doll illustrated his point that in the Dymaxion house bedclothes were not needed as the "air is always perfect."[4]

Some accounts in the press focused on peripheral elements of the house, particularly elements Fuller added later. The "fog gun" was one such gadget. As he envisioned it, a fog gun "loaded with 90 percent compressed air, ten percent atomized water, and a small amount of solvent" would wash the dishes. A similar gun in the bathroom would supply an hour's bath with a pint of water.[5]

Others, however, understood that the true significance of the house had nothing to do with inflatable floors and fog guns. *Fortune* magazine retraced the steps through which Fuller came to the basic design: "Mr. Fuller's diagnosis of modern shelter led him to a fundamental distinction. He observed that modern housing combines two elements—the housing of utilities such as plumbing, heating, lighting, etc., and the housing of people. The first must be strong…the second may be light." The conclusion Fuller reached from this starting point was that "if the housing of the utilities was to be strong and rigid, and if the housing of people was to be light, then the first might be used for the support of the second. The development of this idea produced the Dymaxion House."[6]

Like a number of architects of his generation, Fuller took the automobile industry as his model for the housing industry of the future. Once a prototype had been developed and tested, mass production could begin. By offering mass-produced machines, rather than expensive, individually designed, and laboriously built houses, the supplier could free people from the drudgery involved in purchasing and maintaining a traditional home. The mass production of good, cheap, scientific housing would be as liberating as the automobile had been to a nation of horse owners. With houses (or their parts) rolling off the assembly line, the cost per house would decrease rapidly, just as in the case of the automobile. But the analogy with the auto industry went beyond mere production. Fuller envisioned that each Dymaxion "unit" would be delivered and built by a crew connected with a local Dymaxion service station. The service station would also make repairs, replace worn-out or broken parts, and install new options as they were developed by the parent company.

Yet the truly revolutionary significance of the Dymaxion house went beyond construction techniques, beyond gadgets, beyond the new building and service industries it would call forth. Several contemporaries extolled the freedom the house offered. "Its function," wrote one, "is to aid living."[7] As another put it, the house offered "no arbitrary partitionings; instead, the things you use in the house form partitions of themselves. Bookcases, pianos, laundry, closet space, you move them around to suit the need, with the result that you run the house, it doesn't run you."[8] Hugh Kenner, writing in *Bucky: A Guided Tour of Buckminster Fuller*, stated, "The house was to do the laundry and the dishes. It was to warm and circulate the air.... The idea was not silly luxury, but the canceling of silly toil. The directness seems nearly insane. What is really unsettling about the Dymaxion House is that it doesn't tell you what to do with yourself, doesn't give you so much as a hint. That's up to you." The owner would be free to live, rather than to keep house.

The liberation offered by the Dymaxion house inevitably involved social and even political dimensions. As *Fortune* saw it, "The whole house...is as nearly self-sufficient and as nearly free from the political nuisances of city water and city sewage and city electricity and city light as may be." Fuller, writing in 1934, five years after his department-store lectures, attributed his failure at attracting the interest of "profit-minded" private capital to the Dymaxion house's social implications.[9]

The point was largely moot, though, because the house could not have been built, and Fuller knew it. He also knew exactly how long it would take to bring the house into production, for as a "statistician of technological history he had observed a steady 22½ year lag—unique to the world of building—between the inception of a new industrial idea and its general adoption."[10] He not only knew the Dymaxion house would not be built for 20 or more years, he claimed that the house was "a theory only," and "despite pragmatic criticism it has conscientiously been kept so." The house, he went on, "has been merely an attitude. An attitude of willingness to think truthfully. To think truthfully of the general problem of life's survival and its potential solutions in the terms of the latest achievements of the intellect, quite unfettered by history's relatively temporary national, political and aesthetic bonds."[11] The attitude embodied in the house became a system, the Dymaxion philosophy, which "aims to harness on a non-profit basis the maximum technological resources for the greatest number of people."[12]

The Dymaxion Bathroom

The Dymaxion bathroom was initially developed in 1931 for the American Radiator Company. Made of Monel-coated copper, it was intended to be die-stamped like automobile bodies. The economy of production and installation, however, was so great that any hope for production was destroyed by opposition from the plumbers' union, concerned about the loss of jobs to a prefabricated unit that could be installed in minutes. In 1936 Fuller succeeded in interesting the Phelps-Dodge Research Laboratories in the bathroom, which became known, because of its dimensions, as the "Five by Five." It consisted of two chambers of equal size—one housing the bath and the other a sink and toilet—which could be locked together by a U-piece door frame. Special features included:

- Indirect lighting at the bottom of the tub to illuminate the water and the floor, serving to prevent accidents;

- A lavatory drain located on the side of the basin nearest the user so that the water would spout away from the user without splashing;

- An electric heating system between the two chambers that warmed all metal surfaces;

- Sliding, rather than swinging, doors to maximize space;

- Removable panels under the toilet and lavatory to permit full access to all pipe connections.

The whole assembly—shell, fixtures, heating system, forced ventilation unit, and all—weighed only 420 pounds. Although several prototype units were completed in 1937, full production of the Five by Five never occurred.

While the Dymaxion house of 1929 remained a model, Fuller did not abandon his Dymaxion philosophy. In the next few years, he designed and built a Dymaxion bathroom, a Dymaxion car, and a Dymaxion map. He even developed—and practiced for several years—a Dymaxion system of sleeping: 30 minutes every six hours. In its own way, each invention was every bit as revolutionary as the Dymaxion house.

The Dymaxion bathroom was
a marvel of efficiency.
(©1960 The Estate of
Buckminster Fuller. Courtesy
Buckminster Fuller Institute,
Los Angeles)

The Dymaxion Car

While the Dymaxion bathroom drew few raves from the public, the Dymaxion car drew crowds. Indeed, so many people showed up to watch a July 1933 track test of the "Model C2 Dymaxion Transport" that the test was hampered by the press of people hedged around the track. The car was a streamlined affair, variously described as shaped like a fish, a tear, or a pear. It was definitely not car-shaped. Rounded like an airplane cockpit in the front, and tapered in the rear, the Dymaxion car had only three wheels. The single rear wheel produced an incredibly small turning radius and helped make the efficient shape possible. As with the Dymaxion house, the shape of the Model C2 Dymaxion Transport was dictated by physics, not fashion. The vehicle was hailed by *Business Week* as possibly heralding the "beginning of the end of the automobile as we know it." It could do 120 miles per hour with its Ford V-8 engine; got 40 miles to the gallon; and had a periscope instead of a rear-view mirror.

Unluckily for Fuller, an accident involving the car drew unfavorable publicity, and an interested consortium of British investors backed off. The car was not forgotten, however, and as late as 1964 *Time* magazine called it "one of the most dramatic leaps forward in automobile design that has ever been made."

The Dymaxion car, in front of Keck's Crystal House at the Century of Progress Exposition, 1934. (© 1960 The Estate of Buckminster Fuller. Courtesy Buckminster Fuller Institute, Los Angeles)

A cartoon, originally published in Architectural Record, *pokes gentle fun at Fuller's industrial-looking house. (Alan Dunn,* The Last Lath, *1947. Reproduced with permission.)*

During World War II Fuller worked at the Foreign Economic Administration in Washington, D.C., where a variety of circumstances led to the rebirth of his first and greatest Dymaxion idea. Looking ahead to the end of the war, Fuller and others began to

Dymaxion Deployment Unit, 1941, shown with a bathroom addition. Fuller developed these "units" during the war for the federal government as inexpensive, portable housing. (© 1960 The Estate of Buckminster Fuller. Courtesy Buckminster Fuller Institute, Los Angeles)

turn their attention to housing the returning veterans. Although the *New York Times* predicted that few changes would be seen in postwar houses, it had not counted on Buckminster Fuller. In late 1945 he unveiled his new and improved Dymaxion Dwelling Machine.

The house was circular. Its walls and roof were aluminum. It had plexiglass windows that remained fixed and a rooftop ventilator with fins that rotated in the wind like a weather vane, assuring a continuous supply of fresh air. Like its predecessor, it was suspended from a central mast. But unlike the first Dymaxion house, and perhaps most important, it had a producer: the Beech Aircraft Company of Wichita, Kansas.

The road to Wichita had been a circuitous one. It had begun according to *Business Week*, in the Washington office of Rep. Clare Boothe Luce, where Fuller went to meet a friend for lunch and encountered two young union men who had come to discuss labor legislation: Gregory Bardacke and Herman Wolf. Both had backgrounds as officials in the labor movement—Bardacke with the milliners' union, Wolf with the ladies' garment workers.

As always, Fuller had ideas. The nation had a housing shortage of immense proportions. He had a house that could be mass-produced in immense quantities. With the war almost over, the nation had excess aircraft-producing capacity. He had a house that could be built in an aircraft factory. As always, Fuller conveyed his ideas with brilliance and great force. Bardacke and Wolf were won over. Fuller had converts, but he still had problems—money, for one; labor unions, for another.

The money problem would be tackled in the conventional way by lining up outside investors. Fuller started with Philadelphia capitalist William S. Wasserman, who became a director of the fledgling company. Other directors were Lawrence Hartness, president of General Motors of Australia, and T. K. Quinn, a former advertising executive.

The labor problem, on the other hand, was treated quite unconventionally: Fuller adopted the unheard-of approach of taking organized labor into partnership in the production of his new Dymaxion house. *Business Week* commented upon the radical approach of the new company, which called itself Dymaxion Dwelling Machines, Inc.: "For perhaps the first time in the history of American business, a corporation has been established which, in its certificate of incorporation, asserts that it will 'provide through a corporate medium an organization to be managed and directed by labor, capital, and science to their collective profit.'"[13]

The logical starting place was with the International Association of Machinists, because the union had large numbers of members employed in the war-swollen aircraft industry who would lose their jobs with the coming of peace. Thanks to the efforts of Gregory Bardacke, now a vice president of Dymaxion Dwelling Machines, Inc., a director's seat in the company was given to Harvey Brown, president of the American Federation of Labor's biggest union, the machinists'.

Casting about for the most appropriate aircraft company to involve in the enterprise, Bardacke asked Brown which firm had the best relationship with the machinists. The answer was Beech Aircraft of Wichita, Kansas. From these contacts eventually came the deal: Beech would manufacture houses to Fuller's specifications and Dymaxion Dwelling Machines, Inc., would market the houses. The chief executive of Beech Aircraft, John P. Gaty, was an aggressive but likable executive who had no hesitation about producing Fuller's houses. The winning combination of men, money, and ideas was the principal reason behind the headline of an April 1946 *Fortune* feature article: "Fuller's House: It Has a Better Than Even Chance of Upsetting the Building Industry."

And what a house it was! The prototype, manufactured and erected by Beech Aircraft, was a round house, 36 feet in diameter (giving

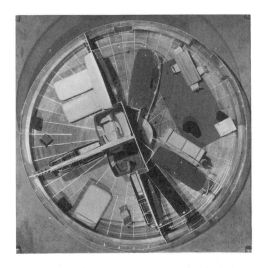

an area of 1,017 square feet). It came complete with a living-dining room, two bedrooms, two Dymaxion bathrooms, and a kitchen equipped with an electric refrigerator, deep-freeze storage unit, range, washing machine, sink, laun-

Model of the Dymaxion Dwelling Machine developed for Beech Aircraft showing the organization of space. (© 1960 The Estate of Buckminster Fuller. Courtesy Buckminster Fuller Institute, Los Angeles)

The prototype Dymaxion house erected by Beech Aircraft in Wichita, Kansas, in the 1940s. (Kansas State Historical Society)

dry bin, and waste disposal unit, according to an enthusiastic article in the March 22, 1946, issue of Beech Aircraft's company publication, the *Beech Log*.

The company had reason to like the house. Initial plans called for Beech to manufacture approximately 50,000 of them (200 a day) in the first year of its agreement with Fuller. Yet the company was not alone in its enthusiasm. *Interiors* magazine remarked that if the house were actually produced as promised, "it will be the biggest bargain in packaged housing

Cables anchor the aluminum frame of the prototype Dymaxion house in Wichita, Kansas, to the ground (© 1960 The Estate of Buckminster Fuller. Courtesy Buckminster Fuller Institute, Los Angeles)

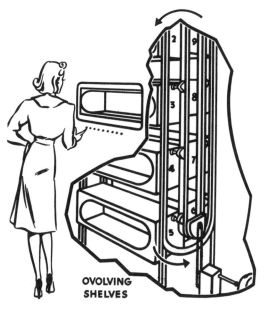

OVOLVING SHELVES

Ovolving shelves, shown here in a drawing, operated at the touch of a switch. (© 1960 The Estate of Buckminster Fuller. Courtesy Buckminster Fuller Institute, Los Angeles)

The claim was justified. As with the first Dymaxion house, the house used tension, rather than compression, as its fundamental structural principle. This meant that the walls did not hold up anything; instead they were held up. The *Beech Log* explained that, freed from load-bearing functions, the walls could serve more useful needs, such as providing closet space. The house had closets that pivoted to reveal clothing and shoe racks. And, of course, being a Dymaxion Dwelling Machine, it had "ovolving" shelves. They rotated vertically, at the push of a button, until the desired shelf could be reached. In April 1946 *Architectural Forum* enumerated the advantages of Fuller's closet and shelf systems: the closets swung out into the room, offering easy access, while the ovolving shelves allowed the full partition to be used for storage, with easy— and equal—access to each shelf. Meanwhile, the *Beech Log* extolled the capacity of the shelf system: the 24 cubic feet of storage space in each ovolving shelf system was "three times the space in an average bureau."

Fuller had promised years before in his Dymaxion lectures that the Dymaxion house would feature rooms with adjustable translucent light emanating from ceilings or partitions. The Dymaxion Dwelling Machine delivered on this promise.

A Dymaxion closet included a swivel door and built-in hat rack. (© 1960 The Estate of Buckminster Fuller. Courtesy Buckminster Fuller Institute, Los Angeles)

Prototype of ovolving shelves. ©1960 The Estate of Buckminster Fuller. Courtesy Buckminster Fuller Institute, Los Angeles)

that this department has yet seen."[14] *Fortune* registered the most sweeping praise: "…when you go into the house it feels as if, for the first time in your life, you had walked into the twentieth century. This is the industrially produced house. No other dwelling in existence is even remotely like it."[15]

Unlike the first design for the Dymaxion house, however, the prototype built by Beech had windows that could be opened. The transparent window panels themselves were fixed shut, but the wall panels beneath the windows could be lowered on the exterior. A plastic curtain covered the wall panel from the inside. When the outer wall panel was lowered and the inner curtain was raised, air could flow freely through a screened opening.

More than one observer mentioned the pleasing effect the gently curving walls gave to the interior. The *Beech Log* was typical in its praise: "The circumference of the house is great enough so that walls curve gently and the arrangement of the dividing partitions and facilities coupled with the high dome of the ceiling gives a feeling of unusual spaciousness." The sweep of the walls and the curve of the domed roof produced another remarkable effect: the acoustics, reportedly, were wonderful. They were tested by the great contralto Marian Anderson, who said that "neverbefore had she heard the sound of her voice flow *around* a room."[16]

Even more remarkable is how fully the Dymaxion Dwelling Machine met the breathless claims that had been made for industrially produced housing years before. It could be

A continuous band of windows and radiating plywood flooring were distinctive features on the interior of the Dymaxion house. (© 1960 The Estate of Buckminster Fuller. Courtesy Buckminster Fuller Institute, Los Angeles)

machine-made, and quickly, in vast quantities. *Fortune* estimated that the aircraft factories in Wichita alone could produce 250,000 dwelling machines a year. It was cheap. At $6,500, or "about a dollar pound," the Dymaxion Dwelling Machine could be purchased for approximately the cost of a Cadillac at that time. In another comparison that gives a sense of the relative cost of the house, *Architectural Record* noted that the house "will be more than 50 percent larger than the conventional house selling in the same price class."[17] As low as the initial projected purchase price was, the cost was expected to go down when mass production began in earnest: "When they are produced in volume—say 500,000 a year—the price to the consumer may get as low as 50 cents a pound, or $3,700 at the present weight."[18]

Fulfilling another promise, this industrially produced house was easily transportable. As it came off the assembly line, the entire house fit into a 16-by-4½-foot shipping tube. Eight "units" could fit into a single railroad car. The Dymaxion house could be built anywhere in a hurry. The *Beech Log* reported that the house could be assembled in 200 hours, "two days' work for a 16-man crew."

The technical innovations of the house extended not merely to its form, but also to its materials, many of which were a direct result of the tremendous boost that the war gave to technology and mass production. These included aluminum, transparent plastic windows, plastic screen, copper wire and tubing, plastic and rubberized fabric, synthetic rubber, fiberglass, plywood, stainless steel, galvanized steel strand cables, cadmium plating, magnesium, and nylon.

For all its newness, the house had one unexpected traditional feature: a fireplace (albeit a stainless steel fireplace). It was included "because Bucky loved open fires and recognized their contribution to the ambiance of a house."[19]

Fireplace aside, traditional references to hearth and home were noticeably lacking in what was, after all, a "dwelling machine." In view of this, Dymaxion Dwelling Machines, Inc., took pains in its promotional materials to reassure people who might have qualms about living in a house that was entered through an airplane door and that was described in one (favorable) article as looking "like a squat aluminum silo."[20] A March 1946 issue of the *Beech Log* reported that Dymaxion Dwelling Machines, Inc., was changing its name to Fuller Houses, Inc., "to distinguish the present circular Fuller House from the original hexagonal-shaped house." In reality, the name change was probably prompted as much by the desire not to scare away potential customers.

The corporate window dressing coincided with a more literal window dressing for the benefit of magazine articles and other publicity materials. The first Dymaxion house may have been unveiled in a sales promotion for modern French furniture, but the marketing people for the second house would have none of that. Nor did they use the "special furniture" Fuller had designed. Instead, "they went straight to Wichita's leading department stores and furnished the model house in the best women's magazine taste."[21]

They also furnished the house with professional models posed in self-consciously domestic scenes: a couple with two children at breakfast in the living-dining room (with a coffee table in the foreground, a *Life* magazine prominently displayed, and a child's model airplane on the living room floor); a couple looking at swing-out closets full of conventional clothing; a couple in the bedroom, the husband reading in bed, the wife sitting at the vanity combing her hair. The purpose of these carefully posed domestic scenes, *Interiors* magazine remarked, was to prove that the average Americans could feel at home in the house.

The effect of all this contrived middle-class conventionality was striking; it created a curious incongruity, as if Ward and June Cleaver found themselves living in a space station. Nevertheless, it worked. The public was apparently excited by the potential adventure of living in a radically new house, or by the prospect of paying off a mortgage in a few years rather than over a lifetime. Whatever the reason, the reaction was overwhelming: the prototype Dymaxion Dwelling Machine was exhibited to the public in Wichita in October 1945. Over the next four months, thousands of people from all over the country came to see the Dymaxion and applaud. Publicity was widespread and enthusiastic and produced an amazing flood of 37,000 *unsolicited* orders, many of them accompanied by checks.

Yet the orders went unfilled. The house was never mass-produced. The standard explanation is that money for full-scale production was not forthcoming. In 1948 *Science Illustrated* reported that "at least ten million dollars were required to tool up for large-scale production of the house; with the war over Beech could not raise the money." More than 15 years later, in a cover story on Fuller, *Time* magazine ascribed the failure to produce the house to "the war's end and a changed economic picture." Hugh Kenner subsequently repeated the story, stating that "ten million dollars was not forthcoming." But these explanations raise more questions than they settle, especially since Fuller himself said that "there were a number of people who wanted to come in and take over the business and put up the ten million."[22]

Kenner also hinted at another explanation for the demise of the Dwelling Machine. He reported that "one account of the fiasco has

Bucky refining his designs until even aircraft executives ran out of patience."

Perhaps the most detailed and plausible account was given by Alden Hatch in *Buckminster Fuller: At Home in the Universe.* To mount a full-scale production effort, the financiers proposed a recapitalization plan that would raise a substantial portion of the money (and, incidentally, make a killing for the inner circle of the original Dymaxion group). Fuller apparently was repulsed at the notion of making huge profits from an experiment that was as much social as architectural, especially when, as he saw it, Fuller Houses, Inc., was years away from being able to put the whole system in place: manufacture, delivery, assembly, and service. As he told Hatch:

I said, "It is not ready. Here are all those orders, but who is going to install it? The present building industry won't do it." The plumbers say they are the only ones licensed to hook it up to the city mains and the electricians say they are the only ones licensed to do the wiring. Both unions say: "If you bring in a house with all the plumbing and wiring all done we won't have any business left. We can't handle it unless we can take all the wiring and plumbing apart and put it together again." Also, the houses would have to be delivered by a very special truck, rather like a telephone truck, and we had no such trucks and no capable distributors. Hundreds of people came to us who wanted to be distributors, but I kept showing them that they did not have the capability of putting this thing up. It was not premature as a demonstration of a principle…. It was technically very successful, but we were nowhere near in a position to go into mass production, and sell them to a lot of people. Because we could not deliver. And it's just not honest to sell people something you can't deliver…. I was forced to do just what I had done before…to shut down solvent. Nobody made any money.

Fuller, Hatch wrote, "felt that it would betray his ideals and falsify his covenant with himself to work selflessly to the betterment of mankind."

The failure of the Dymaxion Dwelling Machine was the end of more than just a house design. Fuller never again designed a

Overlooking water, the Dymaxion house in Wichita in the 1950s with its later additions.
(Kansas State Historical Society)

complete working house. The episode did not, however, mark the end of Fuller's determination to use technology to serve humanity. In 1954, ten years after the start of his last Dymaxion venture, the U.S. Patent Office issued Fuller a patent on his geodesic dome. In the nearly 30 years he had left to live, the geodesic dome would make him a world-wide celebrity, secure his fortune and his reputation as an engineering genius, and make him the center of an enormous cultlike following.

In 1948 the model Dymaxion Dwelling Machine was bought for $1,000 by William Graham, Sr., an agreeably eccentric oil and real estate man. Graham moved the house to his property southeast of Wichita and put it down on a street he had named "Easy Street." The house address changed yearly to match the date. Graham added a level beneath the Dymaxion house, built a two-story wing, removed the ventilator hood when he installed air conditioning, and inserted circular stairs. Fuller visited the Graham family in Wichita many times in the ensuing years. Graham's daughter recalled that Fuller "didn't like any of the remodeling we did on the house, and he never hesitated to say so." Mrs. Graham "was never real impressed with the house because it leaked." William Graham, Jr., remembered that, even with the leaks, "it was a wonderful house to grow up in."[23]

Despite its engineering and architectural significance, the Dymaxion House has not yet been listed in the National Register of Historic Places. The house sits vacant and deteriorating. An organization interested in preserving the house is being formed as this book goes to press. ⬗

SPACE OVER
LIVING
ROOM

COLUMN

BOOKS

CLOSET

SHOWER
TOILET
SKYLIGHTS

COUCH

CASE

LIBRARY

BOOKS

DOWN

GUARDRAIL

FLOWER BOX

FLOWER BOX

DUMBWAITER

LAWN

FOLD-UP
TABLE

OPEN

TERRACE

COVERED

COLUMN

LIVING
ROOM

COLUMN

CUPBOARD

EXTENSION
TABLE

DINING
ROOM

CABINET

DUMBWAITER

KITCHEN

BED ROOM

EXERCISE
ROOM

TUB

TOILET

VENT FAN

BATH

COLUMN

COLUMN

OVERHEAD DOOR

GARAGE

OUT

OVERHEAD DOOR

STORAGE

HALL

HAT

DUMBWAITER

HEATER

FLUE

FROSTED GLASS

PORCH

COLUMN

The life of today for the city worker requires a different setting than for the existence of the early American under pioneer conditions. It is only fair to say that the colonial house served its purpose well for the period when it was created, but it is an anachronism to give the city worker the same house that served totally different needs.

The Aluminaire house was designed to meet the needs of present-day life—the life of the near city. It is so devised as to give house dwellers better light and air with mechanical conveniences and efficiency of arrangement that are unheard-of features of the average suburban dwelling.

A promotional brochure for the Aluminaire house, 1931

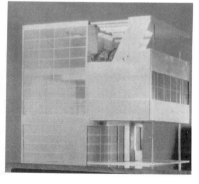

Model of the Aluminaire constructed by Albert Frey. (Colonial Williamsburg Foundation Library, A. Lawrence Kocher Collection)

The Aluminaire was re-erected on the Harrison estate on Long Island in the 1930s. (Palmer Shannon/Colonial Williamsburg Foundation Library, A. Lawrence Kocher Collection)

In 1932 New York's Museum of Modern Art mounted its first architectural exhibition, "The International Style: Architecture Since 1922." Organized by architectural historian Henry-Russell Hitchcock and architect Philip Johnson, the show proved to be a momentous event, introducing Americans to a new "International Style" and the work of Le Corbusier, Gropius, Mies van der Rohe, Aalto, and Oud—European architects whose works were largely unknown in the United States. The exhibition's impact on the course of American architecture over the next 30 years was extraordinary.

Only two American houses were deemed worthy of inclusion in the exhibition and in Hitchcock and Johnson's influential book on the same subject: Lovell House, designed by Richard Neutra and built in California in 1929; and a rather curious-looking aluminum-and-glass box, supported on spindly columns, which featured a drive-through garage on the first floor. Designed by the team of A. Lawrence Kocher and Albert Frey, and dubbed the Aluminaire for its ability "to give light and air to a house, this experimental structure had attracted considerable attention in 1931 at the 50th anniversary show of the New York Architectural League. While the Lovell House has been widely published and praised as one of the first examples of the International Style in the United States, the Aluminaire has been largely, and unjustly, overlooked by architectural historians.

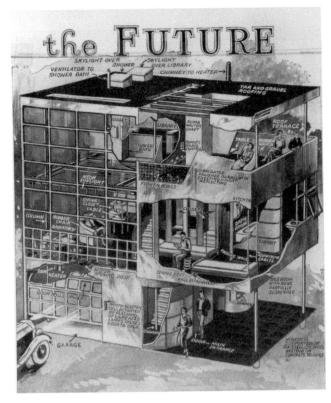

"Cut-away representation of the Home of the Future" from Popular Mechanics *magazine, as drawn by Logan U. Reaves. (Colonial Williamsburg Foundation Library, A. Lawrence Kocher Collection)*

In the 1930s A. Lawrence Kocher was best known to the architectural community as managing editor of the influential *Architectural Record* magazine. Born in 1885, Kocher studied medieval history and architecture at Stanford and Massachusetts Institute of Technology. Under his editorship, which began in 1928, *Architectural Record* became a strong proponent of modernism, encouraging its readers to explore new materials, adopt innovative construction methods, and throw off the mantle of the past. As idea man and master promoter, Kocher would frequently ally himself with other architects to develop designs that, not surprisingly, would then appear in his magazine.

When the Aluminaire came into being, Albert Frey was still new to the American architectural scene. Born in Zurich, Switzerland, in 1903, he earned his diploma at the Institute of Technology at Winterthur in 1924. After designing for firms in Zurich and Brussels in the mid-1920s, he moved to Paris in 1928 and began working at the atelier of Le Corbusier and Pierre Jeanneret. One of the projects Frey worked on was the Villa Savoie, a country house clad in stucco and supported by round posts, today considered by many to be the premier example of the International Style.

Intrigued by advances in American building technology and challenged by "the vast areas and growing populations" of the United States, Frey emigrated to New York in September 1930 and began to look for work. He found the country in a profound economic depression, yet with his experience and contacts he quickly made the acquaintance of New York's most progressive designers and architects, including Lawrence Kocher.

Kocher and Frey freely used the pages of *Architectural Record* to promote their approach to design. The following is extracted from an article by the two men that appeared in the April 1933 issue:

"The more important new materials and methods of construction are derived from efforts to reduce installation labor on the job, to lighten weight of construction and transportation and incidentally to lower cost. These efforts have been particularly directed toward prefabrication of units in floor, wall, roof construction and building parts such as windows and doors that incorporate frame and adjoining wall. It is probable that no new and complete structural system for the house will be devised as an act of design by one individual. New house construction will arise gradually with continued experimentation by architects, engineers and by industry. During the past decade there has been rapid increase in the factory-fabrication of parts of houses and buildings. Wall sections with incorporated window, frame and heating box are now manufactured as units, ready to install. Wall sections, including insulation and exterior and interior facing, are also available for use by architects. Wall sections for the bathroom and kitchen will soon be on the market. These cases are cited as indicative of a trend in building.

"In any fabrication of the house there are certain ideals which should be met. These may be stated in the form of a check list as follows:

• Structural system with prefabricated units joined together by pressure or bolting.   • Materials for walls that effectually exclude heat, cold, dampness and sound.   • Weathertight joints throughout, not subject to deterioration.

• Exterior surface of walls should be hard and durable, requiring little or no maintenance.   • Wall units of uniform size to permit interchange of parts.   • Interior wall surface suited to cleaning with commonly used cleansing powders and soap.   • Structure resistant to corrosion and attack by insects and fungi.   • Absence of projections that gather dust.

• Dry construction.   • Lightweight.   • Minimum flashing.   • Wall structure capable of housing or attaching heating, wiring and lighting pipes and ducts.• Insulation that prevents condensation within interior of house or within walls.

• Parts capable of replacement and addition.   • Erection and installation of units by unskilled labor.

• Possibilities for demolition and re-erection on new site.   • Resistant to earthquake and heavy wind pressure.

• Lightning-proof.   • Fireproof throughout.   • Economical of space because of thinness of walls.   • Possibilities for natural or applied color.   • Windows of uniform and standard size, permitting maximum daylighting and control of fresh air and sunlight.   • Roof drainage through center of house for economy of required piping and to prevent freezing.

• Soundproof partitions.   • Interior partitions flexible and capable of varied arrangements.   • Closets, cabinets and equipment as units.   • Minimum cost of construction and upkeep."

In 1929 Kocher had designed a "modern architect's office" for the Architecture and Allied Arts Exposition, held at Grand Central Palace, an exhibition hall in New York City. His design had attracted such great crowds that the following year he was approached by the exhibits manager to design another attention-getting display for the upcoming Architectural League show. For the previous three years, the league had held a series of modestly scaled shows at the American Fine Arts Society Building on West 57th Street. For its 50th anniversary, however, the league, under the direction of Harvey Corbett, Raymond Hood, and Jacques Ely Kahn, planned to stage a blockbuster at the spacious Grand Central Palace.

Kocher and Frey shared a keen interest in low-cost housing and the possibilities of mass production in solving the housing shortage. They decided that a model single-family house showing the advantages of new maintenance-free materials and prefabrication would not only meet the exhibit manager's needs but also further the cause of true modernism.

Working together, Kocher and Frey developed a comprehensive set of goals and requirements for the Aluminaire that emphasized new materials and improved construction methods.

Aluminum was one of several new metals and alloys beginning to find use in American architecture, and the two men decided that their model house could demonstrate the potential of aluminum to other architects and to the general public. Easily formed into

Le Corbusier's work in the 1920s was an obvious inspiration to Albert Frey. Shown here is the Villa Savoie at Poissy (1929–31), which was designed while Frey was working for Le Corbusier. (John A. Burns, AIA)

Perspective drawing of the Aluminaire's exterior by Albert Frey. (Colonial Williamsburg Foundation Library, A. Lawrence Kocher Collection)

many shapes and patterns, lightweight yet strong, and comparatively low in cost, aluminum had attractive characteristics, many of which had been enumerated in *Architectural Record* as early as October 1929. An article in the December 1931 issue made the case for aluminum in high-rise buildings:

Today a change in [masonry] wall construction seems logical from a purely economic standpoint. The skyscraper came into being in order to make a more profitable use of land. By the use of metal facades it is possible to reduce the thickness of walls 8 to 10 inches. This saving in wall area can be converted into rentable space. With the load on the structural-steel frame reduced by the use of metal in place of masonry, a material saving can be effected in the supporting structure. Again, a metal facade can be erected in approximately one-fifth the time required to erect a masonry wall.

Although Kocher and Frey were given equal credit for the concept of the Aluminaire, it was Kocher who knew of the latest developments in construction materials and techniques. And it was Frey who actually designed the structure and who had to deal with the numerous constraints facing the project. The Aluminaire was Frey's first commission in the United States.

Since the team was allotted limited exhibition space at Grand Central Palace, the structure had to be small. The Aluminaire as designed occupied a space only 22 by 28 feet and stood three stories high. "Only one of each type of room could be included," wrote Frey.[1] Consequently, the Aluminaire was billed as a home for a couple. The structure also had to be assembled and disassembled quickly, given the Grand Central Palace's exhibition schedule.

Frey designed the house in such a way that it could be erected in 10 days—a major accomplishment and a source of real excitement for the architects.

Kocher and Frey succeeded in getting manufacturers to donate materials for the house: Alcoa furnished the aluminum floor joists and pipe columns; Truscon supplied the steel floor decking, projecting steel windows, and steel stairs. Perhaps not surprisingly, the house was sponsored not by the architectural committee of the Architectural League but by a group of manufacturers and industrial contractors.

Frey's design for the Aluminaire clearly reflected his European education and experience, particularly his previous training with the architects Le Corbusier and Jeanneret.

That the Aluminaire exhibited the "new spirit" called for in Le Corbusier's 1923 book

Elevations of the Aluminaire drawn by Albert Frey. (Colonial Williamsburg Foundation Library, A. Lawrence Kocher Collection)

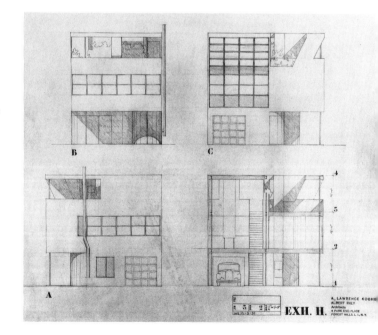

Architect's sketch of the Aluminaire's living area. (Colonial Williamsburg Foundation Library, A. Lawrence Kocher Collection)

From Metal Progress, *the Aluminaire under construction (top) at the Grand Central Palace, April 1931, and the front porch (above) showing a cut-away of the wall and structural system.*

Towards a New Architecture is unquestionable. In this manifesto, Le Corbusier proclaimed that industry "has furnished us with new tools adapted to this new epoch, animated by the new spirit" and that "architecture has for its first duty...that of bringing about a revision of values, a revision of the constituent elements of the house." Le Corbusier eloquently called upon architects to "eliminate from our hearts and minds all dead concepts with regard to the house and look at the question from a critical and objective point of view," arriving at the "House-Machine, the mass-production house, healthy (and morally so too) and beautiful in the same way that the working tools and instruments which accompany our existence are beautiful."

The Aluminaire was designed to be a "machine for living in." Six five-inch aluminum pipe columns set in concrete carried the entire weight of the structure. Steel channel girders, attached to the columns, supported lightweight steel beams, over which was laid light pressed-steel flooring. Because the exterior walls were nonsupporting, they were only three inches thick, built with a light steel frame, two-by-two-inch wood nailers, and two layers of insulation board, each one-half inch thick. On the exterior, the insulation board was covered with a waterproof building paper

The Aluminaire's structural system revealed during its re-erection on Long Island, c. 1935.

and clad with three-by-three-foot corrugated aluminum panels. These panels were fastened to the frame with aluminum screws and washers. The vertical corrugations gave the thin panels added rigidity, and the polished alumi-

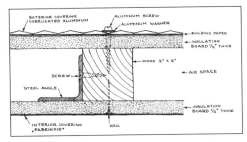

Detail of wall construction. (Colonial Williamsburg Foundation Library, A. Lawrence Kocher Collection)

num surface served to deflect the sun's rays. Large steel windows glazed with ultraviolet glass were grouped together to form continuous ribbons. Sash were designed to be reversible to permit cleaning from inside the house.

The ground floor comprised a drive-through garage with electric overhead doors, the furnace room, a front hall, and steel stairs leading up to the main living space. A dumbwaiter conveniently located near the front door permitted the owner to transport groceries and other goods to the kitchen above and to the terrace on the third level.

A combination living-dining area stretched across the full width of the house; two structural columns and a built-in cupboard and dining room table were the only architectural obstructions in the room. This living-dining

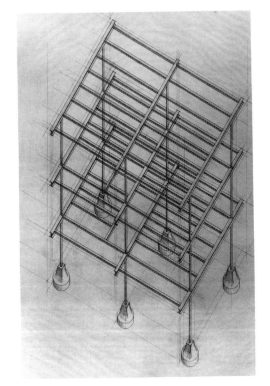

An isometric drawing of the Aluminaire's structural system. (Colonial Williamsburg Foundation Library, A. Lawrence Kocher Collection)

area was two stories high, giving the small house a feeling of openness and space. A small kitchen, separated from the dining area by a swinging door, contained built-in cabinets, an electric stove, a refrigerator, and a Monel

On the third level was a small library, with its own tiny bathroom lit by a skylight. A rooftop terrace with flower boxes and a fold-up table provided additional living space. The terrace, partly covered to provide shade,

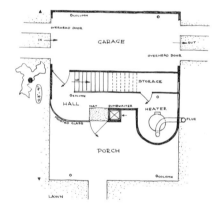 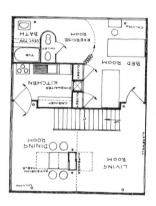 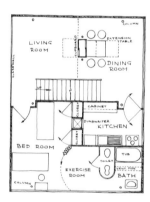

These floor plans show all three levels of the Aluminaire. (Colonial Williamsburg Foundation Library, A. Lawrence Kocher Collection)

metal sink. At the front of the house were the master bedroom suite, with two built-in closets; an exercise room, which could be closed off for privacy by a folding partition on a curved track; a toilet cubicle with a curved wall; and a small bathroom with a tub and a sink.

was similar to terraces found in Le Corbusier's houses of the period, but such private outdoor spaces were new to Americans.

Interior finishes were nontraditional, designed specifically for low maintenance. Most walls were covered with a glazed fabric called

Exterior of curved bathroom wall before disassembly and restoration. (Michael Schwarting)

Fabrikoid, manufactured by the Du Pont Company. The bathroom walls were clad in black Vitrolite, with the exception of the toilet compartment, which was made of a translucent plastic called Lumarith, set in a shiny aluminum frame. Floors were covered with plain black linoleum, and all doors were steel-faced, with chromium handles.

Frey designed the Aluminaire's furnishings to be as innovative as the house itself. Many objects were built in to save valuable space. The expandable dining table, featuring a glass china cupboard above, was covered with a rubber top that rolled on a cylinder in the manner of a window shade. Beds were suspended from cables "to reduce material and bulk."[2] Folding partitions and translucent plastic walls maximized the feeling of space. The library featured a game table with a glass top and chromium-plated tubular legs that ended in rubber feet. Inflatable furniture was also considered for the house but was never fabricated. The house was lit with neon tubes that ran parallel to the window heads. By turning a dial, one could obtain a clear white light, an ultraviolet light, or a selection of colors.

The house was initially designed to be heated by forced air; an oil-burning boiler was placed next to the garage on the ground level.

The Architectural League exhibition opened

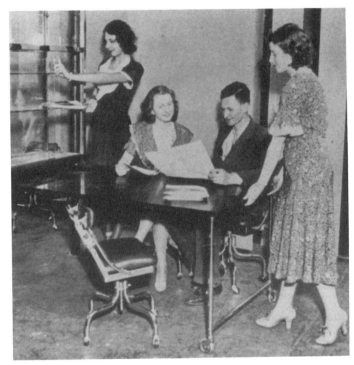

Rolling, expandable dining table, specially designed for the Aluminaire by Kocher and Frey. Frey is shown seated at the table. (Shelter)

on April 19, 1931, to mixed reviews. Henry Saylor, editor of *Architect* magazine, remarked in his diary that "in spite of the fact that the most conservative members of the profession feared that this would be a radical show architecturally, the daily press representatives seemed keenly disappointed over the fact that, as they expressed it, 'it is almost all old stuff.'"[3] Another account stated that one was "immediately struck on entering, with not only an effect of grandeur, but a silence and coldness commensurate with a mortuary chapel. The handful of people wandering apathetically up and down the separate corridors seemed...out of place.... The architectural exhibitions were disappointing, not up to the mark by any means...to us it seemed there was very little interest taken in the show by anyone."[4] The *New York Times*, on the other hand, reported that more than 100,000 people visited the exhibition during its eight-day run. The *New Republic* called the show an "unbelievable hodge-podge," reserving praise only for

Kocher and Frey's house, "a fine and stimulating piece of work...well worth the seventy-five-cent admission."

Reaction to the show by design professionals was swift. Several architects whose work had been omitted staged a rival show "to make the public understand the difference between work in the really modern style and the fantastic creations of 'modernistic' architects so popular in New York."[5] Led by Philip Johnson, these young proponents of the International Style attracted the attention of the press with their own, hastily assembled "Salon des Réfusés" and by picketing in front of the Architectural League's show.

The Salon des Réfusés

The so-called "Salon des Réfusés," organized by young architects unhappy with the Architectural League's show of modern architecture, opened the same week as the league's exposition in April 1931. Housed in a building at 903 Seventh Avenue, near 57th Street, the rival exhibition set out to give "adequate representation to the most progressive side of modern architecture." It featured the work of Clauss and Daub, William Muschenheim, Walter Baermann, Elroy Webber, Richard Wood, and Stonorov and Morgan. Admission was free. The show received wide coverage in the New York papers and in architectural journals; it remained open to the public until May 5.

What's in a Name?

During the eight days it was exhibited at the Grand Central Palace, Kocher and Frey's aluminum house was given many names by the press. The architects, of course, preferred "Aluminaire," which they felt suggested both the material and the design's sense of openness and light. *Time* magazine, in its April 27, 1931, edition, dubbed the Aluminaire the "Magic House" because of its ease of assembly and disassembly and its anticipated low cost. The *Brooklyn Eagle* reported that "vox populi having learned one of its virtues is speed of erection and demolition" promptly decided that "Zipper House" might be more appropriate. Still another newspaper called the house the "Peek-a-Boo Domain." Later, when the house was moved to Long Island and re-erected, it was called the "K-F House," the initials referring to the architects' surnames.

Ironically, Kocher and Frey's Aluminaire House was one of the few displays at Grand Central Palace that received favorable comment. One of the organizers of the Salon des Réfusés exhibition, quoted in the *New York Times*, applauded the Aluminaire as "almost the only modern work in the whole show." In reviewing the Architectural League show, the *New York Times* focused almost exclusively on the "all-metal" house, without, however, mentioning the architects by name. Illustrated with a photograph of the house, the article noted that "the speed with which the house was erected in Grand Central Palace… seemed to indicate that whole subdivisions of metal homes could be put together of standardized parts fabricated in distant factories before the basements of ordinary houses could be completed."[6]

Although Kocher and Frey had hoped to develop similar houses for mass production, they found neither the public interest nor the financing to underwrite such a venture. Contractors resisted their ideas, preferring to stick with traditional building materials and construction techniques. The Aluminaire remained one-of-a-kind.

As a team, Kocher and Frey continued to explore the use of standardized building components in housing. In May 1932 *Architectural Record* published their model low-cost farmhouse, which used readily available building materials. Like the Aluminaire, it had exterior walls and partitions made of insulating board clad in metal. In 1934 another of their revolutionary designs appeared in *Architectural Record*: a weekend house covered in canvas and set on columns. Sponsored by the Cotton-Textile Institute, this house featured a sheltered parking area on the ground floor and living quarters above—similar in concept to the Aluminaire.

Kocher and Frey also designed a small house near Stamford, Connecticut, that appeared in the April 1936 issue of *Architectural Record*. As in the Aluminaire, the principal living rooms of this house were on the second floor (the third floor was a separate

*Designed in 1940, the Frey House, Palm
Springs, California, has walls of corrugated
galvanized iron coated with aluminum paint.*
(Progressive Architecture, *July 1948*)

apartment for guests). More traditional
building materials were used in the Stamford
house: concrete-block construction on the
first floor and wood-frame construction faced
with shingles on the higher floors.

Kocher remained managing editor of
Architectural Record until 1939, when he left
to become a professor of architecture at the
University of Pittsburgh; in later years he was
associated with Colonial Williamsburg. Frey
moved to the West Coast in the late 1930s and
established his own architectural firm in Palm
Springs, California, with John Porter Clark.
Frey has distinguished himself as a versatile
and prolific designer, turning out residences,
schools, hotels, libraries, stores, and office
buildings in the course of his long career. He

has used corrugated metal for exterior walls
on several of his projects, and the residence
he designed for his own use has an aluminum
exterior. Although semiretired, Frey contin-
ues to be active as an architect, working
mostly on small residential projects in the
Palm Springs area.

After the Architectural League show closed
in 1931, Wallace K. Harrison, a distinguished
architect in his own right, purchased the
Aluminaire for just over $1,000. Harrison
had recently purchased 85 acres of land near
Huntington, Long Island, and found himself
with inadequate money to design and build
a new house. The Aluminaire solved his
problem. He had the structure disassembled—
a relatively straightforward procedure—and
moved to his newly acquired property.
Reassembly proved considerably more difficult: the exterior aluminum skin had to be
attached to two layers of insulation in which
wood plugs had been set to take nails. Once
the sheathing was in place, the nail holes were
difficult to locate, and instead of the 18 days
stipulated by Kocher and Frey for erection,
the job required several months. Harrison
designed a large addition to the house in 1932
as his family expanded. In the 1940s the
Aluminaire was moved again; this time the
house was not disassembled but, it is sus-

pected, slid or pushed to a new location on Harrison's estate where it served as a guest house for many years. Unfortunately, during the second move the aluminum pipe columns were chopped off, and the ground floor, which included the drive-through garage, the entry, and the utility room, was demolished. New entrances were cut into the second—now first—floor.

After Harrison's death the estate was sold, and the Aluminaire was rented out, altered, and allowed to deteriorate. Over time the third-floor garden terrace was enclosed to accommodate an additional bedroom, the double-height space was filled in, and other equally unsympathetic alterations were made. Most of the exterior panels lost their shininess, many became dented, and some were replaced. The Aluminaire's last tenant was evicted for nonpayment of rent in 1986.

In the meantime, preservationists surveying the cultural resources in Huntington nominated the Aluminaire to the National Register of Historic Places; it was listed in 1985 and singled out as exemplifying "the principles and design elements of the International Style."

View of the Aluminaire in the late 1980s before disassembly. *(Michael Schwarting)*

The fate of the Aluminaire house was publicly debated in 1987 when its owner, a surgeon, sought to demolish the house to develop the land. Joe Rosa, an architect who was researching the work of Albert Frey and recognized the significance of the structure, did much to publicize the plight of the Aluminaire. State and local preservationists banded together to fight the proposal, and the *New York Times* ominously reported on March 8, 1987, that an "icon of modernism [was] poised for extinction." The savior was the New York Institute of Technology, which came forward and offered to move the house to its Center for Architecture in Central Islip, Long Island. With a sizable grant from the New York State Department of Parks, Recreation, and Historic Preservation, the

The Aluminaire being
dismantled by students.
(Michael Schwarting)

Aluminaire was carefully dismantled by institute students in 1988. Reassembly is expected to begin in 1991.

The Aluminaire, designed as an experimental house to promote new technologies and materials and to generate new ideas, was not without its flaws. As Reyner Banham pointedly noted in his book *The Architecture of the Well-Tempered Environment*, internal acoustic privacy was minimal; a prime culprit was the bathroom on the third level directly above the living area. Banham also criticized the lack of inherent stiffness that made the Aluminaire almost impossible to erect without temporary bracing. And the house was not well insulated by today's standards, although it was lauded at the time of its original construction for its effectiveness in excluding heat and cold.

Nonetheless, the impact of Kocher and Frey's design was not insubstantial. The Aluminaire gave many Americans their first real glimpse of an International Style dwelling: sleek, low-maintenance surfaces; large windows making maximum use of natural daylight; built-ins; and a compact, efficient floor plan. Even if the startling, machinelike appearance of the house was not embraced by the majority of new homeowners and their architects, many of the Aluminaire's features began to appear in American houses in the late 1930s and 1940s. Two-story living spaces, such as the one featured in the Aluminaire, are today commonplace, as are built-in furniture and the use of synthetics to create easy-to-clean, low-maintenance surfaces. The materials used in the house—aluminum and synthetic products—had appeared elsewhere, but their application to residential architecture was new. In the last 50 years aluminum has become a ubiquitous cladding material in America, although not in the form of the square panels envisioned by Kocher and Frey but as horizontal strips that simulate traditional wood clapboarding.

There is no question that the Aluminaire gave many New Yorkers their first look at the potential of standardized construction. The dismantling and reassembly of the house at least three times in its 60-year history is testimony to the soundness of Kocher and Frey's initial concept. A noble experiment utilizing new materials, design principles, and construction techniques, the Aluminaire introduced the American public to the concept of the house as a "machine for living in" and eloquently proclaimed the confidence its designers held for the future of the American house. ⬗

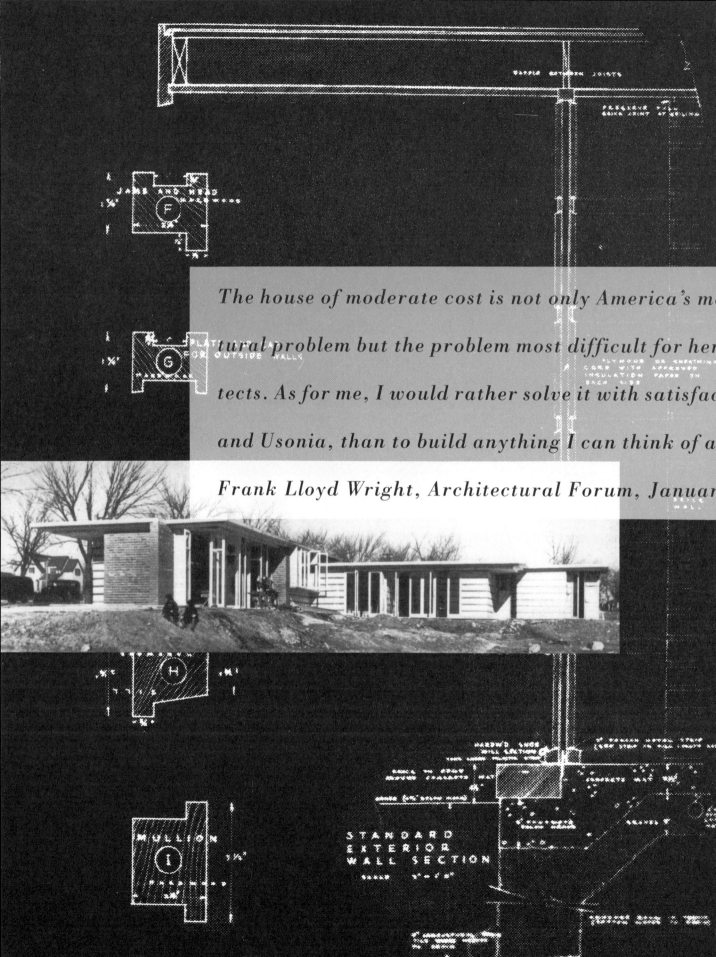

The house of moderate cost is not only America's m[...]

[...]tural problem but the problem most difficult for he[...]

tects. As for me, I would rather solve it with satisfac[...]

and Usonia, than to build anything I can think of a[...]

Frank Lloyd Wright, Architectural Forum, Januar[...]

The house of moderate cost is not only America's major architectural problem but the problem most difficult for her major architects. As for me, I would rather solve it with satisfaction to myself and Usonia, than to build anything I can think of at the moment.

Frank Lloyd Wright, *Architectural Forum*, January 1938

(center left)
Garden facade of the Jacobs
House, Madison, Wisconsin.
(Architectural Forum)

Sash details of one of the working
drawings for the Pope-Leighey
House, Mount Vernon, Virginia.
(Frank Lloyd Wright Foundation)

In August 1936 a young journalist and his wife, Herbert and Katherine Jacobs, drove west from their home in Madison, Wisconsin, to visit Frank Lloyd Wright in his studio at Taliesin. They presented Wright with the bold challenge of designing for them "a decent five-thousand-dollar house." Wright, to their surprise, accepted the challenge. That house became Usonia Number One, the prototype for the roughly two dozen houses that Wright designed over the next several years as cost-effective and efficient homes for the families of average means.

Architects and the construction industry always suffer during economic downturns, and the Depression defined the accomplishments and failings of the 1930s. Wright, faced with a dearth of clients, founded his own architecture school, the Taliesin Fellowship, in 1932. Two years later the *Milwaukee Journal* sent a junior reporter—Jacobs—to check on the progress of the new school. As so often in life, serendipity played a part. Literally at the time Jacobs was interviewing Wright, Katherine Jacobs, back in Milwaukee, was giving birth to their daughter, Susan, who was destined eventually to join the Taliesin Fellowship.

Yet another two years later, a job opportunity brought the Jacobses to Madison, where they were distressed by what they found available in the rental market and decided to build their own house. A cousin's suggestion led them to make the appointment to visit Wright in 1936. The Jacobses, believing they would need to tempt Wright beyond his architectural fee, turned their major limitation—a lack of money—into a plea on behalf of the millions of Americans with similar constraints. Wright, agreeing to undertake the task, realized that this was more than just a commission for a small house. In fact, Wright told the Jacobses that he had wanted for years to design a low-cost house but that no client had ever asked. Wright would ultimately spend more time on the Jacobs House than his fee warranted, but he in turn benefited from the opportunity to experiment with some of his ideas for inexpensive building techniques.

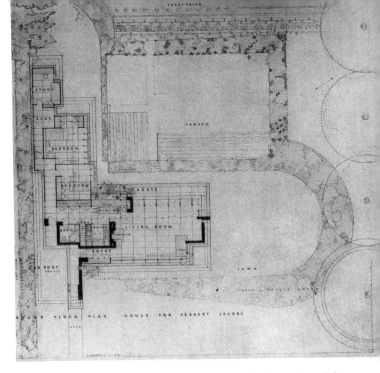

Wright integrated the adjacent landscape into the floor plan of the Jacobs House (1937), making it an extension of the house. (Architectural Forum)

Wright told the Jacobses that most clients would expect a $10,000 house for $5,000. The Jacobses assured him that they understood a budget of $5,000 would require compromises. Wright was fortunate in this respect. His clients had not only a tight budget but also a clearly defined program and realistic expectations. With a large body of work already built, Wright had a firm grasp of the relationship between the role and expense of the various features in a house. The economies he advocated were in two areas: construction and function. The Jacobses would need to pare down to the necessities. From his knowledge of construction costs, Wright quickly ticked off the amenities the Jacobses would have to do without, including a tiled bathroom and fancy cabinetry. Another casualty of economy was a basement; the house was to be built on a concrete slab.

The Jacobses were fortunate in another way: their architect was at a peak of creativity in his career. Already in his sixties, Wright had recently published his autobiography and was enjoying a period of rejuvenation. The Taliesin Fellowship projects—among them Broadacre City, Wright's vision of a suburban utopia—began to attract attention and, ultimately, clients. One of these clients was Pittsburgh retailer Edgar Kaufmann, father of Taliesin apprentice Edgar Kaufmann, Jr.

The younger Kaufmann encouraged his father to commission Wright to design Fallingwater, the family's weekend retreat in the Pennsylvania mountains. Another major client of the 1930s was Herbert F. Johnson of the Johnson Wax Company. Both Fallingwater and the Johnson Wax Administration Building, destined to be among Wright's most famous works, were on the boards at Taliesin when the Jacobs House was designed.

In January 1938, after the Jacobs House was completed, Wright wrote in *Architectural Forum*:

In our country the chief obstacle to any real solution of the moderate-cost house-problem is the fact that our people do not really know how to live, imagining their idiosyncracies to be their "tastes," their prejudices to be their predilections and their ignorance to be virtue where any beauty of living is concerned. To be more specific, a

What Can Be Eliminated from the Typical House?

In the January 1938 issue of *Architectural Forum*, Wright explained how to save money in constructing a house by eliminating unnecessary items:

"1. Visible roofs are expensive and unnecessary.   2. A garage is no longer necessary as cars are made. A carport will do, with liberal overhead shelter and walls on two sides.   3. The old-fashioned basement, except for a fuel and heater space was always a plague spot. A steam-warmed concrete mat four inches thick laid directly on the ground over gravel filling, the walls set upon that, is better.   4. Interior 'trim' is no longer necessary.   5. We need no radiators, no light fixtures. We will heat the house the Roman way—that is to say, in or beneath the floors—and make the wiring system itself to be the light fixtures, throwing light upon the ceiling. Light will thus be indirect except for a few outlets for floor lamps.   6. Furniture, pictures, and bric-a-brac are unnecessary except as the walls can be made to include them or be them.   7. No painting at all. Wood best preserves itself. Only the floor mat need be waxed.   8. No plastering in the building.   9. No gutters, no downspouts."

Many of Wright's suggestions—the carport, slab-on-grade construction with radiant heat, built-in furniture, and indirect lighting—were solid innovations that became widely accepted. However, the list mixes construction economies with stylistic dogma. While all roofs are expensive, Wright objects to visible roofs, not mentioning that flat roofs do not shed water well and are prone to leaks. Gutters cost money to install and are rarely attractive, but they do help prevent water damage to walls and foundations.

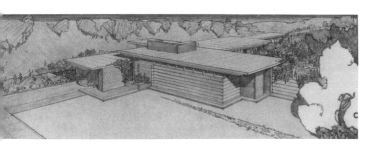

Wright often used perspective drawings such as these of the Jacobs House, because they most closely approximated what the eye would see. (Architectural Forum)

small house on the side street might have charm if it didn't ape the big house on the avenue, just as the Usonian village might have great charm if it didn't ape the big town.

To achieve what Wright intended, people would have to rethink how they lived and adapt to a new social order. Not everyone was up to it—one reason we do not all live in Usonian houses. The Jacobs family, however, was willing to break with tradition. From their perspective, Wright was spectacularly successful; the Jacobses became Wright's devoted clients and friends.

Most people would agree that Wright's work was revolutionary and that he marched to a different drummer. Yet to Wright himself, his work was evolutionary. Ideas evolved over time; favorites were repeated. Concepts were developed, set aside, and later resurrected, sometimes on paper, sometimes only

What Does "Usonian" Mean?

The origin of the term "Usonian" is mysterious. Wright supposedly attributed the word to Samuel Butler's utopian novel *Erewhon,* although "Usonia" does not appear in standard editions of the book. Wright considered "United States of North America" a better and more precise term than "America." The word "America," he reasoned, also includes Canada and Mexico. Just "United States" gives no clue to location, while "United States of America" does not distinguish between North and South America. Further, "USA" could be confused with the then newly formed Union of South Africa. "Usonia" was the term Wright adopted to describe the country and people he was designing for, to give his work an authentic American imprimatur. Through his writings and force of will he made the term part of our vocabulary.

Today "Usonian" is used almost exclusively as a stylistic term associated with the approximately two dozen wooden Wright-designed houses built between the mid-1930s and the early 1940s.

in his mind. Wright indulged his fascination with new materials throughout his career, usually with the client as guinea pig.

Antecedents abound in Wright's work. The Usonian houses were no exception. Like all architectural "firsts," the Jacobs House contained elements from earlier designs. It was, however, the first complete Usonian house and a clear prototype for subsequent Usonian designs. And, like all prototypes, it contained mistakes. But by any commonly accepted measure, the house was a success. It was published, received critical acclaim, brought fame and attention to its architect, pleased the client, and came in on budget. As a result, clients sought Wright out to design more Usonian houses.

Adopting a grid system to establish regular, modular dimensions, Wright organized the concept for Usonian houses to the point that standardized drawings were used for details common among the individual houses. The grid system allowed maximum design flexibility; the standard details gave the Usonian houses a strong family resemblance. Although few would accuse Wright of taking a "cookie-cutter" approach, repeating standardized details also reduced his design costs. There is no evidence that he passed these savings on to his clients in the form of reduced fees. Rather, the clients benefited from savings in construction costs.

What could the client expect in a Usonian house? Typically ground-hugging, the houses were one story, basementless, featuring an overhanging flat roof that contrasted with the verticality of a brick or stone chimney. Walls were a thin sandwich of boards with building paper between layers. Owners of Usonian houses reported that the thin walls made sweaters a standard winter garment. In the summer, natural ventilation had to suffice to keep the house cool. The absence of attic and basement, and the sandwich-wall construction, meant that there was no space to run air-conditioning ducts. Although pine was used for the exposed wall surfaces in the Jacobs House, Wright switched to more rot-resistant cypress and redwood for later Usonian houses. Areas where materials joined were always horizontal, sometimes exagger-

The houses visible in the background give context to the dramatic modernity of the street facade of the Jacobs House. (Roy E. Peterson and Larry Cuneo, Architectural Forum*)*

As seen in the Pope-Leighey House, the living space of a Usonian home typically featured a quiet space with shelves, built-in furniture, a dining area (to the left, defined by a lower ceiling), and the hearth (just visible to the right). (Jack E. Boucher, Historic American Buildings Survey)

ated. Even screw heads were turned so that their slots were horizontal. South or garden-facing walls featured huge expanses of glass that blurred the distinction between inside and outside. North or street-facing walls tended to be nearly solid, with narrow ribbons of windows set high under the roof eaves.

The floor plan radiated from the chimney mass. The hearth was the figurative and literal heart of the house, dominating a large living room that included a dining space and, often, an alcove with built-in shelves and desk. Adjacent, but not separated by a door, was the kitchen. The spaces flowed into one another, defined by function and architectural detailing—i.e., perception—rather than by walls and doors. In the communal areas of the house the effect was of great spaciousness. By contrast, the private spaces were small

The dramatic horizontal emphasis and grain pattern of the cypress siding of the Pope-Leighey House are complemented by the whimsical pattern of the vertical windows lighting the gallery space inside. (Jack E. Boucher, Historic American Buildings Survey)

The Pope-Leighey House

Half a continent away from the Jacobs House, not far from Washington, D.C., another Usonian house was built that was destined to play a role in the emerging historic preservation movement. Designed for Loren Pope in 1939 for a site in Falls Church, Virginia, the house is a "small polliwog-plan" Usonian, the body comprising the main living spaces and the tail, short in this instance, being the private bedroom spaces. The house exhibits typical Usonian features: a single story, slab-on-grade construction, spaces rather than rooms in the public areas of the house, small bedrooms with built-in closets, large expanses of glass. The Pope-Leighey House, as it is now called, was to become the first National Trust for Historic Preservation property that could be called vernacular; that is, the home of an ordinary citizen. Today the house is one of the few Usonian houses open to the public.

The National Trust's involvement with the house began shortly after a July 1963 letter from the Commonwealth of Virginia's Department of Highways informed the owner, Marjorie Leighey, that her house lay in the right-of-way for a planned interstate highway. Mrs. Leighey, determined to fight for the house's survival, sought the assistance of the National Trust for Historic Preservation and the U.S. Department of the Interior. Over the following year, negotiations among federal, state, and local officials and representatives of the National Trust, attended by extensive media coverage, led to the house's rescue from demolition. Still, the highway officials prevailed. The highway could not be moved; the house would have to be.

However, the group that had come together to save the house was later instrumental in helping to force highway officials to take historic values into consideration when planning road construction.

What followed was a unique cooperative effort that brought together Loren Pope; Marjorie Leighey; Gordon Chadwick, the Taliesin apprentice who supervised the original construction; the original builder, Howard Rickert; and officials from the National Park Service and the National Trust. The wooden parts of the house were dismantled and trucked to their new site on the grounds of Woodlawn Plantation, a National Trust property near Mount Vernon; the brick masonry and concrete floor were replaced. As part of the work, documentation of the house was prepared for the Historic American Buildings Survey, a roster of significant structures across the country maintained by the National Park Service; the Pope-Leighey House is one of the youngest buildings ever so honored.

and cramped; they were generally arranged as a wing, or tail, off the main part of the house. Hallways were narrow, bedrooms snug but made efficient by built-in closets.

Wright used the Jacobs House to define his Usonian concept. In his 1954 book *The Natural House*, he wrote:

Notwithstanding all efforts to improve the product, the American "small house" problem is still a pressing, needy, hungry, confused issue. It is only super-common-sense that can take us along the road to the better thing in building.

What would be really sensible in this matter of the modest dwelling for our time and place? Let's see how far the first Herbert Jacobs house at Madison, Wisconsin, is a sensible house. This house for a young journalist, his wife, and small daughter was built in 1937. Cost: Fifty-five hundred dollars, including architect's fee of four hundred and fifty. Contract let to P. B. Grove.

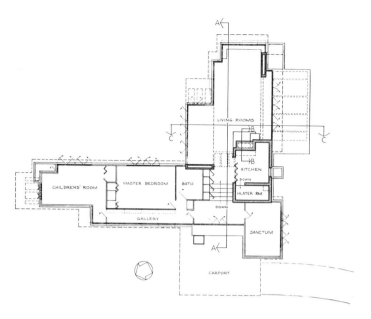

Floor plan of the Pope-Leighey House (1940). (James M. Hamill, Historic American Buildings Survey)

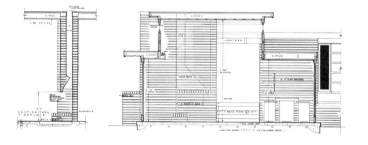

This cross-sectional drawing of the Pope-Leighey House illustrates the geometric complexities of a Usonian house. (Jack E. Schafer, Historic American Buildings Survey)

To give the small Jacobs family the benefit of the advantages of the era in which they live, many simplifications must take place. Mr. and Mrs. Jacobs must themselves see life in somewhat simplified terms. What are the essentials in their case, a typical case? It is not only necessary to get rid of all unnecessary complications in construction, necessary to use work in the mill to good advantage, necessary to eliminate, so far as possible, field

The Pope-Leighey House on its original site in Falls Church, Virginia. (Jack E. Boucher, Historic American Buildings Survey)

labor which is always expensive: it is necessary to consolidate and simplify the three appurtenance systems—heating, lighting, and sanitation. At least this must be our economy if we are to achieve the sense of spaciousness and vista we desire in order to liberate the people living in the house. And it would be ideal to complete the building in one operation as it goes along. Inside and outside should be complete in one operation. The house finished inside as it is completed outside.

Wright's approach to the problem of affordable housing was multifaceted. He used new construction techniques and new materials. Perhaps most boldly, he proposed a new social order, introducing changes in our perception of what a house should look like, how it is arranged, and how we live and function in it. The functional changes he introduced can be seen in today's ubiquitous open-plan houses, in which spaces flow into one another instead of being separated into cubicles by walls and doors.

A narrow gallery with clerestory windows gives access to the bedrooms in the Pope-Leighey House. Wright rationalized the narrow gallery on the basis of the narrow passages in Pullman sleeping cars. (Jack E. Boucher, Historic American Buildings Survey)

Dismantling the Pope-Leighey House in preparation for its move to Woodlawn Plantation, Mount Vernon, Virginia. Usonian walls and roofs were prefabricated units that could be set in place at the job site. (Donald B. Myer, AIA, Historic American Buildings Survey)

Wright-designed dining furniture stands in front of floor-to-ceiling glass doors that open onto the Pope-Leighey House garden. (Jack E. Boucher, Historic American Buildings Survey)

The Pope-Leighey House on its current site at Woodlawn Plantation. (Jack E. Boucher, Historic American Buildings Survey)

Wright's conception of communities of the future was demonstrated in his proposals for Broadacre City developed in the early 1930s: low-density, low-rise, and green. By contrast the French-Swiss architect Le Corbusier's vision of the ideal 20th-century city, *la ville radieuse*, could not have been more different: high-density and high-rise. A large percentage of Wright's built work had been suburban, so it made sense that his city of the future was suburban in character. He envisioned his Usonian homes— Prairie Style houses for the common man— being designed for, and built in, that setting.

Like all revolutionaries, Wright faced resistance. Building-code officials were skeptical of his structural innovations, mortgage lenders wary of his designs. The Jacobs House, because of its flat roof, did not qualify for a Federal Housing Administration mortgage. A sympathetic banker who in his youth had enjoyed Wright's Midway Gardens (an outdoor recreational garden and restaurant in Chicago now demolished) arranged a loan for the Jacobses. Loren Pope had to get his mortgage money from his employer. And Usonia, the very people Wright hoped would embrace his new order, was indifferent. Americans, it seems, preferred saltboxes and colonials. ⬛

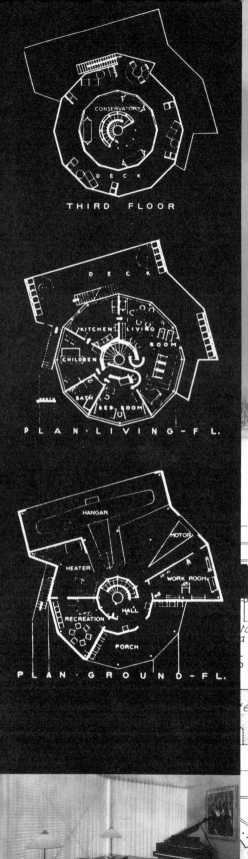

THIRD FLOOR

PLAN·LIVING·FL.

HANGAR

MOTOR

HEATER

WORK ROOM

RECREATION HALL

PORCH

PLAN·GROUND·FL.

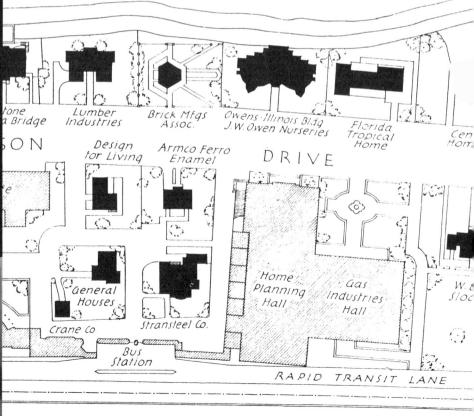

LAKE MICHIGAN

...tone
...a Bridge

Lumber
Industries

Brick Mfgs
Assoc.

Owens-Illinois Bldg
J.W. Owen Nurseries

Florida
Tropical
Home

Cen
Hom

...SON

Design
for Living

Armco Ferro
Enamel

DRIVE

Home
Planning
Hall

Gas
Industries
Hall

W. &
Stoc

General
Houses

Stransteel Co.

Crane Co

Bus
Station

RAPID TRANSIT LANE

INNER DRIVE

The usual house of today is rigid. The House of Tomorrow is flexible. At one moment, with venetian blinds raised and the curtains drawn back, one feels as though he were out of doors, an exhilarating and unusual sensation. In another moment, the room can be entirely enclosed to the point of the most comfortable seclusion. Throughout the house every modern convenience is made available at the touch of a finger. Absolute comfort is assured. One cannot but feel how very practical are the innovations relating to our future mode of home-life.

Home and Furnishings: A Century of Progress, 1934

Conceived in 1927, at a time of great economic prosperity, the Century of Progress International Exposition opened in Chicago in May 1933 to a Depression-weary public. This international fair had been organized to celebrate the centennial of America's largest midwestern city and was intended to depict a "century of progress" in science and technology and its effects on industry and on everyday life. The fair, which was extended through 1934, turned out to be a welcome escape from the grim realities facing many Americans.

Like the Chicago World's Columbian Exposition of 1893, with its strong neoclassical architecture and elaborate site plan, the Century of Progress Exposition made a strong impression on the general public, who flocked to the shores of Lake Michigan to catch a glimpse of the future. There were exhibition halls constructed by the giants of American industry, eager to show their latest, most up-to-date products, and even a complete automobile assembly plant that could be toured by a thousand people at a time. There were pavilions built by such countries as Sweden and Italy; Goodyear blimps; Burlington's streamlined Zephyr train; and exhibits dedicated to science, travel, and transportation. For many, the Century of Progress Exposition represented their first exposure to modern design and technology. As the fair entered its second year—the 1934 season—existing exhibits were modified and new displays created in the hope of sustaining high attendance.

Today the fair has been largely forgotten, dwarfed by a similar but larger extravaganza in New York in 1939. The fair's most spectacular buildings have been razed or moved, its artifacts scattered, and its 427-acre site redeveloped.

Thirteen modern homes were on display when the Century of Progress Exposition opened in 1933. Clustered together along Leif Erickson Drive were:

Howard T. Fisher's General Houses, Inc.

The Design for Living House, designed by John C. B. Moore

The Armco-Ferro Enamel House, designed by Robert Smith, Jr.

The Stran-Steel House, designed by O'Dell and Rowland

The Masonite House, designed by Frazier and Raftery

The Rostone House, designed by Walter Scholer

The Tropical Home, designed by Robert Law Weed

The Lumber Industries House, designed by
    Ernest A. Grunsfeld, Jr.

The Common Brick House, designed by Andrew N. Rebori

The House of Tomorrow, designed by George Fred Keck

The House of Today, designed by Corbett, Harrison and
    MacMurray

Keck's Crystal House was created for the exposition's 1934 season and was located elsewhere on the fairgrounds.

Surprisingly, given the elaborate industrial exhibits and exotic foreign pavilions, one of the Century of Progress Exposition's most popular attractions was a collection of 13 model houses built along the Lake Michigan waterfront. Financed and built by private corporations and trade associations, the houses were intended to show the impact of modern technology on residential architecture and to "present to the layman the *dernier cri* in house design, plan, furnishing, and equipment."[1]

House sponsors went to great lengths to demonstrate new structural and surface materials, old materials put to new uses, the latest heating and air-conditioning units, kitchen equipment, bathroom fixtures, and labor-saving and comfort-providing devices. Such features were, according to one contemporary account, incorporated in the houses "for the edification, education, and stimulation of the prospective homeowner"— in other words, to present new ideas and to promote new products to an eager, if impecunious, public.

One house, in particular, stood out among the others at the crowded site: a starkly modern 12-sided structure, three stories tall, with exterior walls of glass and an airplane hangar on the ground floor. To say that the house was unusual would be an understatement. True to its name, the "House of Tomorrow" bore little resemblance to anything fairgoers had seen before. Its architect, George Fred Keck, was a young Midwesterner who had begun a modest practice in Chicago just seven years earlier.

Keck was born in Watertown, Wisconsin, in 1895, and attended the University of Illinois, where he earned a degree in architectural

Exterior view of the House of Tomorrow in 1933. (Hedrich-Blessing)

engineering. After two years in the Army during World War I and several years as an architectural apprentice, Keck opened his own office in Chicago in 1926. His younger brother, William, born in 1908, joined the firm upon his own graduation from the University of Illinois; he became a full partner after World War II. George Fred Keck's first commissions skillfully synthesized a variety of contemporary American and European influences: Prairie Style, de Stijl, and Art Deco. It seems clear that Keck recognized the Chicago exposition as a great opportunity to promote modern architecture.

Unlike fairs that came before it, the Century of Progress Exposition did not receive city, state, or federal support; rather, it was sponsored entirely by public-spirited citizens and private industry. Concessionaires were contracted to furnish transportation, facilities, conveniences, amusements, and entertainment. Modest admission prices—10 cents for the House of Tomorrow—enabled the concessionaires to recoup their investments. In the case of the House of Tomorrow, Keck applied to the directors of the exposition to construct, maintain, and operate a model house; a

Map showing the locations of the Modern Houses at the Century of Progress Exposition, 1933. (Architectural Forum)

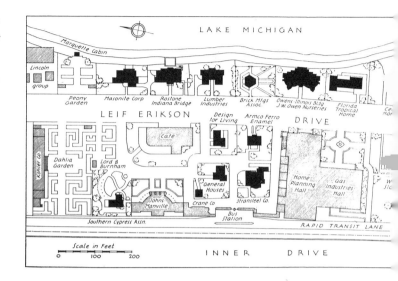

corporation, Century Homes, Inc., was established specifically to facilitate construction and operation. The corporation in turn sold manufacturers the rights to install their materials and products in the house. General Electric, Libbey-Owens-Ford Glass Company, Reynolds Metals, and the Goodyear Tire and Rubber Company were some of the better-known manufacturers whose products were used in the House of Tomorrow and whose names were listed in the promotional leaflet. Pierce-Arrow supplied a sensational Silver Arrow automobile, which was housed in the garage, and Curtiss-Wright donated the small "sport biplane" that sat in the ground-floor hangar.

Ironically, Keck's inspiration for the House of Tomorrow came neither from Buckminster Fuller's Dymaxion, which had appeared in architectural journals in 1929 (see Chapter 5), nor from the Bauhaus designs, which around this time were receiving widespread attention in Europe. Even though Keck had purchased an early translation of *Towards a New Architecture* and was obviously influenced by Le Corbusier's concept of the house as a "machine for living," the inspiration for his particular design can be traced to a building located just half a mile from his childhood home in Watertown, Wisconsin:

the Richards House (see page 53), a three-story octagon constructed in 1853! The promotional leaflet for the House of Tomorrow stated, "If the inventive spirit and direct expression as exemplified in [the Richards House], built in the middle of the last century, had been carried on, we should have escaped the inanities of the post-Civil War period and the last thirty years of this present century. We might now have an architectural technique comparable to the technical development in our industries."

Its polygonal shape aside, the Richards House contained a number of features that found their way into the House of Tomorrow: a centralized heating system, a central staircase, and shading devices on the windows to protect against summer heat.

The promotional brochure provides additional insight into Keck's original concept:

The house of tomorrow is an exhibition house. It was designed to demonstrate mechanical equipment and new building materials that are now on the market. The house of tomorrow is an efficiently designed house. The chief concern of the architect was not to give a specific form to his building, but rather to find a solution to the many and varied new requirements of a residence in a simple and direct manner. The causes were considered first, the effects later. He started from the inside and worked out.

The brochure goes on to give a concise description of the house:

The house is designed around an air-conditioning system. [Such a] system works most efficiently when operated within a closed space, when its balance of air output and intake is not disturbed, as by open windows and doors. Glass is obtainable in such large sizes that, with the use of standard store-front construction and a steel frame to carry floor and roof loads, it is possible to use it as walls, thus doing away with windows and their attendant expense of upkeep and other inefficiencies. By using venetian blinds, roller shades and curtains, these last of almost numberless materials, the light through these glass walls can be controlled from absolute darkness to as full light as nature affords.

One of the most unusual features of the House of Tomorrow was its structural system:

The house is built on a steel frame. Delicately slender columns carry the steel beams, fibre-concrete covered joists and fibre-concrete floor slabs. In many portions of the house the frame-work is left exposed, notably in the central portion around the stair and in the solarium on the top floor. This may appear strange at first glance. Tomorrow we will be accustomed to it and will know it to be as right and proper and beautiful as we now consider Elizabethan exposed half-timbers and ceiling beams of wood.

A series of photographs in the brochure illustrates how the structural framework was erected. First, the central utility stack was constructed; next, the steel framework, including the floor beams, was lifted into place and attached to the central utility stack.

From the House of Tomorrow pamphlet, a series of views demonstrates how the House of Tomorrow was constructed. (William Keck)

With the steel framework complete, the pre-fabricated fibre-concrete floor joists were laid in place and the floor slabs poured. There were no bearing walls or partitions in the house at all; exterior walls were either glass or "phenoloid board," a type of vermiculate board. Interior walls were covered with plasterboard or Carrara glass. For the 1934 season, a more permanent material—standing-seam copper painted black—replaced the "phenoloid board" on the exterior. Cross-bracing at each bay, behind the windows, provided additional stability to the structure.

The plan of the house was unlike any other in the exposition, as the brochure was quick to point out:

The plan of the house is as unusual as it is logical. The utilities, the heat and cold ducts, vents, stack, water-supply pipes and stairs are located in the central portion of the house and the rooms radiate from this central portion. All the living rooms are outside; only the

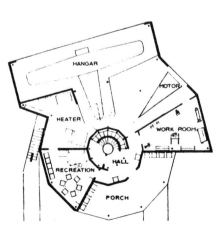

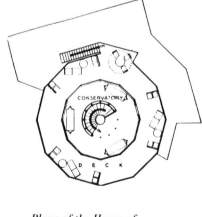

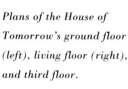

Plans of the House of Tomorrow's ground floor (left), living floor (right), and third floor.

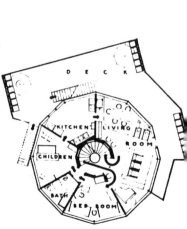

services are inside. The stair in this central portion is equipped with indirect integral lighting. The plan is very flexible, as can be judged by referring to the first floor plan. Notice that the work-room and the garage extend out beyond the volume of the second floor and that the airplane hangar extends out even farther. The third or sun-deck floor can be enlarged and additional bedrooms and bathrooms located there. Complete new floors could be added above as nothing below would be disturbed. The roof over the projected areas is covered with a waterproof compressed asphalt board and serves as a terrace. The house is nearly circular in shape a duodecagon more exactly. This shape was not selected arbitrarily but resulted from the number and sizes of the rooms required on the different floors and from the fact that the glass walls on each of these twelve sides would be of a size that could be installed efficiently. Had this house been smaller or larger the number of sides would accordingly have been decreased or increased.

Additional innovations abounded: Venetian blinds, roller shades, and curtains controlled the amount of light entering the house. At one moment the blinds could be raised and the curtains drawn back to give the sense of being out of doors. The house began Keck's lifelong interest in maximizing the use of the sun's rays (see Afterword). According to his brother William, who helped develop the details of

The House of Tomorrow at the Century of Progress Exposition in 1934. Admission was 10 cents, while children with parents were admitted free. (State Historical Society of Wisconsin)

the plan, the Kecks' firm was unable to interest a glass manufacturer in subsidizing the cost of heating the building during the winter (the house was boarded up in the winter after the fair season was over).

The House of Tomorrow was one of the first houses open to the public that featured central air conditioning. The system was designed to maintain the house at a constant temperature and humidity level; with inoperable windows, the system provided air that was "ever fresh, odorless and dustless."[2] In reality, in the summer months the master bedroom proved impossible to keep cool, and it was closed to visitors.

Keck anticipated that homeowners of the future would use personal automobiles and airplanes to get from place to place and that they would want to store these vehicles nearby. Electric doors in the hangar and garage folded up into the ceiling with the flick of a switch. To fit the plane into its snug hangar, a portion of the floor around the tires was cut away.

Great care was taken in lighting the house; portable and adjustable lamps were used throughout, and dimmer switches were installed on each floor. Illumination in the master bedroom featured colored filters for a more restful light.

Interior view of the dining area. The floor, designed for easy maintenance, is end-grain block wood. (Hedrich-Blessing)

Floors had low-maintenance coverings: rubber tile, end-grain block wood, wood, and concrete. Each flooring material was used where it best served its purpose.

The kitchen design reflected up-to-the-minute mechanical innovations. When the exposition opened in 1933, kitchen appliances were electric. When the exposition reopened in 1934, the kitchen was "gas-powered to the nth degree" with the latest gas range and a gas-fueled, iceless refrigerator.[3]

The house contained no permanent, built-in closets. Rather, movable wardrobes were provided to hold clothes, lending added flexibility to the plan.

Kitchen of the House of Tomorrow. (Iconographic Collections, State Historical Society of Wisconsin)

Living room of the House of Tomorrow. (Iconographic Collections, State Historical Society of Wisconsin)

View of terrace, with a blimp in the background. (Hedrich-Blessing)

Glass was also used extensively on the interior. In the living room the walls were of colored and polished plate glass. The wall around the stairway was of black Carrara glass, while the wall separating the kitchen was soft-gray glass. Bathroom walls were sheathed in frosted glass. Even the legs of the grand piano were constructed of glass. All surfaces could be cleaned easily and required little or no maintenance.

Keck designed the house with large wrap-around decks on two levels that extended the house's living area. He envisioned tremen-

dous use of the decks in the summer months; with their sporty pipe railings, the open terraces gave visitors the impression of being on board the deck of a sleek ocean liner.

The 1933 promotional brochure emphasized that it was impossible to treat the interior as separate from the exterior, as the House of Tomorrow "is so completely a whole, the decorating and the furnishing being but a completing of the house." Furnishings, executed by local firms, were designed by Keck's office to complement the architecture. Lamps, chairs, hammocks, beds, and tables were specially designed to maximize the sense of spaciousness and to fit the somewhat awkward spaces. Although rare and exotic woods, luxurious fabrics, and polished metal were widely used, the overall effect was spare and understated.

One of the most talked-about features of the house was the built-in aquarium in the children's room. One commentator wrote, "Children, according to all reports, are fascinated by the fish and will spend hours quietly watching their movements. Now that, I claim, is a real idea. Anything that will keep kids occupied for hours…quietly…well, that has some merit."[4]

For the 1934 season, the interior was transformed by decorator Mabel Schamberg: overstuffed Moderne chairs, ruffled flounce curtains, and a zebra-skin rug in the newly designated "cocktail room" gave the House of Tomorrow's interior a decidedly Hollywood appearance. Referring to the transformation of a basement room into a lounge area, Schamberg said: "Since the repeal of the Volstead Act, the [new] cocktail room figures largely as a necessary adjunct to the well-equipped home." "Flamingo pink" became one of the dominant colors, introduced in various tones throughout the house to inject a "spirit of gaiety and happiness for the family group." Not surprisingly, the change in decor pleased neither of the Kecks.

More than 750,000 people toured the house in the first year of the exposition. In 1934,

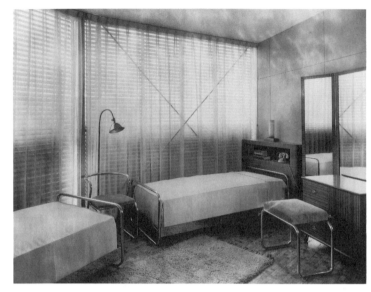

Bedroom in the House of Tomorrow. (Iconographic Collections, State Historical Society of Wisconsin)

after the redecorating, another 500,000 toured the house. While there was never any intention to market the house, the architects stood ready to build one for a prospective client. Alas, for whatever reason, no requests were forthcoming.

Reaction to the fair's architecture, including the 13 model houses, was mixed: Ralph Adams Cram, known for his Gothic university campuses, looked on the architecture of the exposition "as a definite retrogression, a reversal of a fine tendency and a return to the regrettable aberrations of the fifty years of aesthetic 'Dark Ages' in the United States," according to the July 1933 issue of *Architectural Forum*. However, another respected architect, Jacques Ely Kahn, praised the "high standard of accomplishment" and "clarity of presentation" evident in the fair's architecture. Frank Lloyd Wright, perhaps stung because his work was not represented at the exposition, accused the fair's designers of "wholesale imitation" and dismissed "the whole performance...[as] petty, strident, and base."

The reaction among the lay visitors was similar; *Architectural Forum* polled fairgoers and published some of the more colorful comments in its July 1933 issue. Advertising

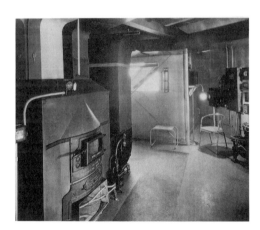

Furnace room of the House of Tomorrow. (Iconographic Collections, State Historical Society of Wisconsin)

executive Joel Newton of Chicago called the House of Tomorrow "very fine and...so very comfortable," while Mrs. J. C. Lawrence, a housewife from Oak Park, Illinois, indicated that the House of Tomorrow and its neighbor, the "Common Brick House," were "too much like prisons." A carpenter from Brooklyn, New York, expressed concern about the flat roofs that were found on many of the houses, including the House of Tomorrow: "You must figure on storms in winter and a flat roof isn't so good."

With the House of Tomorrow a financial success, George Fred Keck submitted a second application to the exposition directors "to construct, equip, maintain and operate a Modern house, charging an admission of ten cents per person." Keck's second design was even more radical than the first: the Crystal House was made entirely of glass and steel; it "combined the ultimate constructivist aesthetic with truly progressive structural and material technology."[5] The house had a totally prefabricated structural frame, which was erected in three days; floors consisted of steel sections bolted in place. The location of the Crystal House, far from the other modern houses in the fair, prevented it from becoming a financial success, and at the close of the 1934 season it was dismantled and the furnishings and materials auctioned off to pay the bills.

The House of Tomorrow was far luckier. After the fair closed in 1934, Chicago developer Robert Bartlett purchased six of the fair's houses for $2,500 apiece. He had them loaded onto a barge and transported 30 miles to Beverly Shores, Indiana, a resort town that he was developing along Lake Michigan.

There the houses stood, open to the public for an additional 10 years to entice prospective buyers to the stucco houses that Bartlett was building elsewhere in Beverly Shores. According to local residents, Bartlett built a 200-foot-long pier on the lake to receive the buildings; the houses were lifted by giant cranes onto the pier and then rolled across the dunes on timbers to their new locations. In the mid-1940s the Century of Progress houses were sold as private residences. When the Indiana Dunes National Lakeshore was established in 1966 as a unit of the National Park system, it included the houses within its boundaries. An agreement with the National Park Service will keep the House of Tomorrow in private hands until 1995.

Since its relocation to Beverly Shores, the House of Tomorrow has undergone a number of changes, the most radical being the replacement of the large plate-glass windows with smaller, operable sash. Presumably the

Crystal House, 1934. (Hedrich-Blessing)

alteration was made for reasons of economy; large sheets of glass are not energy-efficient in the cold midwestern winters. Many of the house's original interior finishes, however, are still present: the black pigmented glass in the living room, the end-grain block wood flooring in the bedrooms, and the banded synthetic flooring in the third floor sunroom. As the carpenter from Brooklyn predicted, the house has been plagued by a leaky roof. Nonetheless, the future of the House of Tomorrow looks good: it and the remaining houses from the Century of Progress Exposition were listed in the National Register of Historic Places in 1986.

George Fred Keck and his brother William went on to build up a well-respected architectural firm, active throughout the Midwest. Many of the ideas introduced in the House of

*The House of Tomorrow, now part of the
Indiana Dunes National Lakeshore.
(H. Ward Jandl)*

Tomorrow—the use of passive solar energy, large expanses of glass, and central air conditioning—found their way into later Keck and Keck designs. During World War II the brothers designed prefabricated houses, and their residential work, much of it making use of passive solar concepts, was published frequently in the 1960s. In addition to his extensive practice, George Fred Keck headed the department of architecture at Chicago's Institute of Design from 1937 until 1944. At age 85 he received an award from the American Institute of Architects, Chicago Chapter, for his 50 years of "distinguished architectural practice which pioneered many new concepts in design and technology."[6] William Keck, who helped translate his brother's ideas for the House of Tomorrow into working drawings, still maintains an office in Chicago.

One of George Fred Keck's principal concerns throughout the 1930s and early 1940s was to familiarize the public with modern design and technology. The House of Tomorrow did much to achieve this goal. According to his brother, Keck did not expect people to request copies of the Century of Progress houses. Rather, for clients Keck took a practical approach, designing houses that employed current technologies and contemporary principles yet that were relatively traditional in appearance.

The Chicago writer Joseph C. Folsom neatly summed up what the Kecks were able to achieve in his article, "The House of Tomorrow":

…the house as it stands is certainly the answer to a desire on the part of the public to see what architects are thinking about. I don't know. Probably the House of Tomorrow is just a pipe dream. Probably none of us will ever live in a house like that. But there are a multitude of things there that we will all want to incorporate in the next house we build, and it is certainly a tonic to run into something new and original for a change. ♨

KITCHEN

LIVING R

EQUIPMENT ROOM

BATH

BEDROOM N

CLOSET

"Anne, will you come shopping with me this afternoon? I'm going to buy a house." This is what you may expect to hear one woman say to another in the next few weeks as you walk down the street, or perhaps you yourself may be saying, "Thank you very much, it's just the kind of house I want. Please send it to this address and charge it," for the packaged house is here and will soon be exhibited in your favorite department store. Imagine being able to buy your home as you would buy a package of cereal or face powder—a home complete in every minute detail, that you can actually see, touch, examine, and discuss before you buy it and above all know exactly what it is going to cost, down to the last penny, before you move in.

With this tantalizing opener, the May 1935 issue of Woman's Home Companion heralded the extraordinary Motohome, the brainchild of architect Robert W. McLaughlin, Jr., and promoter Foster Gunnison. Years of planning had preceded the Motohome's introduction into the rapidly expanding prefabricated housing market. A month earlier, this remarkable prefabricated house had been introduced to the general public at Wanamaker's department store in New York City. Wrapped in cellophane and tied with a huge red ribbon, the house had been unveiled in a special ceremony by none other than the president's mother, Sara Delano Roosevelt, who called it "science's answer to the housing problem." The New York Times reported that Mrs. Roosevelt expressed the fervent hope that the "women of America will more and more have good homes, well planned, such as this."

McLaughlin, born in Kalamazoo, Michigan, in 1900 to a prominent minister and his wife, served in the U.S. Navy during World War I and graduated from Princeton University with a master's degree in fine arts in 1926. After completing a traveling fellowship to study architecture in Italy, France, and England, he moved to New York and formed a partnership with Arthur C. Holden, another Princeton graduate and a vigorous advocate of community planning. The two quickly developed a "thriving business in designing conventional country homes for socially prominent squires and dowagers."[1]

Like many other architects during the Depression, McLaughlin saw exciting opportunities in the field of low-cost housing, and, in association with engineer John B. Lewis, he began to explore the feasibility of marketing prefabricated dwellings nationwide.

One of the team's first objectives was to analyze various materials and types of construction and the ways in which they could be used to speed assembly: framed and frameless

The prototype for the Motohome was the Hazelton, Pennsylvania, house constructed for Donald Markle in 1933.

systems; lumber, steel, and concrete; wall and insulating boards—all were carefully examined to determine the best-for-all-purposes method of construction. After months of research, McLaughlin and Lewis determined that the most cost-effective house would be one framed in steel and clad with wall panels composed of concrete and asbestos.

McLaughlin shared these ideas with Donald Markle, president of the Jeddo-Highland Coal Company in Hazelton, Pennsylvania, who was interested in providing affordable housing for his 4,000 miners—and, not coincidentally, in finding a new outlet for his firm's anthracite-burning furnaces. Markle liked what he heard and ordered a house.

Constructed in the fall of 1932, the house became a prototype for the Motohome. Resting on a cement foundation with a three-foot air space, the four-and-a-half room house was constructed by six unskilled laborers in one month's time. Modular wall panels were bolted onto a steel frame. Vertical sheets of fiber insulating board, faced on each side with asbestos cement, formed the 2 ¼ inch-thick walls. The flat steel roof was insulated with a paper-thin sheet of aluminum. Floors were supported by open-truss steel joists, overlaid with gypsum planks and a wood finish. The finished house, while modest in

To downplay the stark modernity of McLaughlin's architecture, the interior of this Motohome was furnished with traditional furniture.

size and simply detailed, was not without character; its soft-green exterior, highlighted with black bands at the top and bottom and with shining verticals of aluminum, stood in striking contrast to the staid clapboard cottages that lined Hazelton's streets.

The house was deemed a technological success after its thermal abilities were subjected to a series of rigorous tests, but Markle apparently did not order additional units. Nonetheless, satisfied with the performance of his prototype, McLaughlin formed a corporation called American Houses, rented office space in New York City, and purchased a 15,000-square-foot plant in Kearny, New Jersey, to begin production. Using standardized components and a grid system, McLaughlin was able to create approximately 120 different models, ranging from one-room cottages to large, two-story residences complete with maid's quarters and a two-car garage.

McLaughlin proposed to market the houses through a network of dealerships; by December 1933 offices in Houston, Boston, and Orlando, Florida, had been established. The Boston dealers, Frederick B. Taylor and Thomas H. Burchard, were young entrepreneurs fresh out of college. Their incorporation papers declared that their partnership would "act as distributor and/or agent and/or dealer…finance and arrange for financ-

ing…deal in contracts…buy, sell and hold land for itself or others…transport necessary materials, supplies and equipment by road, rail, steam, truck, air or water."[2] The breadth of these activities suggests that many of the details for manufacturing and marketing American Houses were not yet worked out; it also indicates that the company was being set up to do volume business.

By the end of 1933, American Houses, Inc.,

The living and dining area of a Motohome decorated with more modern furniture.

had built approximately a dozen model homes throughout the Northeast for testing and marketing purposes and had generated some positive press in national architectural magazines. In January 1934 *Architectural Record* reported that the company offered some 30 standard houses of prefabricated construction, ranging in price from $1,975 to $15,000, not including the cost of land or erection.

Architectural Forum noted in April 1934 that "while most prefabricators strive to produce a house for the masses, American Houses subscribes to the old doctrine that 'style percolates downward.'" The company's

Six unskilled laborers constructed the four-and-a-half room house in one month. Wall panels of insulating board faced on both sides with asbestos cement board were attached to a steel frame, secured with exterior aluminum pilasters.

goal was not to liberate the slum dweller but to supply distinctive, well-built houses for families in the middle income bracket.

Like the original model in Hazelton, McLaughlin's new houses were all steel-framed, on four-foot centers, with exterior wall panels of asbestos cement and flat roofs. Standard equipment for the houses included a stove, water heater, and furnace; air

humidity control and circulation features; interior wiring; interior plumbing; and complete interior and exterior decoration. Outside walls were painted, and interior walls were finished with a covering material available in a variety of colors and patterns. All of the houses featured steel casement sash with inside screens.

The materials and equipment for the houses came from a variety of existing sources. Established companies supplied the various components—doors, hardware, window sash, plumbing fixtures—based on specifications prepared by American Houses, Inc. The wall panels themselves were fabricated in the New Jersey factory, which also served as a centralized distribution center. This concept of using outside suppliers, initiated with the first house at Hazelton to reduce overhead, was an important tenet of the company's approach to mass-produced housing throughout its 15-year history.

It was in 1934 that American Houses, Inc., affiliated itself with Houses, Inc., an organization founded by General Electric for the prime purpose of "cooperating in the encouragement of house-building of all worthy types."[3] Houses, Inc., was unique to the housing industry. A holding company, it had no houses of its own, it manufactured nothing, it had no plants. Instead, it promised to do what American Houses, Inc., had heretofore been unable to do: invest money in the company to enable it to perfect its product and manufacture houses on a large scale.

At the helm of Houses, Inc., was Foster Gunnison, a 38-year-old Brooklyn native who, as junior partner of the lighting firm Cox, Nostrand & Gunnison, had sold fixtures to the Empire State Building and Rockefeller Center. Although he barely knew the difference between a stud and a joist, he was called by *Architectural Forum* in May 1935 "a creative salesman, a man who concocts glorious schemes on the basis of which is always the de-sire to sell a load of brick or something just as tangible." While at college, Gunnison had befriended Owen D. Young, chairman of the board of General Electric; both men were intrigued with the possibilities of prefabrication, and Young encouraged his protégé to pursue his interests. Gunnison sold his family interest in the *Brooklyn Eagle*, a well-respected local newspaper, and entered the housing business.

With informal assurances that he could count on Young and General Electric for assistance, Gunnison cast around for someone with construction experience to help in this new venture. As a lighting-fixture sales agent he had often dealt with the Fred F. French Companies, developers of Tudor City and Knickerbocker Village in New York City; from this organization he tapped Arthur Olsen, a senior executive with more than 20 years of building experience. Together Gunnison and Olsen probed virtually every development in the field of prefabrication, and stopped when they discovered American Houses.

American Houses, Inc., had by 1934 become a relative veteran in the prefabrication field; in fact, with 20 houses to its credit, the company was the leading housing prefabricator in the

The Motohome bathroom was, according to promotional literature, "a symbol of cleanliness and health." An equipment room, located between the bathroom and kitchen, was dubbed the "moto-heart" by Motohome promoters; it contained the house's oil burner, air conditioner, air filters, and hot-water supply.

country. It had gained practical experience through actual construction, yet still lacked sufficient funding to go into large-scale production. McLaughlin knew his company's weaknesses and saw in Houses, Inc., an opportunity to greatly expand operations. Gunnison, impressed with the strides that American Houses had made toward affordable housing in just a few short years, moved quickly and decisively. The two companies joined forces.

With engineers borrowed from the General Electric Company and the American Radiator Company, money from Houses, Inc., and McLaughlin's technical know-how, Gunnison set up shop. In the fall of 1934 he rented half a floor in Grand Central Palace, an exhibit hall in New York City, and set up the smallest unit that American Houses made. Aside from the rent, there was no overhead; according to *Architectural Forum*, everyone involved was working for nothing except the promise of a great future if their venture was a success.

Throughout the remainder of 1934, Gunnison and Olsen focused on the problems of perfecting manufacture: where to buy materials, how best to distribute their products, and how to finance them. McLaughlin and his staff used this time to select from the 120 house plans the 12 best. Gunnison clearly recognized that the cost of the completed houses depended

on the speed with which the houses could be fabricated; prices given out to the press were tentative, ranging from $3,800 to $9,900 in the January 1935 issue of *Westchester Magazine*, and from $4,900 to $15,000 in the May 1935 *Architectural Forum*.

What made the Motohome different from other steel-frame, prefabricated houses of the period—and from the earlier houses constructed by American Houses—was what McLaughlin termed the "moto-unit." This mechanical core—"the thing that makes the house go"—contained all the plumbing, heating, electrical, and mechanical devices for the house. It was this moto-unit that gave the Motohome its name. The moto-unit was installed in an "equipment room" that served the kitchen on one side and the bathroom on the other. In a two-story house, the upstairs bathroom was set directly above the moto-unit. The unit was designed to be preassembled, arriving at the site ready for simple connections to pipes and ducts. The specially designed furnace could be heated by gas, oil, coal, or electricity, "enabling the homeowner to choose the fuel best suited to his needs and the contents of his purse."[4]

Included in the basic price of the house were all materials and equipment, delivery, and erection, but not the cost of the lot or landscaping. By the time of the unveiling at Wanamaker's, Gunnison threw in the home furnishings, books in the living room, *and* a two-day supply of groceries—a shrewd piece

SG, Series 100." Again, this may have been a marketing ploy; Gunnison assured prospective buyers that the various models would be issued in limited quantities and that changes in design would be made as the production of each series was completed.

In 1935 *Westchester Magazine* reported that, during the early stages, the houses would be sold under various financial plans to determine which was most acceptable to

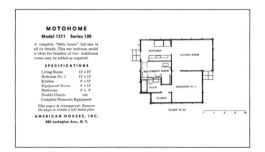

Illustrations from the Motohome catalog showing Model 1311, Series 100 R. The smallest model offered by American Houses, Inc., it was considered ideal for families of two. The floor plan was printed on transparent paper and could be reversed if prospective purchasers so desired.

of promotion that added to the futuristic aura surrounding the Motohome. Gunnison's gimmick did not go unnoticed in magazine and newspaper accounts.

Unlike the precut Sears Roebuck houses, which had evocative names such as "the Avon" or "the Princeton," Motohomes were listed according to model and series, such as "1421

the homeowner. The article stated that the houses would likely be sold on a monthly installment basis extending over a period of 15 years; the installments were to include life insurance so that if the owner should die, his family would have free title to the house.

Monthly payments could be as low as $38 for a bottom-of-the-line, three-room model. Gunnison persuaded the Federal Housing Administration, which had agreed to loan to one of Howard Fisher's prefabricated homes (see page 165), to ensure mortgages on Motohomes and sought commitments from local banks and insurance companies as well.

Parts for the houses were to be shipped by rail or boat to distribution centers. From these centers, the parts would be loaded onto trucks and shipped to the individual sites, accompanied by a construction supervisor and a mechanical superintendent. It was estimated that smaller houses could be erected in two weeks, using local labor, while large models would require three weeks. As part of their promotional materials, Gunnison and McLaughlin showed a futuristic six-wheel truck with an enormous glazed cab; emblazoned on the truck's side was the slogan "THIS CONTAINS ONE AMERICAN HOUSE."

While at this stage Motohomes were available in only 12 models, McLaughlin envisioned prospective buyers eventually being able to design their own custom-built homes using standardized components. "If you are interested in buying a house," he told reporter Katherine Bissell of *Woman's Home Companion* in May 1935, "the first thing that is given you is a box containing little models of exteriors with windows, doors and so on, interiors with various-sized rooms, and landscaping with trees and shrubs. Then with your very own hands you can build your home and see for yourself exactly what it is going to look like on your particular lot which you own or are hoping to own." But in 1935 any deviation from the 12 basic patterns—such as a basement, a pitched roof, or changes in fenestration—would necessarily increase the cost. If a Motohome owner wanted additional space at a later date, the sides and corners of the house could be "unbuttoned"—that is, taken down and re-erected—without loss of building materials.

The Motohome that was unveiled at Wanamaker's in April 1935 was one of the smallest models that American Houses offered. Despite its modest size—just four rooms— Joseph Appel, executive director of Wanamaker's, compared the house to "the introduction of the electric light, the wireless, and the automobile."[5] The house bore a striking resemblance to houses previously constructed by American Houses, Inc.: gray exterior walls made of cement and asbestos and trimmed in aluminum, metal casement windows, a flat roof, and a canopy over the front door with a scalloped fascia. McLaughlin

One of the most complete—and entertaining—descriptions of the Motohome's interior can be found in the May 1935 issue of *Woman's Home Companion:*

"Through the front door we entered directly into the living-room. What impressed me immediately was its sense of space, even though the room measures only twelve by sixteen feet. Mr. McLaughlin explained that this effect was achieved by the placement of the windows in one corner of the room. The room was so quietly and tastefully furnished in this demonstration house that one felt like sitting down in it immediately, which we did—

chose the color gray for the exterior to eliminate the need to paint and to reduce maintenance costs. He claimed, according to *Woman's Home Companion*, that the neutral shade of gray would "weather down to resemble lovely old pewter, taking on the blues and greens of the surrounding landscape."

These three Motohomes were constructed in White Plains, New York, in 1935 and were open to the public as model homes.

A month after the unveiling at Wanamaker's, three new model Motohomes were opened for public inspection on a naturally wooded site in Westchester County, New York. Gunnison told reporters that the site had been chosen "because we wish to prove [the houses'] acceptance in the highest class of community." The houses caused a sensation in White Plains, the town where they were erected: 4,000 people

that is, as soon as Mr. McLaughlin had turned on the air conditioner!

"When he came back, I was looking for the electric clock and the radio which he had previously mentioned. It took me several minutes to find them because they had been so well placed as to blend into the interior.

"'And there is also to be an electric cigarette-lighter,' he said, 'so that a busy woman can rush in the front door, or in from the kitchen, glance at the clock and with one switch light her cigarette and turn on the radio.'

"'He then called my attention to the following important features of the room:

• The floor of compressed hardwood beautifully waxed to resemble old timbers shiny with age.

• The ceilings marked off in large squares to look like lovely old plaster, of patented acoustical material, as are all the walls throughout the house.

• The casement windows with their cranked handles as in automobiles and with either screens or storm windows which button in so neatly and so compactly one can hardly see how and where it is done.

• The soft-toned wallpaper background from which spots can be removed with soap and water.

• The artificial lighting, which is always a bone of contention in any house, because the woman likes soft lighting over her chairs and the man a very bright light by which to read or play cards. So with each one of these houses goes a patented floor lamp; as it overhangs the back of a chair it is soft and subdued, but turned upward it becomes very bright, indirectly lighting the whole room.

• The dining corner with table and chairs, which immediately after dinner becomes an important part of the living-room.

"Through a door at the left we entered the kitchen—to me the most exciting room in the house. Here, encased in a large long cabinet of insulated steel along one side of the room, is the domestic moto-unit. This unit contains all the plumbing, heating, electrical and mechanical devices for the kitchen and bath. Indirect lighting enables the housekeeper to work without ever being in her own light. At the extreme left in the ceiling is an electrical exhaust which takes out every bit of the cooking fumes. The same exhaust can draw the cool night air into the roof compartment, so that in warmer climates it is not necessary to run the air conditioner at night.

"Immediately below all the interesting utility cupboards is an electrical refrigerator, an electric stove, and a sink with beautiful drainboards, one of which when opened shows an electric clothes-washer. The working counter is covered with dull polished metal and—wonder of wonders—all along the foot of the cabinet there is a space of about two inches from the floor up, which enables one to stand at the sink and work without scraping the toes of one's shoes.

"The furnace is a wonderful new invention and can run with coal, oil, gas or electricity. There are no radiators in any of the rooms because of the air-conditioning system.

"Immediately behind this cupboard is a closet for housing the hot water unit with an opening from the hall, thus completing the working unit of the house all in one compact square.

"The bathroom side of this mechanical unit has many novel features such as a new lavatory—a little longer and much narrower than usual, but of a size which enables one to bathe a baby in it as comfortably as in a small tub. Over the lavatory is a new triplicate mirror-faced cupboard with large spaces for storing everything from safety razors to face powder.

"The hall has a large cedar-lined closet for linens and blankets, and every closet has an electric light in it.

Each Motohome kitchen was completely furnished with a large refrigerator, Monel metal sink and counter, and four-burner gas or electric range.

"A complete set of books telling how to get the most out of life in the house is another unique feature. These tell how to maintain and take care of the house, how to decorate it, how to landscape it, how to bring up the babies and even how to set the table and cook. Etiquette and budgets are also carefully explained.

"The whole house is built on a concrete foundation, every four feet having sixteen-inch floor joists of steel over which a steel rein-forced termike is laid, then a mastic and then the floors. There is a three-foot air space under the house. A cellar is not necessary but you can have one if you wish by paying a little more.

"Above the fireproof walls and ceilings are sixteen-inch steel beams, and then termike and finally a fireproof sun deck. The house can stand twenty-six feet of snow on the roof and a one hundred and fifty mile an hour wind, is a perfect lightning arrester and will withstand shocks of earthquake. The house is also fireproof, soundproof and termite-proof."

About the only detail omitted from this description was the patented toilet that hung from the wall; its seat automatically registered the sitter's weight.

Many of the larger two-story Motohomes had roof decks such as this.

a week trooped through, at 25 cents a head, with profits being donated to charity. The smallest home was a single-story, two-bedroom model with a built-in garage. The second model was slightly more spacious, with three bedrooms and a larger living room. The third model had two stories, with three bedrooms, two baths, and a separate dining room.

Initial reactions in the news media and in architectural journals were positive—writers and critics saw the Motohome as the beginning of "a new epoch in American architecture."[6] In reporting on the progress of the Motohome, the July 1935 issue of *Architectural Forum* stated that 4,950 people had been seriously enough interested to sign a purchase contract, "if and when contracts are being accepted." The same article went on to mention that 40 Motohomes had been built or were in the process of erection, most as private residences.

This series of aerial views shows three Motohomes being constructed in Boston; again, while all three utilize the same building components, each model is distinctly different.

Additional model homes were built in Boston, Staten Island, and Garden City, New York, in an effort to stimulate sales. The Staten Island model Motohome, sponsored by the local chamber of commerce, was given away at the end of the exposition.

Despite strong interest on the part of prospective home buyers—model homes seemed to attract large and enthusiastic crowds—actual sales were sluggish and profits were nonexistent. Only 150 or so Motohomes were built between 1934 and 1936. Most of them were constructed in the suburbs of New York: White Plains, Oyster Bay, Little Neck, and New Canaan, although company records show that Motohomes were also built in such places as Caldwell, Kansas, and Sarasota, Florida.

What caused the Motohome to falter? Clearly McLaughlin and his colleagues had designed an innovative series of houses, combining the latest technology with the concepts

of mass production. Each model was solidly built and carefully designed to reduce maintenance costs and make the homemaker's job easier. While rooms tended to be small (particularly the bedrooms), the houses were well organized and functional. The Motohome may have had some gimmicks, such as the built-in cigarette lighter, but most of the featured appliances and equipment were true labor-saving devices that are today found in most American houses.

Failure of the Motohome to revolutionize the housing industry can be attributed to several factors: the extreme novelty of the product, its relatively high cost, and the lack of capitalization. From its inception the Motohome was radically different from typical houses of the period. Its boxy shape, flat roof, corner windows, and industrial appear-

Model 21064GG, Series 100 L, one of the largest Motohomes offered. It featured a two-car garage, four bathrooms, and six bedrooms.

The Model 21064GG, constructed in a suburb of Washington, D.C. This winter view shows the house shortly after construction.

The same Motohome 50 years later with minor modifications that left the house basically unaltered. In 1988 the house was radically altered and its Motohome details discarded. (John A. Burns, AIA)

ance set it apart from its Colonial Revival and bungalow neighbors. Its materials—steel, aluminum, plywood, concrete, and asbestos—were new to residential construction and were decidedly untraditional. Its method of construction—relying largely on prefabrication—was different from what most homeowners were familiar with. And its price was beyond the reach of the majority of American families. Motohomes were introduced to the public just as the United States was recovering from a severe economic depression, and while there was widespread interest in acquiring new houses, few families could afford the downpayment necessary to make ownership a reality. Sales of the Motohome were focused in the New York area, where low-cost speculative houses were widely available; in short, the Motohome was not competitive.

The funds needed to permit full-scale production of Motohomes simply were not forthcoming. Perhaps made nervous by the lack of immediate sales, General Electric and Houses, Inc., withdrew their support within two years of the exhibit at Wanamaker's. "Creative differences" may be one way to characterize the dissolution of the partnership. Without outside financial support, American Houses, Inc., was unable to produce and market the Motohome.

McLaughlin had hoped to produce a house that was both cheaper and of higher quality than the competition. This had not been possible, he reported to the board of directors of American Houses in early 1938, because "the labor economies of prefabrication have been confused and offset by the development and use of new materials." McLaughlin recom-

mended that American Houses, Inc., refocus
its efforts to concentrate solely on low-cost
prefabricated housing, using traditional
designs and traditional materials. "If our
primary reason for being is not to produce a
better house but as good a house that is
cheaper," McLaughlin argued, "then we
should immediately so plan our activities as
to take full advantage of savings in labor
without then penalizing ourselves by using
more expensive materials." Supported by
pages of financial data, McLaughlin's recommendations were apparently accepted by the
board. In the summer of 1938 the company
abandoned its previous approach and reverted to the use of conventional designs,
platform-frame construction, and traditional
materials. One of its first projects was the
construction of 136 precut, partially prefabricated houses in Dundalk, Maryland, for
Bethlehem Steel; ironically, this single project
produced more compact Cape Cod houses
than all the Motohomes sold in the previous
two years.

Subsequent endeavors of American
Houses, Inc., were written up in American
architectural journals, but the company's
later products tended to be conservative in
design, materials, and appearance. During
World War II the company was actively in-

*Although American Houses, Inc., stopped production of the
Motohome, it continued to experiment with prefabrication. Here, in
Dundalk, Maryland, more than 100 prefabricated wood-frame units
were built for Bethlehem Steel.*

volved in the production of demountable housing—buildings that could be disassembled
quickly and re-erected on another site—and
in licensing other companies to manufacture
prefabricated housing parts. Robert
McLaughlin continued as chairman of the
board of American Houses until 1945; in 1952
he assumed directorship of Princeton
University's School of Architecture, where
he remained until his retirement in 1965.
McLaughlin died in 1989.

Late in 1935, Foster Gunnison from Houses,
Inc., founded his own company, Gunnison

"Going... going..."

In 1936 a Washington, D.C., automobile distributor named Lee D. Butler placed an order for a two-story Motohome. The house was erected at the site Butler selected: a prominent corner in Kenwood, an exclusive neighborhood of colonial and Tudor Revival homes in the Washington suburb of Bethesda, Maryland (see illustrations on page 153). With its flat roof, panel walls, and metal casement sash, Butler's Motohome stood out from the gable roofs and brick walls of its neighbors and was featured in the real estate pages of the *Washington Star*.

Homes, with headquarters in New Albany, Indiana. The company produced what was called "the first commercially successful mass-produced house in the United States."[7] Gunnison Homes built thousands of houses nationwide and achieved a staggering production rate of one house every 16 minutes. In 1953 Gunnison's company was taken over by U.S. Steel. Gunnison died eight years later in Florida. ⬙

In 1984 the house was purchased by a couple committed to preserving the house's Bauhaus look yet eager to update its mechanical systems and increase the size and number of windows. The resulting renovation respected the front elevation, with its characteristic panels and corner windows, and maintained much of the original plan. At the same time, the interior was given an airier feel with two-story spaces and larger rooms. The rear elevation was transformed by large expanses of glazing and a new stucco surface. Shortly after the project's completion—and renewed publicity in Washington newspapers—the couple separated and the house was sold.

Not satisfied with the recent renovation, the new owners decided that further expansion was needed. The front elevation was rebuilt in 1988, and all of the surviving, characteristic Motohome details were eliminated. The end result was a house that offers no clues to its distinguished and unique origins.

A two-story Motohome built for Advanced Homes, Inc., in Madison, Wisconsin. The garage has been converted into an extra room and solar panels have been added along one wall; despite these alterations the house is clearly recognizable as a Motohome. (H. Ward Jandl)

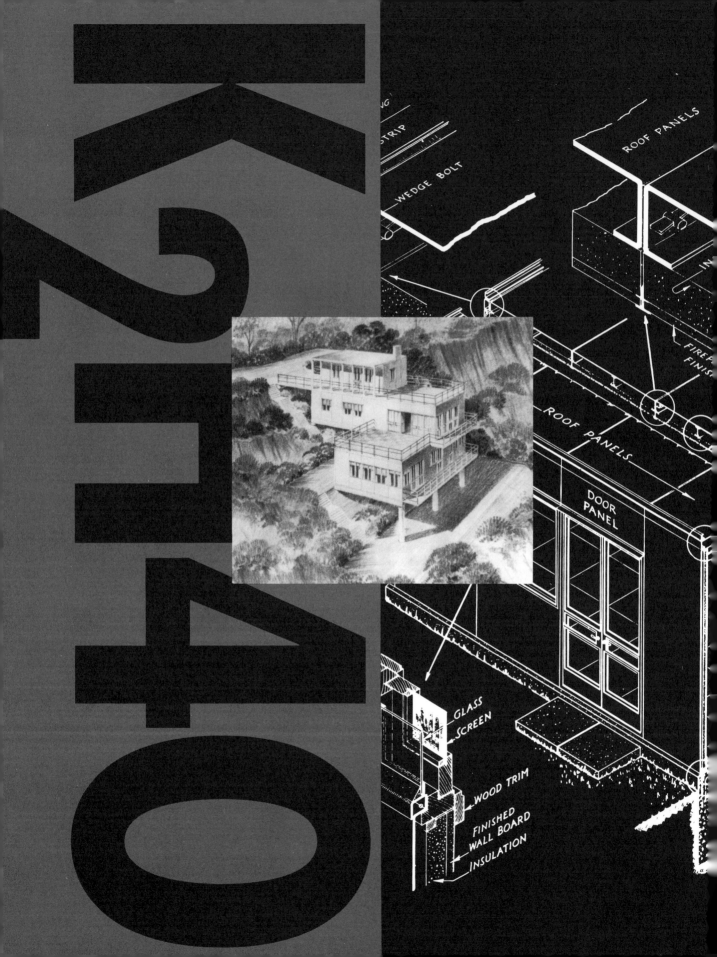

K2 1940

ROOF PANELS

WEDGE BOLT

STRIP

ROOF PANELS

DOOR PANEL

GLASS SCREEN

WOOD TRIM

FINISHED WALL BOARD

INSULATION

Ten   K₂H40: THE PROMISE OF PREFABRICATION

The house, among all the important tools of the twentieth century, is unique in the inefficiency and clumsiness of its design. The age that has produced the ocean liner, the skyscraper and the zeppelin has as yet done but little towards solving one of the most important and basic needs of mankind.... Of all the productions of our present day, the house alone is considered in terms of the past. We do not ride in Louis XIV stage coaches, or wear Elizabethan ruffles—why then should we live in imitations of Cotswold cottages or French eighteenth-century chateaux?

At the time he penned these words for *Architectural Record* in 1929, Howard T. Fisher was just 26, a year out of the Harvard University Graduate School of Design. His article predicted how improved technologies, materials, and methods of construction would make future houses more comfortable and convenient. Many of Fisher's predictions came true. New homes would be climate-controlled, the air warmed and humidified in the winter, cooled and dehumidified in the summer; walls would be well insulated, large windows would have "vacuumized" (double-glazed) panes; outlets for telephones would be in every room; bedrooms would have private baths, which Fisher considered "no extravagant luxury but an absolute basic minimum"; and dressing rooms would be "the place for the latest fad in health and athletic equipment— the Indian clubs, the ultra-violet lamp, the electric vibrator, or whatever it will be in the future."[1] Curiously, unlike many proponents of industrialized housing, Fisher was not an advocate of a new social order. He cautioned that the latest contraptions should "take into account the human elements of the servant problem," and noted that "many appliances are lying idle today not on account of any defects but simply because servants will not use them."[2]

On the Formula

K₂H4O is an architectural formula used to describe a specific General Houses model. "K" represents the basic house design, "₂" is a subdivision of the K design, "H" stands for a hall entrance, "4" means that there is room for four beds (but in only two bedrooms), and "O" indicates an optional extra room. Fisher chose alphanumeric formulas, rather than names, to identify the designs in order to give them a scientific aura. Models were given popular names only for purposes of marketing.

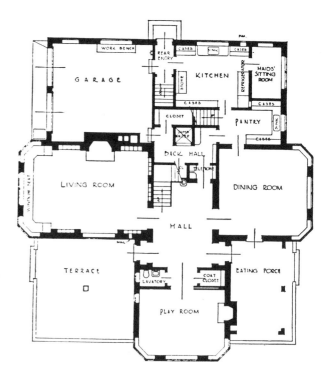

Between 1929 and 1932 Fisher expanded and developed his ideas into a new approach to housing that utilized a completely integrated, industrialized process patterned on the production of automobiles. In 1932 Fisher founded his own company, General Houses, Inc. But before doing so he solicited the support of several of the nation's leading industrialists.

How did someone so young and with so few built works get the ear of Charles A. Liddle, president of the Pullman Car and Manufacturing Corporation; Owen D. Young, president of General Electric; Harry S. Wherrett, president of Pittsburgh Plate Glass; and Lloyd R. Smith, president of the A. O. Smith Corporation? It certainly helped that one of Fisher's first commissions, a house for his older brother, Walter, received wide critical acclaim. Designed while Howard Fisher was still in school, the house is a large, imposing brick structure strongly reminiscent of modern Dutch housing of the period. The house's design was published in the United States and England shortly after its completion in 1929; the house still stands in the exclusive Chicago suburb of Winnetka, Illinois. Henry-Russell Hitchcock declared in the February 1930 issue of *The Arts* (two years before he and

The Walter T. Fisher House and its first-floor plan, 1929. (Howard T. Fisher, Architectural Record)

On Garages

Not all of Fisher's predictions came true. He was by no means alone among architects in promoting flat roofs, but the American public did and still does prefer sloped—or what Frank Lloyd Wright called "visible"—roofs. Another of Fisher's suggested improvements, that the garage should be adjacent to the front entrance, logical as it seems, has been only infrequently adopted. Garages were at first sited like the stables they replaced, away from the house, generally at the rear of a lot. Fisher wrote:

"In the past the garage has been built separate from the house, or where it is attached to the house has been placed as far as possible from the front door and connected through the kitchen or back hall. This was done on the theory that the garage was a dirty and perhaps even a noisy place. But it need not be, and where members of the family drive the car there seems to be no reason to make them go through the kitchen every time they want to go in or out. For the greatest convenience the garage should be located either near the front door or in such a way as to connect directly with the front hall."[3]

Despite Fisher's suggestion, the automobile and its attendant garage continue to deprive the suburban homeowner of the pride and enjoyment of entering through his own front door. Most of us still clomp from the garage into the house through the kitchen or, worse, the laundry room, just as the servants and chauffeurs used to. Front entrances are reserved for guests and salespeople. Fisher had better luck with some of his other ideas for garages:

"To avoid the necessity of having to get in and out of an automobile to operate garage doors they should be controlled by means of a switch placed on a post which the driver can reach without getting out of the car. Doors which roll up take the least space and are least affected by snow. There is no way of predicting what the future requirements for privately owned airplanes will be, but for automobiles it will seldom be advisable to build a garage that will hold less than two cars and most larger houses will require space for three or more."

Today the two-car garage with remote controlled overhead doors is a ubiquitous part of the suburban scene.

What Makes a House Prefabricated

Just what is a prefabricated house? Traditional home builders construct each house on-site, taking raw materials, cutting them to fit, and assembling the structure piece by piece, a slow and labor-intensive process. Prefabrication is meant to industrialize the construction process, making it more efficient and therefore less costly. The U.S. Department of Commerce officially defined prefabrication:

"A prefabricated home is one having walls, partitions, floors, ceilings, and/or roof composed of sections or panels varying in size which have been fabricated in a factory prior to erection on the building foundation. This is in contrast to the conventionally built home which is constructed piece by piece on the site."[4]

Philip Johnson organized the famous Museum of Modern Art exhibition on International Style architecture) that the house "is very nearly the first in America to which the most rigid international standards of architectural criticism may be profitably applied."

It also probably helped that Fisher was from a prominent Chicago family. His father, Walter Lowrie Fisher, was one of Chicago's leading lawyers and Secretary of the Interior under President Taft. Howard's brother, Walter, was a lawyer and president of the Amalgamated Trust and Savings Bank. There are other indications that Fisher moved in high social circles. In its July 4, 1932, issue, *Time* magazine, for instance, after describing young Fisher as "both a technician and theorist in architecture"—perhaps a polite way of saying un- or underemployed, not an uncommon status for architects in the Depression—went on to say that he was "considered an expert on designing squash courts."

Whatever the impact of family connections and commissions, however, it was Howard Fisher who conceived the ambitious proposal to found a construction company that would be the housing-industry equivalent of General Motors, and it was Howard Fisher who convinced corporate leaders to participate in the venture. Even the name of the organization, General Houses, Inc., consciously imitated the industrial giant.

Manufacturers, faced with underutilized production capacity because of dwindling demand, sought new markets for their wares. Even in the depths of the Depression, the housing industry was a considerable market; selling a few pounds of a product for every new home could return a sizable profit. Major industries thus consistently directed some of their research and development efforts toward the housing market. The housing industry, buffeted by similar economic woes, was constantly looking for innovations that could make homes affordable. Traditionally a fragmented industry made up of hundreds of small companies, the housing industry welcomed the vast resources that major corporations could bring to bear on a problem.

Time magazine assessed the situation:

It is notorious that the U.S., most precocious child of the Industrial Revolution, is a laggard in Housing—the business of furnishing cheap and comfortable shelter. Less than half the homes in the U.S. measure up to

Howard Fisher further explained the essentials of prefabrication:

"If you *shove* and *snap* a product into place in the field, that is prefabrication. If you mix, cut, spread, fit, and patch—that's not prefabrication. If the field operation is essentially *assembly*, rather than *manufacture*, you have prefabrication. A brick and plaster wall, of course, employs manufactured ingredients, but such a wall is really manufactured in the field. The amount of scrap and waste that must be cleaned up and removed from a building site may be taken as a rough index of the degree of prefabrication employed in any given building operation, since waste results principally from a manufacturing process and not an assembly process."[5]

To some extent, prefabrication is common in house construction today. Windows and doors come preassembled in their frames, ready to be fitted into rough openings. The most obvious example of prefabricated housing is the mobile home, which arrives at the site on wheels and needs merely to be placed on its foundation and connected to utility lines. That is as far as prefabrication can go, however. No one has yet been able to prefabricate foundations.

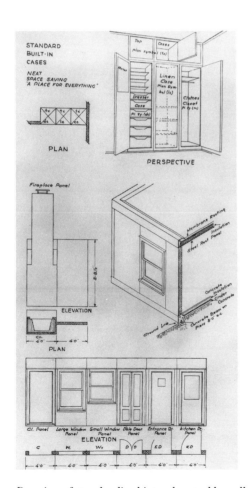

Drawing of standardized interchangeable wall units and built-in cases. (Howard T. Fisher, Architectural Record)

minimum standards of decency.... In measuring how far the housing industry has lagged behind the Industrial Revolution, Fortune found that whereas the $5,000 automobile of 1911 now sells for $2,000, the $20,000 house of 1911 still sells for $40,000.

There have been stirrings indicative of the application of science and scientific methods to shelter just as there have been to transportation.... A special committee of United States Steel Corp. has studied steel houses. American Rolling Mill Co. sees a future where steel will be used for streets as well as for houses. McClintic-Marshall has tried a small steel frame house division. In the secret laboratories of A. O. Smith Corp. of Milwaukee (largest maker of automobile frames and a leading manufacturer of welded steel pipes) engineers are known to be at work on housing.

Fisher's genius was in refining the idea of assembling houses from standardized prefabricated parts—that is, building houses the way General Motors assembled automobiles. The idea presented a challenge to Fisher's

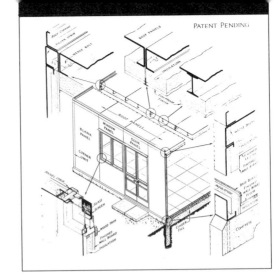

Details of prefabricated construction show the original panel designs used in the Page House and in the 1933 Century of Progress houses.(F. J. Wilder, Architectural Forum)

The Ruth Page House, 1929, was the first prefabricated house built by General Houses, Inc. Ruth Page was Fisher's sister-in-law. (Architectural Record)

talents both as an architect and as an engineer. The form and fit of all the individual components were critical to the success of the system. The houses should not be standardized, just the component pieces, so that there could be an almost infinite variety of house designs. Individual houses would be custom built on-site using stock components delivered by various suppliers from their warehouses. The companies Fisher initially lined up represented an impressive array of American industries:

American Radiator and Standard Sanitary Corporation: heating and plumbing

Concrete Engineering Company: design of concrete foundation

Container Corporation of America: insulation

Curtis Companies, Inc.: windows, cabinets, and millwork

General Electric Company: wiring and appliances

Pittsburgh Plate Glass Company: glass and paint

Pullman Car and Manufacturing Corporation: four-foot-wide pressed-steel panels for walls and "battle-deck" floors and roofs

Thomas A. Edison, Inc.: cement

In July 1932, even before General Houses completed its first house, *Fortune* magazine proclaimed, "It is now at last possible to announce that an integration of manufacturers, architects, engineers, and bankers has been effected with the early production of a low-cost, prefabricated house of excellent design and quick construction as its purpose." The house referred to was another family commission for Fisher, a small, single-story prefabricated house in Winnetka for his sister-in-law, the dancer Ruth Page.

General Houses, Inc., contracted to build a model home at the 1933 Century of Progress Exposition in Chicago. The housing exhibit at the fair was, in fact, a showcase of prefabrication; eight of the eleven houses were prefabricated. The particular General Houses model

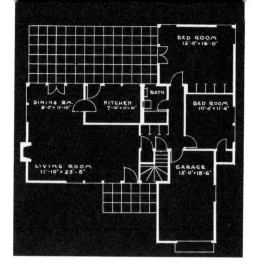

Floor plan and rendering of the General House erected for the 1933 Century of Progress Exposition— the Elmhurst K_3H4DP. (Kaufmann and Fabry/Hedrich-Blessing)

erected was a K_3H4DP "Elmhurst," a one-story, two-bedroom, single-bath house with a fireplace and a flat roof that retailed for $5,450.[6] The foundation was a turned-down concrete slab on a cinder fill. (The foundation got its name from the fact that the floor slab "turned down" around its perimeter and at other structural bearing points both for additional strength and to get below the frost line.) Bolts were set in the wet concrete to anchor the wall panels. The load-bearing wall panels were four feet wide and nine feet

The K_3H4DP, its rear terrace, and living room. (Kaufmann & Fabry)

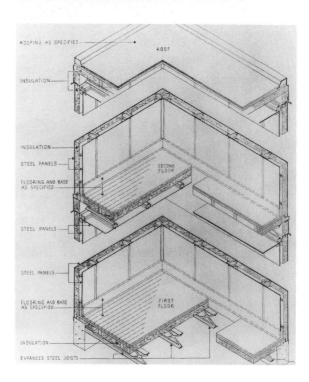

*Details of prefabricated construction show the new panel designs of the 1934 Century of Progress house. (*Architectural Forum*)*

tall, fabricated by Pullman from 14-gauge, rust-resisting, copper-bearing sheet steel, shop-finished with red lead. The panels were simply designed, easy to form on bending jigs, and thus did not require expensive custom tooling. Joints were made by bolting through the turned edges of the panels. Mastic was used to waterproof the joints. Roof panels were similar, but of "battle-deck" construction, with an I-beam welded at the midpoint to lend additional strength, and long enough to span the width of the house. The large and heavy roof panels had to be lifted into place with a crane, an expensive limitation. Interior surfaces of the wall and roof panels were finished with rigid insulation covered by wallboard. Interior partitions were sandwiches of rigid insulation faced with wallboard. The floor came in two-foot-square sections with a backing of two inches of insulation.

In 1934 General Houses, Inc., erected a second demonstration home for the Century of Progress Exposition. The new house was different from the 1933 model. (Models of prefabricated houses were constantly changing because manufacturers continuously tinkered with their designs.) Open-web steel joists supported the roof and floors, eliminating the need for a crane to erect the house. The furnace was relegated to a basement. A garage,

opening into the front hall, was added. Both exterior and interior wall surfaces were sheet steel with either Celotex or rock wool batt insulation; the total thickness of the walls was slightly more than four inches. The walls were described as similar to those of a refrigerator. Full-length windows were installed. The entire house, except for interior furnishings and equipment, was assembled on its foundation in 200 hours. Most of the 25,000 pounds of steel was bolted together with just a socket wrench.

Some of the suppliers changed, too. The open web joists and steel panels were fabricated by Kalman Steel Corporation, a subsidiary of Bethlehem Steel. Insulation came from the Celotex Company and General Insulating and Manufacturing Company. The window glass came from American Window Glass Company, although the paint still came from the Pitts-

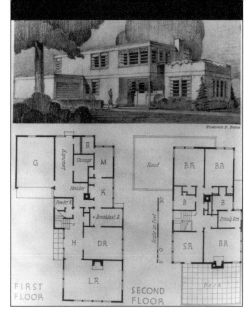

FIRST FLOOR   SECOND FLOOR

Rendering and floor plans of the first
speculatively built prefabricated house in
River Forest, Illinois. It was also the first
"prefab" to receive a Federal Housing
Administration–insured mortgage.
(Frederick D. Petrie, Architectural Forum)

The house in River Forest today.
(John A. Burns, AIA)

burgh Plate Glass Company. Some suppliers
were unchanged, including Curtis (windows
and millwork), General Electric (appliances),
and American Standard (plumbing fixtures).

The Century of Progress Exposition may
indeed have marked the high point of the prefabricated-housing movement in the United
States: by the time of the New York World's
Fair in 1939, traditional design and construction dominated the demonstration houses.
After the intense publicity surrounding
General Houses that started with the 1932
Fortune magazine article and ended when
the Century of Progress Exposition closed in
1934, the company settled down to work on
its goal of mass producing affordable homes.
The designs, materials, and suppliers continued to evolve over the next few years, but the
original concept remained intact. Most of the
sales of General Houses concentrated in the
Midwest; a few models were shipped overseas.
In 1935 the company became the first prefabricator to wholesale houses to a speculative
builder. The first house sold at wholesale,
purchased by developer Frank P. Ross of
Oak Park, Illinois, and erected in nearby
River Forest, received the first Federal
Housing Administration–insured loan on a
prefabricated steel dwelling. By 1936 General
Houses, Inc., had switched to a system of
steel-frame construction similar to the
Motohome's, with wall panels consisting of
cement-asbestos sheet siding, insulation, and
a plywood interior finish. General Houses,

Rendering of the dramatic house Fisher hoped
to build for himself. It was never constructed.
The house was likened to a Cadillac or
Lincoln, unlike the other General Houses,
which were compared to a Ford.
(Charles H. Dornbusch, Fortune)

Inc., built several hundred of its modern-looking houses before World War II, but the company's output was far below what could be considered mass production. In 1940 the company lost its founder when Fisher moved to Washington, D.C., where he worked for the National Housing Agency. In the late 1940s he resumed his architectural practice; in 1964 he became a professor at his alma mater, Harvard University.

Faced with public indifference to steel houses and flat roofs and encountering resistance not only from mortgage lenders but also from building and zoning officials and the craft trades, General Houses, Inc., eventually produced what the customer wanted as a means of survival. The company abandoned its primary material—steel—and its characteristic modern, flat-roofed styling in favor of more commercially popular designs and materials. After intensive development work at the end of the decade, the company introduced wooden homes of conventional architectural appearance, with sloping roofs, but still constructed of prefabricated panels. Undoubtedly, some of the changes resulted from Fisher's work for Sears Roebuck, the well-known Chicago-based manufacturer of precut houses. In 1935 Fisher designed a flat-roofed Sears house using prefabricated plywood wall panels. The new General Houses wall panels had two-by-four-inch frames with vertical, V-jointed tongue-and-groove siding, insulation, and gypsum board interior finish. Roof and ceiling panels were similar but had two-by-six-inch framing members.

Howard T. Fisher and General Houses, Inc., were prime movers in the development of the prefabricated-housing industry in the United States. The company even became one of the first prefabricators to participate in the housing program initiated by the Department of Defense in anticipation of World War II. Using modified versions of its new wooden designs, General Houses, Inc., erected five large developments to house defense workers during the build-up for the war. After the war, the company sold its wood-panel houses through lumberyards and materials dealers, and survived through the late 1940s.

General Houses, Inc., had a great deal in common with American Houses, Inc., developer of the Motohome (see page 141). The founders of both companies were idealistic, well connected, and Ivy League educated. Although the companies operated independently, they nevertheless seem intertwined. Certainly after the first published articles about their designs, each must have known about the other. General Houses, Inc., was the first to produce a steel-panel design. The steel-frame/cement-asbestos-panel Motohome was remarkably similar to a design subsequently adopted by General Houses. Both companies sought out large manufacturers as suppliers. American Houses operated its own factory; General Houses relied on components ordered from the manufacturers'inventory. General Houses got the first nationwide publicity; American Houses succeeded in signing on Wanamaker's and General Electric as corporate sponsors. Facing similar regulatory and marketing problems, both companies were ultimately forced to switch to traditional designs executed in wood in order to survive economically.

The group of talented architects Fisher recruited to work with him at General Houses, Inc., included Lawrence Perkins, Todd Wheeler, Philip Will, Jr., Charles S. Dornbusch, and Edward Larrabee Barnes. Perkins, Wheeler, and Will eventually founded their own highly successful architectural firm. Perkins, who worked on the first home General Houses built, later became famous for his school designs. Wheeler, Fisher's chief draftsman, became a hospital designer. From 1960 to 1962 Will served as president of the American Institute of Architects. Dornbusch, who produced many of the renderings that appeared in the 1932 *Fortune* magazine article, later taught at the Illinois Institute of Technology under Mies van der Rohe, where he won a Langley Fellowship from the American Institute of Architects in 1941 to study the German barns of southeastern Pennsylvania for the Historic American Buildings Survey, an early study of that vernacular building type. Barnes carried his experience to his own firm in New York, where he worked with industrial designer Henry Dreyfuss to design a prefabricated house for Consolidated Vultee in 1947. That project, like the more famous Lustron houses (see page 183), was one of the postwar efforts to redirect excess aircraft-production capacity to the pent-up demand for housing. ♣

John Farley

2"MOSAIC CONCRETE
LATH AND PLASTER WOOD FRAME
LEAD FOIL PENCIL RODS
HOOKED ANCHOR LEAD FOIL
RUBBER GASKET
4"4" MESH

WOOD FLOOR & JOISTS

WALL OF COLORED
SMALL STONE AGGREGATE

The present social movement is a leveling one and it is entirely possible that we all will come to understand that the security we desire for ourselves and our dependents lies in the nation's ability to provide food and shelter for everyone. It seems to me that the simplest way in which such security can be achieved is to enable everyone to procure a small house and a plot of ground, which can be cultivated and which will produce sustenance.

John J. Earley, *Journal of the American Concrete Institute,* **1935**

John Joseph Earley was born in New York City on December 12, 1881, to James Farrington Earley and his wife, Mary Kelly. James Earley was a fourth-generation stone carver who had emigrated to Boston from Dublin. In 1890 he traveled to Washington, D.C., to supervise a contract for his employer. Eventually he took over the contract himself and his family joined him in Washington, where he opened the Earley Studio, a stone carving and modeling business. A steady stream of commissions allowed the Earley Studio to establish its still-standing office at 2131 G Street, NW, in Washington's Foggy Bottom neighborhood. One of James Earley's carvings is the Monk of Dahlgren at Georgetown University's Dahlgren Chapel. His most widely known work is almost anonymous: he designed the buffalo nickel for the United States Mint.

John Joseph Earley was educated in Washington's parochial schools and at St. John's College. He apprenticed with his father at age 17 and began to learn the crafts of stone carving, sculpture, and model making.

In his father's studio he met Basil Gordon Taylor, who had started in the studio as a handyman but quickly earned more responsible positions. Upon James Earley's death in 1906, John Earley inherited the studio and began to run it with Taylor's assistance. Over the next decade, the firm would concentrate increasingly on plaster and stucco work.

Concrete and stucco, both historic materials, were rediscovered and became newly popular after the turn of the century. In the 1910s it became apparent that one of the modern variants of these materials, portland cement stucco applied over metal lath, deteriorated rapidly due to

Meridian Hill Park and Architectural Concrete

In 1916 the Earley Studio was contracted to perform the stucco work at Meridian Hill Park, a new park planned for a fashionable neighborhood north of the White House in Washington, D.C. The contract called for a full-scale stucco panel sample to be made for approval by the architect, Horace Peaslee, and the U.S. Commission of the Fine Arts. The first sample was rejected as drab and uninteresting. A second, textured sample was flawed by the dull gray color of the portland cement. The chairman of the commission, architect Cass Gilbert, suggested pressing pebbles into the soft stucco before it hardened—a possible solution, but costly because of the amount of labor it would require. Earley came up with the idea of using pebbles already in the mix—the aggregate—to achieve the same effect. The outer surface of concrete could be brushed away before it hardened completely and the aggregate revealed.

A new sample was cast, the formwork stripped off while the mix was green, and the still-soft surface of sand and cement was brushed away. The resulting panel was a rich, creamy tan, the natural color of the Potomac River gravel that had been used as the aggregate. The finished panels, which Earley called "architectural concrete," received rapid approval. Initial problems with the evenness of the appearance were solved by carefully controlling the size of the aggregate so that it would be distributed evenly throughout the mix.

A further problem developed when the Studio tried to strip away the intricate mold used to cast the balusters. Suction pulled pieces off of the soft castings, ruining most of them. In order to conform to the mold, the mix had to be so runny that it gained strength slowly. The green castings were too weak to hold together. Applying knowledge gained from the Bureau of Standards experiments, Earley instructed his crew to use old newspapers to soak up excess water from the castings. The technique worked. The castings could be stripped green without harm, and brushed to expose the aggregate finish.

Thus refined, Earley's techniques were used to produce the architectural elements of Meridian Hill Park still enjoyed today.

rusting. The Association of Metal Lath Manufacturers asked the National Bureau of Standards to research the problem. The bureau's research included the erection of test panels using different types of metal lath and various stucco formulas. The Earley Studio was apparently one of the contractors chosen to produce test panels for these experiments, which continued into the 1920s and attracted widespread interest from the building community. What the tests quickly showed was that reducing the excess water in the mix strengthened the material and reduced the likelihood of cracking or crazing in the finish. This finding would prove important in Earley's subsequent work with architectural concrete.

Earley was among the first to find practical applications for the National Bureau of Standards' scientific research. In his stucco work at Meridian Hill Park in Washington, D.C., he arrived at two essential elements of his future work with stucco and precast con-

Earley first used his exposed aggregate concrete extensively in Meridian Hill Park in Washington, D.C., as seen here in the Palladian fountain. (Jack E. Boucher, Historic American Buildings Survey)

crete and the basis for a highly successful business: careful grading of aggregate sizes to assure a uniform appearance when the surface is brushed and removing of excess water from the setting mix to achieve early strength.

The next important step came when Earley and J. C. Pearson, who was in charge of conducting the Bureau of Standards experiments, decided to collaborate in developing a new type of stucco with aggregate a tenth the

size of that found in structural concrete. Their idea was to use colored aggregates and Earley's brushed-surface technique to produce a permanently colored stucco finish. By 1919 they were confident enough in their process to employ it in the Earley Studio's stucco work on a field house in Washington's Potomac Park. The series of experiments and the practical experience gained in his work on the field house led Earley to secure several patents that formed the core of the "Earley Process," which his firm would use for the next 40 years.

The success of the Potomac Park field house also led to a commission that was to further the Earley Process. The congregation of the Church of the Sacred Heart, a Roman Catholic parish in Washington, D.C., was planning to build a Romanesque basilica with an elaborate and colorful interior. Since marble mosaics were so expensive, the church leaders approached the Earley Studio in the hope that colored concrete could somehow be used in imitation of traditional mosaics. Intrigued, Earley set to work. He accumulated aggregates in 200 different colors, from as far away as Italy and France, all carefully cataloged using the Munsell system. Next, he developed a technique to separate adjacent colors. Plaster molds were made from the architect's drawings, with thin plaster ridges defining the extent of each colored concrete poured into the mold. Ordinary concrete reinforced with steel mesh was poured over the back of the mosaic for support. Newspapers were used to draw off the excess water, providing the necessary strength so the molds could be stripped off and the surface wire-brushed before hardening. For wall and ceiling surfaces, negative-image molds were made and pressed into a coat of brown plaster applied to the surface; the molds left thin ridges into which the colored concrete could be troweled. After hardening sufficiently, these molded concrete forms could also be brushed to expose the aggregate. Installing the entire concrete mosaic took a year; the results were spectacular. When the church was consecrated in mid-1923, Earley's labors received critical acclaim. Thereafter, for many years, the Earley Studio would seldom lack for work. In 1936 the American Institute of Architects awarded Earley its medal for craftsmanship for his work at the church.

Other significant commissions of the 1920s included a replica of the Parthenon in Nashville, Tennessee; buildings for the new campus of Louisiana State University in Baton Rouge; and the Baha'i World Faith Temple of Light in Wilmette, Illinois, the most technically difficult project the Earley Studio would ever undertake. Earley was involved in the building of the temple from 1920, when the temple's architect, Louis Bourgeois, paid Earley an initial visit, until the completion of the project in 1941. There were smaller projects, too, including a mosaic scene of

The thin, precast panels Earley developed were first used in this concrete mosaic ceiling at the U.S. Department of Justice. (Jack E. Boucher, Historic American Buildings Survey)

a stegosaurus and a palm tree over the entrance to the Reptile House at the National Zoo in Washington, D.C. For the Department of Justice, the Earley Studio fabricated 11,000 square feet of thin, brightly colored, concrete mosaic ceiling panels that were so strong they were used as the formwork for the structural concrete they were meant to cover. Earley's work for the Justice Department earned him the 1934 Turner Gold Medal from the American Concrete Institute for "making concrete an architectural medium."[1]

Economic and social upheavals associated with the Depression prompted Earley to investigate ways in which his concrete process could be used to manufacture affordable housing. Attempts at concrete houses had been made before, of course, from William Ward's Castle to the experiments of Grosvenor Atterbury and Thomas Edison. Atterbury's precast components required the use of a large crane. Edison's poured-in-place structures required heavy formwork and specialized equipment at the site. Most concrete houses were exceptionally heavy and looked as if they were made from—well, concrete. Earley and Taylor hoped to devise a system whereby attractive, relatively lightweight, precast concrete panels could be assembled on a traditional wood frame. The panels were to be sized so that a small contractor could erect them, as Earley saw himself as a manufacturer, not a contractor. Indeed, Earley's panels for the first experimental house, erected on Colesville Road in Silver Spring, Maryland, were trucked to the site in pairs on the back of a small truck and set into place with an A-frame beam hoist.

Earley was a craftsman—he referred to himself as an architectural sculptor—and the system he developed did not supplant the traditional craft trades. Earley's technological advances were designed to integrate with existing construction practices. Thus Earley did not encounter the resistance from the building trades that plagued other prefabri-cators, whose products tended to replace craftsmen with mechanics. Further, Earley contended that his system would put architects in a competitive position with nonarchitectural pre-fabricators. He meant to improve house building, not revolutionize it.

The house on Colesville Road designed to Earley's specifications by
Washington architect J. R. Kennedy, was a single-story, L-shaped, five-
room house with a hipped roof. Completed in late 1934, the house was
known as Polychrome House Number One on account of its colorful
appearance. The exterior comprised 32 precast panels, each four to eight
feet wide and nine feet tall, of three basic types: plain panels, panels with
door or window openings, and corner panels. The plain panels were a
pinkish beige, from the red jasperite aggregate. Corner panels, in the
form of fluted pilasters, contained cream-colored quartz aggregate.
Window and door surrounds were also cream, with a cobalt blue ceramic
aggregate panel set under each window. Every panel was topped by a
decorative frieze consisting of a narrow cobalt blue band over a geometric
zigzag-and-arrow pattern in red, black, and cream. The front door
featured three inset panels in an intricate red-and-black design. Even the
edge of the door sill had a red-and-black mosaic pattern. The house's
foundation and floor slab were poured-in-place concrete with the vis-
ibleperimeter brushed to expose a light brown aggregate. The whole
construction was crowned by a precast chimney trimmed in red and
black. In February 1935 *Architectural Forum* described the startling and
colorful effect as "Hittite," but it might be more accurately called Art
Deco. The interior of the house was conventionally finished, with two
exceptions: a decorative floor-to-ceiling mantelpiece and the concrete
trim around each window, cast as an integral part of the panels. A detached garage was built in the back yard using monochromatic panels.

Earley's system was indeed well thought out. The panels were cast in man-
ageable sizes. Adjacent panels were designed so that there was a change in
color and/or plane at each vertical joint, effectively hiding the joints. As a
result, the house did not look as if it was made of repetitive panels—a ma-

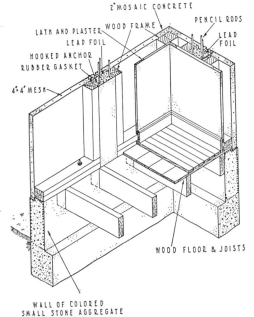

2" MOSAIC CONCRETE
WOOD FRAME
LATH AND PLASTER
PENCIL RODS
LEAD FOIL
LEAD FOIL
HOOKED ANCHOR
RUBBER GASKET
4"x4" MESH

This drawing shows how the precast panels fit together and were locked into place by a concrete column. (Bemis Foundation, Massachusetts Institute of Technology)

WOOD FLOOR & JOISTS

WALL OF COLORED SMALL STONE AGGREGATE

The garage for Polychrome House Number One was constructed of simpler, less expensive panels. (Architectural Forum)

The Earley Polychrome House panels were complete wall units. The windows were cast within the wall panel so that no field fabrication was required. (Architectural Forum)

The concrete panels were erected over a conventional wood frame. Here, five panels have been set in place: three wall panels, a window, and a corner. (Architectural Forum)

The Earley Process

Earley's precast panels were made from cement, graduated aggregate, and water. His standard mix was 94 pounds of Atlas white portland cement, 300 pounds of coarse aggregate, and 110 pounds of fine aggregate, mixed with five gallons of water. The color of the coarse aggregate, revealed after the surface had been brushed, determined the panel color. Once a panel was cast, excess water was drawn off by blotting the back of the casting with old newspapers. Removing the excess water made the concrete both denser and stronger. At a time when most concrete had a compressive strength of 3,000 pounds per square inch, Earley's castings routinely achieved a compressive strength of 5,000 pounds per square inch. Tensile strength was provided by welded wire mesh with a four-inch grid. Each panel was approximately two inches thick and thicker at the edges.

U-shaped hangers were cast into the back of each panel for lifting and anchoring the panels to the structural frame. Adjacent panels were set in place on shims and braced. Vertical reinforcing rods were threaded through the anchors at the edges. Lead foil and a rubber gasket covered the joint, then a concrete column was poured around the reinforcing bars, locking the whole system together. The foil and rubber gasket allowed for expansion and contraction while maintaining a weathertight seal. Once the concrete column had set, the shims and bracing were removed, leaving the panels hanging from the columns independent of the wood frame. Earley and Taylor were granted U.S. Patent No. 2,050,290 on August 11, 1936, for their technique of tying precast panels together.

jor drawback of most panel construction. Another feature indicative of the care taken with the design was the way the copper gutter formed a logical and integral part of the wall. In Earley's house the gutter became a decorative asset, a comment one can rarely make about gutters.

The panels of the Polychrome House were erected over a conventional wood frame with concrete columns cast in place behind each joint. Earley described the polychrome panels as replacing the diagonal sheathing and siding on a typical wood-frame house. The panels' major advantage over wood was that they required no maintenance. Admitting an initial cost $300 higher than a comparable speculatively built wooden house, Earley contended that by the time the exterior of the wooden house needed a second paint job, the costs would be even.

On January 5, 1935, Earley, Basil Taylor, and Oswald F. Schuette chartered the Earley Process Corporation in the District of Columbia. (Schuette, an old friend of Earley's, was a Washington newspaperman known for his anti-monopoly reporting of radio and copyright issues.) The corporation, with offices in the National Press Building, the Earley Studio in Foggy Bottom, and a concrete plant across

The panels, light enough to be delivered in pairs on the back of a small truck, could be erected using a simple beam hoist. Here workmen adjust placement of a panel for the small open porch of Polychrome House Number Two. (Architectural Forum)

The same open porch 50 years after its construction. (John A. Burns, AIA)

*This two-story house was one of three built by
Earley near his two single-story Polychrome
Houses. Skeptics at first believed that Earley's
concrete process was not suitable for two-story
structures. (John A. Burns, AIA)*

*The Fealy House was the first prefabricated
house built in the District of Columbia. (John
A. Burns, AIA)*

*The formal facade of this Earley house is
rooted in traditional Virginia house forms. To
make his later houses more marketable, Earley
experimented with more popular traditional
housing designs to disguise the houses'
prefabricated nature. (John A. Burns, AIA)*

the Potomac River in Rosslyn, Virginia, proposed to market affordable housing using precast concrete mosaic wall panels. Polychrome House Number One was opened to the public in January 1935 as a demonstration house.

Earley described the endeavor:

We have developed a new architectural medium, which we call mosaic concrete. It is our contribution to the construction of small houses. We know it very well. We are not deceived about its value relative to other materials, nor about the probable extension of its use. It will make strong and beautiful walls, which we are sure will receive popular approval. They can be prefabricated with high perfection and great economy and they can be assembled in place by any practical builder…. Our experience in the execution of many interesting problems indicates that our type of architectural concrete may be best applied to small houses in the form of thin precast slabs or panels, made in the Studio,

taken to the building, and erected in place…. Prefabricated thin slabs…flexibly attached to reinforced concrete skeletons as in our small house, offer an architectural medium, the like of which has been never known, and the limits of which are the limits of the human ingenuity.[2]

If successful, Earley planned to license other crushing and casting plants to produce aggregate and polychrome panels nationwide. He estimated that one crushing plant could serve a 300-mile radius, and a casting plant a 50-mile radius. He did not intend to build houses himself, but only to sell the panels.

Polychrome House Number Two was erected next door to Number One in 1935. Number Two demonstrated an even more economical version of the Earley Process. Its panels were simpler, with built-in corner returns, fewer changes of plane, no special door and window surrounds, and only one aggregate color, a rosy pink. The vertical joints were openly expressed. Perhaps to attract attention, two of the house's large front windows were circular. A small cornice formed the top of each panel, above which ran a continuous copper gutter. At each gable end the gutter served to hide the horizontal joint between the wall panels and the gable panels above. The gable had a stylized motif of diagonal bands and a circular attic vent with a V-shaped grille. The house's foundation was similar to Number One's. A few months later, three two-story houses were built around the corner from the first two houses. All three houses were essentially of the same design, differing only in detail and color.

Earley's craftsmanship is still widely visible in the Washington area. In addition to the five houses in Silver Spring, several houses using the Earley Process were built in Virginia and the District of Columbia. One of them, the Fealy House, designed by University of Pennsylvania architect Harry Sternfeld, received the first building permit ever issued by the District of Columbia for a prefabricated house.

In retrospect, the Polychrome Houses might be seen as the proving ground for the viability of Earley Process panels in curtain-wall construction. The houses' walls were detailed so that the panels were suspended on the structural columns and did not rest directly on the foundation—conditions similar to what one would find in a curtain-wall office building. Earley's hopes for the precast technology came true, but not in the field of housing. Limited by high delivery costs, Earley himself licensed the technology to other companies. Over the years precast architectural concrete became a major exterior cladding material and has been used in buildings nationwide. Indeed, thousands upon thousands of buildings across America can trace their lineage to the little houses in Silver Spring.

The Earley Studio enjoyed its greatest fame in the 1930s, with important commissions, honors, and prosperity. Earley was a respected figure in the concrete industry. In 1938 he was elected president of the American Concrete Institute, the first non-engineer to be so honored. The Universal Atlas Cement Company, whose white portland cement

Earley always used, featured his work prominently in its advertisements. When the architects of the Thomas Alva Edison Tower in Menlo Park, New Jersey, decided to use concrete in recognition of Edison's contributions in that field, they solicited Earley's services.

The Earley studio survived the war years by producing mundane concrete pieces; there was no market for mosaic work. At the end of the war, as business was beginning to pick up, Earley suffered a stroke on a job site and died several weeks later. His biographer, Frederick Cron, wrote:

John Earley was the last of the concrete pioneers. Others before him had discovered how to produce the "magic powder"—portland cement—how to mix it with stone and sand to make concrete, and how to use concrete as a structural material. But Earley was the first to control the exterior appearance of concrete in an important way and to impart brilliant permanent color to the surface. His contribution was unique: he was the one who made concrete beautiful.

The Earley Studio continued under Basil Taylor until his retirement in 1952, when his son Vernon took over the business. In 1962 the company moved from Rosslyn to Man-assas, Virginia, displaced by the same interstate highway that forced the move of Frank Lloyd Wright's Pope-Leighey House. Business in the 1950s and 1960s consisted almost exclusively of precast panels and architectural concrete products. Since there was little financial incentive to train younger employees in the intricacies of mosaic concrete, Earley's art gradually died out as the older employees retired. The Earley Studio, faced with a slow economic decline, was liquidated in 1973 after 84 years of service.

In an age of decaying infrastructure and crumbling concrete highways and bridges, Earley's work remains as bright and crisp as when it was first built, a legacy that will endure.

wall studs

interior
wall panel

reinforcemen
base retaine
4" asphalt til

cinder bl
anchor b

THE *Lustron* HOM

Twelve LUSTRON: THE ALL-METAL DREAM HOUSE

Imagine a two bedroom one-floor plan ranch-type home that has more than 1,000 square feet of floor space.... An all-steel porcelain enameled—inside and out—mass-produced house that is well within the income of home buyers.... A home that is built in a factory by the same mass-production methods that have made the motor car industry the outstanding economic achievement of the century.... A home that is speedily assembled on the site by a local builder-dealer under factory trained supervision.... One that provides durability and permanence in construction and is almost maintenance free.

That's something, isn't it? And, it's past the imagination stage. Read further! Then, you'll want to take the first opportunity—if you haven't already—to look at the Lustron Home. We think that you'll agree that we've brought Mr. Average American's dream right down to earth—within his reach.

A promotional brochure for the Lustron house

Carl Strandlund, c. 1947, stands outside the Lustron plant in Columbus, Ohio. (Architectural Forum)

The idea of a prefabricated, all-steel dwelling did not originate with the Lustron house; indeed, demountable corrugated metal structures had appeared nearly 100 years earlier in boom towns both in the United States and abroad. And fairgoers at Chicago's Century of Progress Exposition in 1933 had been introduced to steel-clad residences in two model houses: the Armco-Ferro Enamel House, designed by Robert Smith, Jr., and sponsored by the Insulated Steel Construction Corporation; and the Stran-Steel House, designed by O'Dell and Rowland and sponsored by the Stran-Steel Corporation. Both of these blocklike structures featured walls constructed of enameled metal panels that were bolted or screwed together. It took the genius of Carl Gunnard Strandlund, however, to see the potential for such construction and to market it nationally in an aggressive and systematic manner.

In 1946 Strandlund, a middle-aged, $100,000-a-year vice president and general manager of the Chicago Vitreous Enamel Products Company, traveled to Washington, D.C., in search of steel to build more gas stations. World War II had made steel scarce, and the federal government regulated the distribution of the precious material to private industry.

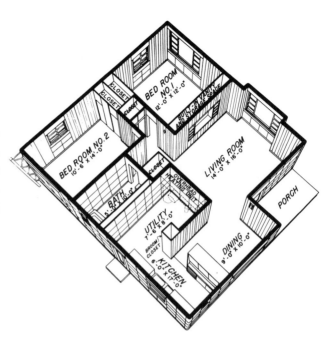

Floor plan of the Lustron. Rooms, while not large, were well laid out; built-ins and closets abounded. (Ohio Historical Society)

Strandlund quickly found that Washington Fair Dealers were not interested in gas stations, but they were eager to help reduce the severe housing shortage that was beginning to arise as American GIs returned home from Europe and the Pacific.

Since the mid-1930s Chicago Vitreous had been manufacturing porcelain-enameled steel panels for gas stations in the Midwest, including those of Standard Oil of Indiana. The panels simplified gas-station construction, proved easy to clean, retained their fresh appearance, and seemed almost indestructible. A consummate entrepreneur and promoter, Strandlund was quick to grasp the panels' possibilities in residential construction and he made some preliminary sketches for a steel-and-enamel house that he took with him to Washington.

Before this fateful trip, Strandlund claimed not even to have known the name of his congressman. He had trained as an industrial engineer and had been in business in the Midwest all his life; before joining Chicago Vitreous he had run a farm equipment company. Over the next several years, however, Strandlund would catch up for lost time, making many influential friends. One of these was Wilson Wyatt, Truman's dynamic young housing administrator; another was Henry A. Wallace, the secretary of commerce. Strandlund

Exterior view of the two-bedroom Lustron. This was Lustron's most popular model, available in a variety of pastel colors. (Ohio Historical Society)

captured Washington's interest when he pulled out his sketches for an all-metal house and boldly promised full production of 100 houses a day within nine months at the affordable retail price of $7,000 per house!

With encouragement from key members of the Truman administration, Strandlund returned home to draw up detailed plans. Using the technology perfected at Chicago Vitreous, a small team of architects and stylists came up with a complete set of working drawings within a few months. The man responsible for the actual design that became the Lustron house was Morris H. Beckman, a young architect who had graduated from MIT in 1938 and had served as chief draftsman at Skidmore, Owings and Merrill. Beckman and his partner, Roy Burton Blass, had recently opened their own office in Chicago, and Blass, through his connections with Chicago Vitreous, landed the job. Beckman, despite his lack of experience with prefabricated housing, took on the design assignment.

What emerged in short order from the drafting table was a rectangular, one-story, two-bedroom house with a low-pitched roof and a recessed front porch. Stylistically it was on the conservative side: contemporary in appearance yet conventional in most respects save its materials. Standard features included four large picture windows (one in each bedroom and in the living and dining rooms), radiant heating panels in the ceiling, plenty of closets, and built-ins galore: cabinets in the kitchen, bookcases in the living room, and a

vanity for the master bedroom. With the exception of the floor, which was asphalt tile on a concrete slab, all surfaces were of porcelain enamel on steel.

The Lustron living room and built-in bookcase. Pictures were hung with magnets rather than nails. (Ohio Historical Society)

View of the Lustron's all-electric kitchen, with its combination dishwasher and washing machine. The kitchen was efficiently organized to make maximum use of the limited space. (Ohio Historical Society)

The plan itself made excellent use of rather limited space—slightly more than 1,000 square feet. A feeling of spaciousness was achieved by opening a dining alcove off the 14-by-16-foot living room. Food prepared in the fully equipped galley kitchen could be passed across a built-in counter into the din-

The Lustron dining room, with a pass-through to the kitchen. The pass-through became a common feature in houses built after World War II. (Harold Denton)

View of the master bedroom, with its wall of built-in closets and mirrored vanity table, both popular features with first-time home buyers. (Ohio Historical Society)

ing area. Both bedrooms featured large closets with sliding doors, and one wall of the master bedroom was taken up with a built-in vanity flanked by drawers. To conserve space, interior doors slid into pockets in the walls. The need for a basement was eliminated by creating a utility room off the kitchen;

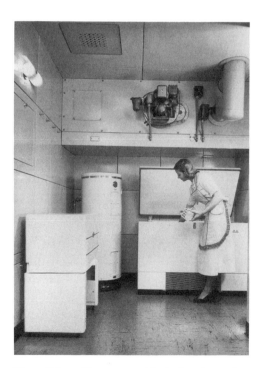

View of the utility room, with the heating unit below the roof and a handy deep freezer. (Ohio Historical Society)

here ironing and sewing could be done, and miscellaneous items could be stored. Access to the radiant heating equipment in the attic was also through this room.

With detailed plans and a whopping $52 million budget (to permit full-scale production) in hand, Strandlund returned to Wilson Wyatt in Washington. Wyatt, impressed with Strandlund's rapid progress and undaunted by the price tag, used his influence to help find a plant suitable for production of 100 houses a day. When it turned out that Strandlund's first choice, a Dodge aircraft-engine plant in Chicago, had already been leased to the ill-fated Tucker Motor Company, Wyatt persuaded the War Assets Administration to lease an almost new aircraft plant in Columbus, Ohio, for $425,000 a year to the Lustron Corporation. The plant, which had been used briefly to build Curtiss-Wright fighter planes for the war effort, fit Strandlund's needs beautifully: it covered more than 23 acres, was modern in design, and was centrally located in a major city.

Next, Wyatt approached George Allen, head of the Reconstruction Finance Corporation, for the capital required to begin production. The RFC had been set up after the war to facilitate the country's transition from a wartime to a peacetime economy. Allen balked when he learned that Strandlund had no personal assets invested in the project other than his infectious optimism and determination, but Allen promised to reconsider if Strandlund could raise $3.6 million on his own.

Over the next few months the Chicago-based firm of Hornblower and Weeks mobilized to sell stock in the new company. Sales, however, were slow: only $840,000 were raised, mostly from would-be suppliers to Lustron. *Fortune* magazine reported that Strandlund himself put up only $1,000, for which he got all 86,000 shares of the voting stock. (His substantial stock in Chicago Vitreous was exchanged for the Lustron patents, according to his colleague Harold Denton.)

Despite the sluggish stock sales, Wyatt continued to press Lustron's case within the Truman administration, eventually forcing a showdown at the White House between the Federal Housing Administration and the recalcitrant RFC. Allen came away the winner in the skirmish. Wyatt resigned his position shortly thereafter, citing the termination of guaranteed markets for factory-produced housing.

With Wyatt out of the picture, and no new doors opening to him, a discouraged Strandlund was packing his bags for the trip home to Chicago when a friend, Lewis E. Starr, national commander of the Veterans of Foreign Wars, called and urged him to see just one more man. That individual was Sen. Ralph Flanders of Vermont, who turned out to be a fellow engineer and an enthusiastic supporter of prefabricated housing. Flanders's immediate support for the venture set the stage for a full review by the Senate Banking and Currency Committee.

Overnight Strandlund's luck began to change. The White House discreetly made known its interest in having the Lustron project proceed. George Allen—Strandlund's primary detractor—unexpectedly resigned his post as head of the RFC. And banking committees in both the Senate and the House lined up in support of Lustron. In June 1947 hastily drafted legislation was passed authorizing the RFC to issue up to $50 million in loans specifically for prefabricated housing. Acting on a note from the White House, on June 30 the RFC passed a $15.5 million loan for Lustron, just 15 minutes before its emergency lending powers were to expire. The significance of the event did not go unnoticed in the press: it marked the first time since the war that the federal government had appropriated money specifically for private venture capital. Strandlund had his start-up capital at last.

The fledgling Lustron Corporation moved quickly to build on the momentum. Strandlund wanted to show Washington skeptics—and the general public—that an all-steel house was, in fact, within reach. Assembled from parts manufactured at the Chicago Vitreous plant in Cicero, Illinois, the first Lustron had been constructed in Hinsdale, a suburb of Chicago, in late 1946. Appropriately enough, the house's occupant was a former Seabee who was now a horticulture student at Michigan State College—reinforcing Strandlund's claim that Lustron would make home-ownership affordable to returning veterans.

Determined to model Lustron's operations on those of General Motors and the Ford Corporation, Strandlund hired many veterans of the automobile industry to fill jobs as stylists, production managers, machinists, and salesmen. The complex machinery needed to fabricate the Lustron was designed and tooled, and the huge factory in Columbus was fitted out with conveyor belts, welding rigs, punching and stamping machines, sheet-metal presses, frit grinders, enamel sprayers, and drying ovens. Lustron and the labor unions signed a contract to cover the complete manufacturing process, and a work force—reaching a peak of 3,400 in mid-1949—was hired to run the complex machinery.

Rather than starting slowly in one region of the country, Lustron took the bold step of marketing its product nationwide, and publicists began the important job of promoting the Lustron home in major magazines and newspapers.

Again taking his cue from the automobile industry, Strandlund set out to establish a network of qualified builder-dealers. Rather than setting new dealers up in business (Lustron apparently received more than 10,000 requests for franchises), the company made the wise decision to work with known commodities. Lustron's franchise policy was

Advertisement that appeared in color for Lustron houses in the November 1, 1948, issue of Life *magazine.*

incorporated into advertising aimed specifically at architects and contractors: "It is the policy of Lustron to enfranchise well-established construction organizations capable of demonstrating to Lustron their financial, construction, merchandising, and land development qualifications." The advertisement went on to note that thousands of applications had been received and were under consideration. By May 1949 some 143 dealers—concentrated in the eastern two-thirds of the country—held Lustron franchises.

Forum noted that on opening day in Chicago, "lines formed early, were four abreast, four blocks long when police were asked to limit [the] crowd since all could not go through before closing time." In Milwaukee, according

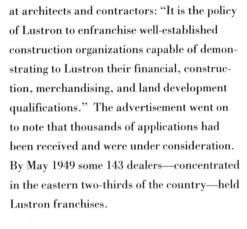

Assembly of a Lustron house in Bradford, Pennsylvania. (Vincent Kohler)

In 1947 demonstration houses began to open; eventually they reached some 100 cities and attracted long lines of potential buyers. Thanks to an all-out advertising campaign in *Life*, *McCall's*, and other magazines and newspapers, the level of interest was extraordinarily high. A January 1949 ad in *Architectural*

to the same ad, "They came...they saw...they liked it! More than 90% of [the] people interviewed approved new advantages of Lustron's basic ideas." And in Miami: "Florida likes the idea of a house impervious to scorching sunlight, salt air, [and] termites. Lustron's porcelain enamel steel construction is a

According to one of the Lustron Corporation's promotional leaflets, the colors of the Lustron house were chosen by leading designers and color experts. The exterior colors were distinctive pastels: pink, surf blue, dove gray, desert tan, maize yellow, blue-green, green, and white. Interior colors were chosen to make furnishing and decorating easy, "permitting the widest possible variation in choice of draperies, rugs, and individual decorating schemes." Prospective owners were encouraged to make their selections carefully: the colors, baked onto the steel panels, were permanent.

'natural' here." Visitors were intrigued by the all-metal construction that required magnets to hang pictures and were enticed by the prospect of low maintenance. What other house could be washed clean with a garden hose and never needed painting? The kitchen, equipped with numerous built-ins, was also an attention-getter, and it was particularly popular with first-time homeowners.

Despite the enormous interest generated by Lustron's demonstration houses, the new company encountered serious problems

almost immediately. Not surprisingly, given Strandlund's proposed $52 million budget, the initial $15.5 million loan from the RFC proved inadequate to underwrite start-up costs. It turned out that more than 3,000 parts, totaling more than 12 tons of steel, were needed for each Lustron house produced,

Lustron's erection manuals were highly detailed; this manual for the 02 model contained more than 160 drawings. (Vincent Kohler)

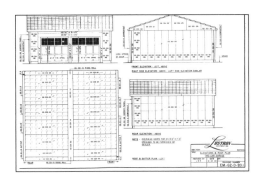

This sheet shows three elevations of the Lustron two-car garage and the roof plan. The design made use of existing Lustron parts. (Vincent Kohler)

and the job of tooling up the plant proved more difficult and costly than production managers had anticipated.

Equally troublesome were the obstacles facing the newly enfranchised Lustron dealers; according to a story in the November 1949 issue of *Fortune* magazine, dealers needed sufficient capital up front to purchase lots, pour concrete foundations, and bring in utilities. In addition, houses that cost the dealer $6,000 wholesale had to be purchased in large lots from the factory. From the outset Strandlund recognized that steel and steel-working machinery were profitable only in volume production; single-house orders did not fit this scheme. This meant that dealers needed between $50,000 and $100,000 in working capital to get started. Rigidity of FHA financing procedures slowed mortgage approvals, making it difficult for dealers to turn over houses quickly. Adding to Lustron's woes were the conservative building codes and deed restrictions in some communities that proved impossible to overcome.

Production costs had raised the retail price of a Lustron house from $7,000 to $9,000 or $10,000, depending on location. While the price (particularly given the large number of standard features in a Lustron) was competi-

Metal panels emerge from the drying ovens in this interior view of the Lustron plant. (Ohio Historical Society)

The Lustron plant at Columbus, Ohio, formerly built Curtiss-Wright fighter planes. (Ohio Historical Society)

tive with the prices of tract houses being built at the same time, the Lustron was not within reach of all first-time home buyers. Nonetheless, back orders for the new houses quickly piled up, and prospective owners experienced long delivery delays.

Thanks to friends in the right places, the troubled Lustron Corporation succeeded in obtaining two additional loans from the RFC—$10 million in 1948 and $7 million in early 1949, bringing the company's total indebted-ness to the federal government to a staggering $37,500,000. Having made a substantial financial commitment to the project, the government was not eager to see Lustron flounder.

Although the first Lustron house rolled off the assembly line in Columbus in March 1948, the enormous plant did not become fully operational until November of that year. At its peak, the factory was able to produce 26 houses a day—a number far short of the 100 envisioned by the optimistic Strandlund in 1946 and far short of the 50 a day needed to break even.

Production problems plagued Lustron throughout its four-year history, but the scale of the Columbus operations was awe-inspiring. The architect Carl Koch, one of the country's leading experts in prefabricated housing, stated: "I remember…our first tour through the premises on a motor wagon, gazing at acres of machinery. Even by American mass-production standards, it was an impressive layout. With everything going at once, [the factory] used as much electric current as Columbus proper. The houses themselves started at one end as rolls of steel, bar stock, or other elementary shapes, and from there were moved by conveyor; sliced, punched, stamped, or otherwise bashed; welded, riveted, bolted as the case might be; or sprayed and backed—finally issuing at the other end as packages of 3,000 component parts, loaded on special trailers and ready to go."[1]

Technologically, the Lustron house was remarkable in a number of respects, most notably its all-steel design. All surfaces, exterior and interior, were covered with porcelainized sheet-metal panels with a matte finish. Exterior panels and those comprising the bathroom and utility room walls were two feet square and had a one-inch-thick layer of fiberglass insulation glued to their inner face. Ceiling panels were four feet square, and all other interior walls consisted of two-by-eight-foot vertical panels. Pinched channel wall studs that supported the panels were spaced on two-foot centers. Rather than spanning the full depth of the wall, the studs were paired in

*Lustron components were carefully loaded onto
a flatbed truck for delivery to the building site.
Assembly took approximately 350 hours.
(Ohio Historical Society)*

such a way as to provide a needed thermal break between exterior and interior walls. Diagonal braces between the studs provided racking resistance. Panels were screwed into the studs, and joints were sealed with plastic gaskets at the construction site. A series of specially designed roof trusses eliminated the need for rafters and ceiling joists. The roof consisted of overlapping porcelainized steel shingles. Only the window frames were not steel: these were aluminum and were manufactured off-site.

Another innovation in the Lustron house was its radiant heating system, which consisted of two basic components: a forced-air furnace located in the utility room and a plenum nearly seven inches thick that hung from the roof trusses above the ceiling. The plenum was insulated from above by both rigid insulation board and six inches of poured insulation. Heat radiated through uninsulated ceiling panels to the rooms below. In moderate climates the system worked as planned, spreading heat evenly. In colder climates, however, the system proved less effective, given the minimal wall insulation, the concrete-slab floor, and single-glazed windows.

*A Lustron home on its way from the factory to
the building site. (Ohio Historical Society)*

A curious feature of the Lustron house that attracted great attention, at least initially, was the combination dishwasher and clothes washer that was installed next to the sink in every kitchen. In 1947 automatic dishwashers were still considered novelties, and few homes contained one. Unfortunately, the new appliance, which was specially manufactured by the Hurley Company, performed neither of its tasks well.

The completed building components were loaded onto a tractor trailer in reverse order of assembly and driven directly to the construction site, where a concrete slab had already been poured. (In theory, the process eliminated the need for an extensive warehouse; as soon as a house rolled off the assembly line, it was sped to a new owner.) On-site the builder-dealer took over, assembling walls and roof trusses first, then exterior panels and the roof. Interior panels, built-ins, and mechanical equipment came last.

Preliminary estimates called for 150 hours of labor to construct a single house; in reality, the job took a skilled crew closer to 350 hours. Lustron provided training at its Columbus plant in how to erect the houses quickly and efficiently; the goal was to have a core of skilled workers at each dealership. But some of the local workmen lacked experience and were unaccustomed to the precise tolerances of machine-made parts; in such situations, construction inevitably took longer than it should. Even so, assembly time—once the various components were delivered to the site—was still far less than for a conventional wood-frame or masonry house.

Initially Lustron marketed only one basic model: the two-bedroom, five-room house that

had been designed in 1946. Company officials recognized, however, that a three-bedroom model would be more practical for larger families, and Lustron began offering a larger version in late 1949. "Standard" and "Deluxe" versions (Models 021 and 02) were offered of the Westchester, the 31-by-35-foot house. Two smaller models, the Newport and the Meadowbrook (Models 032 and 022), were 23 by 31 feet and 25 by 31 feet, respectively; these were also offered in three-bedroom versions. A later offering by Lustron featured a matching garage and an optional connecting breezeway. Both were designed to use existing Lustron panels, but the garage had a wood (rather than steel) frame; apparently no additional tooling was needed for their fabrication.

A Lustron house with matching garage. The Lustron garage used building components from other models. (Collection of Harold Denton)

Lustron recognized that one of the reasons the automobile industry was successful was that it offered the public new, improved models practically every year. In an effort to emulate this approach, in 1949 Lustron officials invited Carl Koch and several of his associates to revamp the Lustron. Although impressed with the scale of Lustron's operations, Koch was appalled that so little serious thought had apparently been given to the preassembly of parts at the factory. He and his associates began to question the quantity and the overdesigned quality of some of the house's parts, which complicated and slowed production. Koch described one such part in his book *At Home with Tomorrow*:

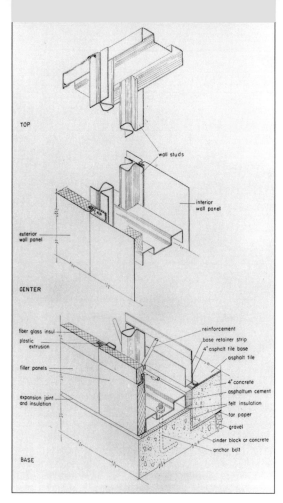

Details of the Lustron's all-metal wall. Twelve tons of steel went into every Lustron house. (Architectural Forum)

The bathtub machine, a giant press, set square in the middle of the works. It was the largest contrivance I had ever seen, reaching about three stories above ground and two below. What it did, as you might suppose, was to take a single, flat piece of metal, make preliminary whirring sounds, and then wallop it decisively into a complete bathtub shape. Its music was impressive.

This press had been procured at enormous expense to turn out individual tubs very cheaply, something like $15 as opposed to a wholesale lot price of around $45. But it soon developed that in order to operate efficiently, and amortize its original cost, it would have to turn out 120,000 tubs a year—40,000 of them for Lustron houses, the rest to be sold on the open market. However, the tubs it made to fit the Lustron house were five feet, one and a half inches long. And almost nowhere in the world can you sell a bathtub of that size. Five feet even, yes. Five feet, one and a half inches, no. At that point, as at several others, Lustron experienced a change of production managers.*

Other weaknesses in the original Lustron design were also identified. Although steel itself is a structural material with great strength in both tension and compression, the Lustron system of two-foot-square exterior panels wasted its strength. Koch was convinced that the house used far more steel than it needed, needlessly jacking up the price. Some of his first recommendations were to increase the size of the standard exterior panel to two by eight feet —the size of the interior panels— and to roll the panels out and cut them to lengths in a continuous-line process. These modifications alone would reduce the amount of steel needed from 12 to nine tons and save the company precious time and money. Koch also designed a system of vertical creasing, or ribbing, that would increase the strength of the panels as load-bearing members and do away with the steel studs. Because of the ribbing, joints would be concealed and the need for gaskets eliminated.

Other recommendations followed: Reduce the four different window sizes to a single unit interchangeable with the wall panels. Offer a variety of interior floor plans by rearranging the component parts. Undertake more assembly work at the factory (cutting the number of components arriving at the construction site from 3,000 to 37). Make the interior wall col-

Model of Carl Koch's revamped Lustron house, which was never built. Standard panels were increased to two by eight feet, joints were concealed, and window units were simplified. (Carl Koch)

ors as unobtrusive as possible, so that the decorating motif of the house could be readily changed.

The Lustron model that Koch and his team devised for introduction in 1950 was a clear improvement over the original; it reflected a sophisticated understanding of the fabrication process and exploited the positive qualities of steel as a building material. In addition to being handsomer than its predecessor, the Koch design was simpler and more versatile. Unfortunately, Koch's ideas for Lustron never got beyond the drawing board.

With available capital quickly drying up and Lustron losing upwards of $1 million per month, Strandlund found himself in Washington defending his floundering corporation and pleading for more time and money. This time, however, he faced an unfriendly Congress and an increasingly nervous Reconstruction Finance Corporation. Close scrutiny of Lustron's finances by a congressional subcommittee in 1948 had revealed several disturbing irregularities, among them the fact that Strandlund had never bothered to file a financial statement with the RFC. Also damaging were rumors of Lustron payoffs to key players in Washington, including none other than Sen. Joseph R. McCarthy. Strandlund's initial promise to

Congress of 17,000 houses by January 1949 came back to haunt him as Congress turned down an appropriation that would have helped solve Lustron's dealer-financing problems.

The press, which had been generally enthusiastic about the Lustron venture, began to publish less-than-glowing reports. In its July 4, 1949, issue *Time* magazine published an article entitled "Bathtub Blues" that detailed some of Lustron's production and financial problems and concluded that the company was far from a success. Other magazines and newspapers followed suit, questioning the future of the company with headlines such as "Whither Lustron?" (*Newsweek*, February 27, 1950) and "What's Stalling Lustron?" (*Business Week*, October 29, 1949).

As if these problems were not enough, Lustron's management suffered a series of devastating losses. *Business Week* reported that more than a half-dozen Lustron vice presidents, including Joseph Tucker, Strandlund's right-hand man, had come and gone in a two-year period, and concluded that Lustron was "up to its neck in trouble." In late 1949, the RFC issued an ultimatum to Lustron: reorganize immediately or face foreclosure.

Plans to sell 60,000 shares of Lustron stock held by Strandlund failed as negotiations with interested parties broke down. In February

1950 the RFC ordered its lawyers to file fore-closure action against Lustron. In March a court-appointed receiver unceremoniously ousted Strandlund and other top officials. By summer the huge plant in Columbus, Ohio, lay idle.

In its three years of operation, Lustron produced approximately 2,500 homes, many of which are still standing in towns across the country. The vast majority were two-bed-room models; several hundred three-bedroom models were constructed in late 1949 and early 1950. Sixty Lustrons, representing the company's largest single order, continue to be inhabited at Quantico Naval Base in Virginia. Two Lustrons, included within the boundaries of the Indiana Dunes National Lakeshore, form part of a historic district listed in the National Register. Lustron building compo-nents purchased after the company closed its doors were used to build the Top of the Mark, a motel in Canton, Ohio, which, although greatly altered, is still standing. Other Lustrons have reportedly been cannibalized for spare parts to aid in remodeling projects.

While not as maintenance-free or inde-structible as promised in the promotional litera-ture, Lustron houses have held up remarkably well. Owners today praise many of the same features that captivated America in the late 1940s: the compact, open plan; the sturdy steel construction; the numerous built-ins and closets; and surfaces that can be washed down with soap and water.

Perhaps the most eloquent epitaph for the Lustron house was written at the height of the political battle to save the company from bankruptcy; it came in the form of a letter to the editor of *Business Week*, published in the February 25, 1950, issue from a reader in Cuba City, Wisconsin:

The fury of the press and political circles of Washington is focused on the failure of Lustron Corporation to meet its RFC obliga-tions. The general attitude is vindictive: another government venture has failed.

Lustron enabled the home buyer in small towns and villages to obtain a home with con-struction qualities beyond the scope of a few local builders. No congressmen have con-tacted Lustron home owners to obtain these sentiments…Lustron has improved the lot of many an American family. I bought one of the first 3 bedroom models in this section of the country…absolute satisfaction is my verdict on every count.

PLAN AFTER FOLDING

Closets stored here in transit

LIVING

DINING

B

HTR

K

BEDROOM

BEDROOM

PLAN SHOWING FOLDING

"Houses of tomorrow" continue to be designed, built, and extolled. While the designs may be new, many of the driving forces behind today's forward-looking houses are not. These prototypes attempt to fill perceived needs of the American public: through the use of new materials and construction technologies, to provide decent, affordable shelter for all citizens and, through good design, to improve the quality of our lives.

Like their predecessors, today's "houses of tomorrow" aspire to solve real and complex housing problems. They continue to promise ease of construction through standardization and prefabrication; ease of maintenance through "miracle" materials and finishes; low construction cost through mass production; greater efficiency through careful engineering and design; and the improved well-being of the occupants through innovative technology and labor-saving devices. Additional concerns—with diminishing natural resources and the rising costs of heating and cooling, particularly in the past 20 years—have also helped shape these houses.

Designers of today's "houses of tomorrow" tend to approach the problem in one of two basic ways. Some designers take traditional construction technologies and materials and use them in innovative ways. Their designs tend to be consciously modern, independent of the past. Other designers, engineers, and companies focus on developing new materials and technologies. Ironically, the houses that these innovators promote are frequently, although not exclusively, traditional in outward appearance and design.

The following is a brief sample of innovative post–World War II houses.

SOLAR HOUSES

Keck and Keck designed what is generally acknowledged to be the first "solar house," constructed in Glenview, Illinois, in 1940. The architects attempted to harness readily available energy from the sun to make the house function more efficiently and less expensively than conventional houses. The house's owner, Howard M. Sloan, was so impressed with the

Keck and Keck built its first solar house in 1940 for Howard M. Sloan in Glenview, Illinois. The major spaces faced south, with the overhanging roof providing shade from the summer sun and allowing the low-angle winter sun to warm the house. (Hedrich-Blessing)

The Massachusetts Institute of Technology built an experimental solar house in 1939. Here a workman installs flat-plate solar collectors. (MIT Historical Collection)

In 1958 the Massachusetts Institute of Technology constructed another solar house in Lexington, Massachusetts. A solar hot dog roaster is in the foreground. (Michael Vaccaro)

design that he developed a subdivision nearby called Solar Park. The research of the Keck brothers in Chicago, the Olgyay brothers in Princeton, New Jersey, and a host of others led to a proliferation of so-called "solar homes" in the 1960s and early 1970s. Glass, clear acrylic, and fiberglass became ubiquitous in the effort to harness the sun. Not surprisingly, there were as many failures as there were successes; one particularly interesting example was the "envelope house," also known as the "double-loop house." In theory, solar-heated air circulated around a continuous air passage between two shells; rising from a south-facing "sunspace," warm air would move up under the rafters of the house, down the north side, under the main floor, and back to the sunspace. While poor heat distribution and high construction costs made the original envelope houses impractical, numerous other configurations combining solar technology with improvements in insulation have proven successful.

EARTH HOUSES

Built into sides of hills or dug into the ground, earth houses were another attempt at making houses more energy efficient. Drawing on the natural insulating qualities of earth, these houses owed much to the sod houses built by immigrants to the United States in the late 19th century. Frank Lloyd Wright and other noted architects experimented with the concept, but it has not been widely emulated.

This earth house, built into the side of a steep hill, is located in Washington, D.C. (H. Ward Jandl)

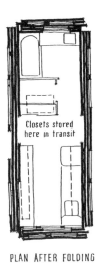

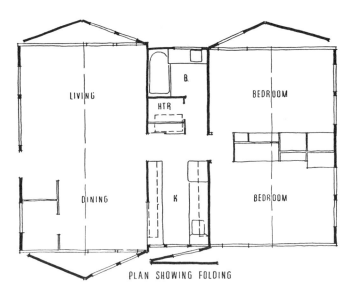

Closets stored here in transit

PLAN AFTER FOLDING

LIVING

B.

HTR

BEDROOM

DINING

K

BEDROOM

PLAN SHOWING FOLDING

This illustration shows the Acorn before and after folding. When fully opened, the Acorn contained two bedrooms, a living and dining area, a bathroom, and a kitchen.

The Acorn House was designed to be demountable: it could be set up, taken down, trucked a thousand miles away, and set up again. The first Acorn House was constructed in Concord, Massachusetts, not far from where its designer-promoters, Carl Koch and John Bemis, had their offices. (Acorn Structures, Inc.)

THE ACORN HOUSE

Initially designed by Carl Koch, Huson Jackson, and John Callender in 1945 as the "ultimate prefab," this one-story dwelling was fully demountable. Four workers could remove the house from the delivery truck, set it up, bolt it together, install its innards, connect the utilities, and make it ready to live in—all in one day. The house was distinguished from other prefabrication efforts of the 1940s in three respects: the high degree of factory completion; demountability; and the low cost of erection at the site. Although the first Acorn House attracted extensive coverage in *Life* magazine, which called it "handsome, cheap and sensible," the company that developed the Acorn, headed by Koch and John Bemis, was unsuccessful in obtaining necessary funding, and the venture failed.

THE TECHBUILT HOUSE

In the early 1950s Koch and Bemis had success with their line of Techbuilt Houses, which took advantage of prefabrication technology but permitted a variety of designs and layouts. Koch himself recalled: "In 1953 came the Techbuilt House, and our ten-year record of mishap, rude practical education, and artistic successes qualified by insolvency was spotted unexpectedly by something that worked—and worked well…. One model of a house, first planned in spare time, fabricated in an overgrown carpentry shop in Acton, Massachusetts, built speculatively in West Concord, varied and built again in Weston, turned into twenty-two models of a house, a corporation, four factories, and a system of ninety franchised builder-dealers from New York to California." By the end of 1957 Techbuilts had been constructed in 32 states. Architectural components of the Techbuilt House were based on a four-foot module; panels consisted of plywood sheets bonded to wood frame members. Modular furniture was specially designed for the Techbuilt House to increase livability and flexibility.

Techbuilt houses utilized prefabrication technology yet did not appear to be "factory-made." Crisp, clean lines and efficient floor plans contributed to the Techbuilt's popularity in the 1950s and 1960s.

THE CASE STUDY HOUSE PROGRAM

At the end of World War II, John Entenza, editor of *Arts and Architecture* magazine, began a program to encourage modernism in residential architecture and to promote mass production, experimental planning, and new materials. Thirty-six Case Study houses were designed between 1945 and 1966 by such distinguished architects as Charles and Ray Eames and Ralph Rapson; 26 of the experimental houses were actually built in the Los Angeles area. Publicized through *Arts and Architecture*, many of the houses were architecturally and technologically innovative, using steel, plastic, plywood, concrete, and

The concept of geodesic domes originated with R. Buckminster Fuller and was promoted as energy efficient and economical. Despite their futuristic, space-colony appearance, geodesic domes are not particularly well suited to residential architecture given the awkwardly shaped openings and lack of flat walls.

expanses of glass, and equipped with the best new designs in refrigerators, ranges, and heating units. Contemporary furniture filled the rooms. Although none of the prototype houses was subsequently built on a mass scale, the Case Study houses influenced a generation of architects and homeowners.

DOME HOUSES

Dome houses originated with Buckminster Fuller as an energy-efficient alternative to wood balloon-frame houses. The Fuller-designed U.S. pavilion at the Montreal World's Fair of 1967 helped to popularize the geodesic dome, which consists of a rigid geometric frame of metal, wood, or plastic covered by either a flexible skin or rigid panels. Although promoted as "completely affordable," and "remarkably beautiful," geodesic domes have had only limited acceptance to date. In the 1970s and 1980s several companies sold kits from which geodesic domes could be constructed for residential use; many of these companies, however, have since gone out of business.

THE MONSANTO HOUSE OF THE FUTURE

Designed as a collaborative effort between Monsanto's plastics division and the Massachusetts Institute of Technology, this distinctive cross-shaped, single-story house was erected at Disneyland in 1957 where it exemplified the sponsoring company's motto, "Better Living Through Chemistry." Without a doubt it was the most celebrated all-plastic house in America. The chemical materials used in its construction included: Polyflex, Resinox, Resimene, Scriptite, Resloom, Stymer, Lauxite, Lauxein, Rez, Gelvatex, Lustrex, Lytron, Vuepak, Opalon, Ultron, Nitron, Salfex, Acrilan, Nokorode, and Teraise. The key to the house's design was an L-shaped structural panel made of overlays of fiberglass matting impregnated with synthetic resin. Filled with foam insulation and given a contoured shape, these modular panels were joined together at the site to form walls, ceilings, and floors. Until it was demolished in 1967, the house attracted thousands of visitors each year who marveled at the push-button telephones, adjustable sinks, climate-control center, and molded plastic furniture.

The Monsanto House of the Future was seen by millions of Disneyland visitors between 1957 and 1967; for many, it exemplified the house of tomorrow with its molded fiberglass walls and push-button technology. (Monsanto)

THE JETSON HOUSE

The house created in 1962 for the television cartoon series "The Jetsons" became for many a strong image of the house of the future. "Designed" by William Hanna and Joseph Barbera, the house was elevated on stilts and was appointed with beds that collapsed and disappeared into the floor, doors that descended from the ceiling, and chairs that moved by conveyor belt to wherever they were needed. Although the house was never built, its whimsical design and myriad gadgets delighted a generation of television watchers. The Jetson House was also featured in the 1990 movie *The Jetsons.*

The Century 21 Plywood Home of Living Light was constructed for the Seattle World's Fair in 1962. Designed by Liddle and Jones and built by the Douglas Fir Plywood Association, the house was, according to promotional literature, "a serious attempt to predict adjustments housing may make in the coming years."

THE CENTURY 21 PLYWOOD HOME OF LIVING LIGHT

This home of the future was exhibited at the Seattle World's Fair in 1962. With its distinctive "roof domes" and undulating walls, the house was consciously futuristic in appearance yet featured materials and products readily available to the homeowner. "It is not likely that space age man will retain the prison of today's straightline architecture," according to the house's promotional literature. "Instead, he will yearn for exotic surroundings like those in the Home of Tomorrow." This popular attraction, designed by the architectural firm of Liddle and Jones, was dismantled after the fair closed, and portions of it have since been incorporated into a restaurant.

The Living Environments Concept House by General Electric Plastics, shown here from the back, currently serves as a development center and marketing tool for both G.E. Plastics and its partner companies. (General Electric Plastics)

XANADU

Designed by Roy Mason, Xanadu was developed in 1983 utilizing inflated balloon-like forms that were sprayed with a fast-setting polyurethane foam to create a rigid shell. The finished house, located in Wisconsin Dells, Wisconsin, resembled a series of plastic igloos. Advertised as an example of low-cost, energy-efficient housing, Xanadu included such features as a sauna, tanning and steam rooms, and holographic television.

Xanadu was constructed in Wisconsin Dells, Wisconsin, in the early 1980s and today is a popular tourist attraction. Its unusual design can be attributed to the use of inflated forms which were sprayed with a fast-setting polyurethane foam.

THE WORLD HOUSE

The World House was a 600-square-foot dwelling fabricated in 1988 of structural foam panels sprayed with stucco on the exterior and textured paint on the interior. A prototype of the World House was erected by World Housing, Inc., of Boca Raton, Florida. Claiming as his business model the McDonald's hamburger chain, promoter Walter Feuchs reduced construction costs by eliminating studs, rafters, timbers, and trusses; rather than being hidden inside the walls, all electrical wiring was covered by molding and sprayed with the same textured paint.

THE LIVING ENVIRONMENTS CONCEPT HOUSE

The General Electric Company built this 2,900-square-foot structure in 1989 in Pittsfield, Massachusetts, as a living laboratory. Designed to demonstrate the numerous uses of plastics in construction, the house is contemporary in appearance yet experimental in its use of standardized modular components designed to work together in flexible ways. Its technology draws upon modular construction techniques developed in Japan. Floors, roofs, and walls can be assembled, disassembled, and reconfigured as family needs and lifestyles change. Plug-in/plug-out kitchen modules make it easy to replace outmoded appliances. Plastics are used extensively in the house's structural components; in its utility systems, mechanical equipment, and nonstructural components such as cabinets, doors, and fixtures; and in the interior and exterior surfaces and trim.

THE SMART HOUSE

Conceived in 1989, the Smart House is engineer-entrepreneur Ross Heitzmann's attempt to bring automation technology to the American home in a systematic manner. More than 20 manufacturers in the home-building industry have committed to developing compatible products. Smart House technology allows the homeowner to program all automated features from a central location, including security, safety, energy management, entertainment, communications, and lighting. Special cable packages that carry electric lines, computer data, telephone lines, and two-way coaxial cables to sockets throughout the house enable appliances to interact with each other. A central controller dispatches instructions to each appliance plugged into one of the sockets. Although technically just one component of a "house of tomorrow," the Smart House's hardware has the potential to improve domestic efficiency and help fulfill Le Corbusier's definition of the house as a "machine for living." ⬛

FURTHER READING

GENERAL

Banham, Reyner. *The Architecture of the Well-Tempered Environment*. London: Architectural Press, 1969.

Bernhardt, Arthur D. *Building Tomorrow: the Mobile/Manufactured Housing Industry*. Cambridge, Mass.: MIT Press, 1950.

Blueprints for Modern Living: History and Legacy of the Case Study Houses. Cambridge, Mass.: MIT Press, 1989.

Bruce, Alfred, and Harold Sandbank. *A History of Prefabrication*. New York: John B. Pierce Foundation, 1944. Reprinted. New York: Arno Press, 1972.

Burchard, John, and Albert Bush-Brown. *The Architecture of America*. Boston: Little Brown and Company, 1961.

Bush, Donald J. *The Streamlined Decade*. New York: George Braziller, 1975.

Clark, Clifford Edward, Jr. *The American Family Home 1800–1960*. Chapel Hill: University of North Carolina Press, 1986.

Corn, Joseph J., ed. *Imagining Tomorrow: History, Technology, and the American Future*. Cambridge, Mass.: MIT Press, 1986.

Corn, Joseph J., and Brian Horrigan. *Yesterday's Tomorrow: Past Visions of the American Future*. New York: Summit Books, 1984.

Fitch, James Marston. *American Building 1: The Historical Forces That Shaped It*. Boston: Houghton Mifflin Co., 1966.

————. *American Building 2: The Environmental Forces That Shaped It*. Boston: Houghton Mifflin Co., 1972.

Giedion, Siegfried. *Mechanization Takes Command: A Contribution to Anonymous History*. New York: Oxford University Press, 1948.

Graff, Raymond K. *The Prefabricated House: A Practical Guide for the Prospective Buyer*. Garden City, N.Y.: Doubleday and Co., 1947.

Greif, Martin. *Depression Modern: The Thirties Style in America*. New York: Universe Books, 1975.

Hayden, Delores. *Redesigning the American Dream: The Future of Housing, Work, and Family Life*. New York: W. W. Norton and Co., 1984.

Herbert, Gilbert. *The Dream of the Factory-Made House: Walter Gropius and Konrad Wachsmann*. Cambridge, Mass.: MIT Press, 1984.

Howe, Barbara J., Dolores A. Fleming, Emory L. Kemp, and Ruth Ann Overbeck. *Houses and Homes: Exploring Their History*. Nashville, Tenn.: American Association for State and Local History, 1987.

Kelly, Burnham. *The Prefabrication of Houses*. Cambridge, Mass.: MIT Press, 1961.

Maddex, Diane, ed. *Master Builders: A Guide to Famous American Architects*. Washington, D.C.: Preservation Press, 1985.

Mansfield, Howard. *Cosmopolis: Yesterday's Cities of the Future*. New Brunswick, N.J.: Center for Urban Policy Research, 1990.

"The New House 194X." *Architectural Forum*, September 1942.

Wright, Gwendolyn. *Building the Dream: A Social History of Housing in America*. Cambridge, Mass.: MIT Press, 1981.

INTRODUCTION

Albrecht, Donald. *Designing Dreams: Modern Architecture in the Movies*. New York: Harper and Row, 1986.

One CATHARINE BEECHER AND THE AMERICAN WOMAN'S HOME

Beecher, Catharine E. *A Treatise on Domestic Economy*. New York: Harper and Brothers, 1848.

Beecher, Catharine E. *A Treatise on Domestic Economy for the Use of Young Ladies at Home and At School*. Boston: T. H. Webb and Co., 1843.

Beecher, Catharine E., and Harriet B. Stowe. *The American Woman's Home, or Principles of Domestic Science*. New York: J. B. Ford and Co., 1869.

Boydston, Jeanne, Mary Kelley, and Anne Margolis. *The Limits of Sisterhood*. Chapel Hill: University of North Carolina Press, 1988.

Harveson, Mae Elizabeth. *Catharine Esther Beecher, Pioneer Educator*. Philadelphia: Science Printing Co., 1932.

Hayden, Delores. *The Grand Domestic Revolution*. Cambridge, Mass.: MIT Press, 1982.

Sklar, Kathryn Kish. *Catharine Beecher: A Study in American Domesticity*. New Haven: Yale University Press, 1973.

Two THE OCTAGON: A HOME FOR ALL

Blumenson, John J. G. "A Home for All: The Octagon in American Architecture." *Historic Preservation*, July–September 1973.

Creese, Walter. "Fowler and the Domestic Octagon." *Art Bulletin* 28, June 1946.

Davies, John D. *Phrenology, Fad and Science: A 19th Century American Crusade*. New Haven: Yale University Press, 1955.

Fowler, Orson Squire. *The Octagon House: A Home for All*. 1848. Reprinted, with a new introduction by Madeleine B. Stern. New York: Dover Publications, 1973.

Fowler, Orson Squire, and Lorenzo Niles Fowler. *Phrenology: A Practical Guide to Your Head*. Reprinted, with a new introduction by Andrew E. Norman. New York: Chelsea House Publishers, 1980.

Luce, W. Ray. "Squaring the Circle: Octagonal Architecture." *Timeline*, December 1989–January 1990.

Schmidt, Carl F. *The Octagon Fad*. Scottsville, N.Y.: Author, 1958.

Three **WILLIAM WARD'S CONCRETE CASTLE**

Condit, Carl. *American Building Art*. New York: Oxford University Press, 1960.

Coney, William B. *Preservation of Historic Concrete: Problems and General Approaches*. Preservation Briefs 15. Washington, D.C.: Government Printing Office, 1987.

Kramer, Ellen W., and Aly A. Raafat. "The Ward House: a Pioneer Structure of Reinforced Concrete." *Journal of the Society of Architectural Historians* XX, No. 1, March 1961.

Ward, W. E. "Beton in Combination with Iron as a Building Material." *Transactions of the American Society of Mechanical Engineers* IV, 1883.

Wight, Peter B. "The Pioneer Concrete Residence of America." *Architectural Record* 25, May 1909.

Four **THOMAS EDISON'S POURED-CONCRETE HOUSES**

Dyer, Frank Lewis, and Thomas Commerford Martin. *Edison: His Life and Inventions*. New York: Harper and Brothers, 1910.

"Edison's System of Concrete Houses." *Scientific American*, November 1907.

"The Edison Concrete House." *Scientific American*, August 1909.

Josephson, Matthew. *Edison*. New York: McGraw-Hill, 1959.

Larned, E. S. "The Edison Concrete House." *Scientific American Supplement*, No. 1685, 18 April 1908.

Five **THE DYMAXION DWELLING MACHINE**

Fuller, R. Buckminster. "Dymaxion House." *Architectural Forum* 56, March 1932.

———."Dymaxion Houses." *Architectural Record* 75, January 1934.

" Fuller's House: It Has a Better Than Even Chance of Upsetting the Building Industry." *Fortune* 33, April 1946.

Hatch, Alden. *Buckminster Fuller: At Home in the Universe*. New York: Crown Publishers, 1974.

Kenner, Hugh. *Bucky: A Guided Tour of Buckminster Fuller*. New York: William Morrow & Co., 1973.

Marks, Robert W. *The Dymaxion World of Buckminster Fuller*. Carbondale: Southern Illinois University Press, 1960.

"The World of Buckminster Fuller." *Architectural Forum* 136. January–February 1972.

Six **THE ALUMINAIRE: GIVING LIGHT AND AIR TO THE HOUSE**

Frey, Albert. *In Search of a Living Architecture*. New York: Architectural Book Publishing Co., 1939.

Hitchcock, Henry-Russell, and Philip Johnson. *The International Style*. Reprint. New York: W. W. Norton and Co., 1966.

Kocher, A. Lawrence, and Albert Frey. "Aluminaire: A House for Contemporary Life." *Shelter*, May 1932.

Rosa, Joseph. *Albert Frey, Architect*. New York: Rizzoli, 1990.

Schwarting, Michael J. "Aluminaire House Update." *Podium*, Summer 1989.

Stern, Robert A. M., Gregory Gilmartin, and Thomas Mellins. *New York 1930: Architecture and Urbanism between the Two World Wars*. New York: Rizzoli, 1987.

Yorke, F. R. S. *The Modern House*. London: Architectural Press, 1934.

Seven **USONIAN HOUSES: FRANK LLOYD WRIGHT'S VISION OF AFFORDABLE HOUSING**

Ford, Edward R. *The Details of Modern Architecture*. Cambridge, Mass.: MIT Press, 1990.

Jacobs, Herbert, with Katherine Jacobs. *Building with Frank Lloyd Wright: An Illustrated Memoir*. San Francisco: Chronicle Books, 1978.

National Trust for Historic Preservation. *The Pope-Leighey House*. Washington, D.C.: Preservation Press, 1969.

Sergeant, John. *Frank Lloyd Wright's Usonian Houses*. New York: Whitney Library of Design, 1976.

Wright, Frank Lloyd. *An Autobiography*. New York: Horizon Press, 1943.

———."The Architecture of Frank Lloyd Wright." *Architectural Forum*, January 1938.

———.*The Natural House*. New York: Horizon Press, 1954.

Eight THE HOUSE OF TOMORROW: AMERICA'S
FIRST GLASS HOUSE

"Chicago and Tomorrow's House?" *Pencil Points* 14,
June 1933.

Cohen, Stuart E. *Chicago Architects.* Chicago: Swallow
Press, 1976.

The House of Tomorrow: America's First Glass House.
Exhibition pamphlet. Chicago: B. R. Graham, 1933.

Keck and Keck Architects. Introduction by Narciso G.
Menocal. Madison, Wisc.: Elvehjem Museum of Art, 1980.

"Keck & Keck, Architects." *Inland Architect*, July 1965.

Raley, Dorothy, editor. *A Century of Progress: Homes and
Furnishings.* Chicago: M. A. Ring Co., 1934.

"The Modern Houses of the Century of Progress Exposition."
Architectural Forum, July 1933.

Nine THE MOTOHOME: THE HOUSE THAT RUNS ITSELF

"American Houses, Inc." *Architectural Forum*, April 1934.

Bissell, Katherine M. "The New American Home: An
Interview with Robert W. McLaughlin, Jr., Architect."
Woman's Home Companion 62, March 1935.

"Homes of the Future?" *Westchester*, January 1935.

"More Integration, Less Prefabrication Spell Success for
American Houses, Inc." *Architectural Forum*, July 1940.

"Motohomes." *Architectural Forum*, July 1935.

"Steel Houses." *Architectural Forum*, April 1934.

Ten K₂H40: THE PROMISE OF PREFABRICATION

Bemis, Albert Farwell. *The Evolving House, Volume III.*
Cambridge, Mass. : Technology Press, 1936.

"Business and Finance: General Houses." *Time*, 4 July 1932.

Carr, Ante Lee. *A Practical Guide to Prefabricated Houses.*
New York: Harper and Brothers, 1947.

Cohen, Stuart E. *Chicago Architects.* Chicago: Swallow
Press, 1976.

Fisher, Howard T. "New Elements in House Design."
Architectural Record 66, No. 5, November 1929.

————."Prefabrication: What Does It Mean for the Architect?" *Journal of the American Institute of Architects* 10,
November 1948.

————.*Our Homes.* Chicago: General Houses, 1934.

"General Houses, Inc." *Architectural Record* 75, January
1934.

"General Houses, Inc.: The General Motors of the New
Industry of Shelter." *Fortune*, July 1932.

Kelly, Burnham. *The Prefabrication of Houses.* New York:
MIT Press, 1961.

Prefabricated Homes, Commercial Standard CS125-47. 2nd
ed. Washington, D.C.: Prefabricated Home Manufacturers'
Institute and U.S. Department of Commerce, 1947.

"A Product of General Houses." *Architectural Forum* 57,
July 1932.

"Three Speculate on Style." *Architectural Forum* 60,
June 1935.

Eleven THE POLYCHROME HOUSE: MOSAIC CONCRETE AND
THE EARLEY PROCESS

Cron, Frederick W. *The Man Who Made Concrete Beautiful.* Fort Collins, Colo.: Centennial Publications, 1977.

Earley, John J. "Architectural Concrete Makes Prefabricated Houses Possible." *Journal of the American Concrete
Institute* 31, 1935.

"First Prefabricated House in District." *The Evening Star*,
Washington, D.C., June 1935.

Hitchcock, Frank A. "Stucco Investigations at the Bureau of
Standards with Recommendations for Portland Cement
Stucco Construction." National Bureau of Standards
Circular No. 311. Washington, D.C.: Government Printing
Office, 1926.

Pearson, J. C., and J. J. Earley. "New Developments in
Surface Treated Concrete and Stucco." *American Concrete
Institute Proceedings*, 1920.

"Prefabrication for Architects." *Architectural Forum*,
February 1935.

"Products and Practice: Architectural Concrete Slabs."
Architectural Forum, February 1940.

Wirz, Hans, and Richard Striner. *Washington Deco:
Art Deco in the Nation's Capital.* Washington, D.C.:
Smithsonian Institution Press, 1984.

TWELVE LUSTRON: THE ALL-METAL DREAM HOUSE

Koch, Carl. *At Home with Tomorrow.* New York: Rinehart
& Co., 1958.

Koncius, Jura. "Little Metal Houses Maintain Their Mettle."
Washington Post, June 30, 1988.

Snyder, Tim. "Lustron: A Prefabricated Ranch House of
Porcelainized Steel." *Fine Homebuilding* 22, August–
September 1984.

"The Factory-built House is Here . . ." *Architectural Forum*,
May 1949.

"The Industrialized House." *Architectural Forum*, June 1947.

NOTES

The following notes are divided by chapter. When only an author's surname and the book's title are included for a given work, that reference is fully cited in the bibliography beginning on page 210.

INTRODUCTION

[1]Albrecht, *Designing Dreams: Modern Architecture in the Movies*, page 110.

One CATHARINE BEECHER AND THE AMERICAN WOMAN'S HOME

[1]Boydston, Kelley, and Margolis, *The Limits of Sisterhood*, page 16.

[2]Ibid., page 18

[3]Benjamin Andrews, *The Journal of Home Economics*, 1912, page 212.

Four THOMAS EDISON'S POURED-CONCRETE HOUSES

[1]Dyer and Martin, *Edison: His Life and Inventions*, page 507.

[2]Ibid., pages 508–09.

[3]*Scientific American Supplement*, April 18, 1908, page 249.

[4]Ibid., page 250.

[5]Letter from Edison, March 6, 1912, at the Edison National Historic Site, West Orange, N.J.

[6]Letter to J. F. Monnot from Edison's assistant, May 29, 1912, at the Edison National Historic Site, West Orange, N.J.

[7]Letter from Edison, March 6, 1912, at the Edison National Historic Site, West Orange, N.J.

[8]Letter from Frank D. Lambie to W. H. Meadowcroft, December 29, 1916, at the Edison National Historic Site, West Orange, N.J.

[9]Letter from W. H. Meadowcroft to Frank D. Lambie, January 17, 1917, at the Edison National Historic Site, West Orange, N.J.

[10]*Los Angeles Express*, August 15, 1922.

Five THE DYMAXION DWELLING MACHINE

[1]Leigh White. "Buck Fuller and the Dymaxion World," *Saturday Evening Post*, October 14, 1944, pages 22–23, 73.

[2]Ibid, page 72.

[3]"The Dymaxion American," *Time*, 10 January 1964, pages 46–47.

[4]Ibid, page 48.

[5]Janet Mabie, "A House for a God," *Forum and Century* 97, March 1937, pages 141, 142.

[6]"Housing VI: Solutions," *Fortune*, July 1932, pages 61–62.

[7]Theodore Morrison, "The House of the Future," *House Beautiful*, September 1929, page 293.

[8]Janet Mabie, "If Ever Come Dymaxion Days," *Christian Science Monitor Magazine*, September 11, 1935, page 12.

[9]Buckminster Fuller, "Dymaxion Houses: An Attitude," *Architectural Record* 75, January 1934, page 10.

[10]Robert W. Marks, "Bucky Fuller's Dymaxion World," *Science Illustrated*, November 1948, page 62.

[11]Fuller, page 10.

[12]Marks, page 60.

[13]"House United," *Business Week*, 10 February 1945, page 42.

[14]"For Fuller Living," *Interiors*, May 1946, page 118.

[15]"Fuller's House," *Fortune*, April 1946, ppage 169–70.

[16]Hatch, *Buckminster Fuller: At Home in the Universe*, page 177.

[17]"Dwelling Machines," *Architectural Record* 97, April 1945, page 122.

[18]"Fuller's House," page 176.

[19]Hatch, page 176.

[20]"For Fuller Living," page 118.

[21]Ibid, page 118.

[22]Hatch, page 180.

[23]Brian Settle, "Fuller Remembered with Awe, Gentle Skepticism," *Wichita Eagle-Beacon*, July 3, 1983.

Six THE ALUMINAIRE: GIVING LIGHT AND AIR TO THE HOUSE

[1]Letter from Albert Frey to H. Ward Jandl, February 24, 1989.

[2]Ibid.

[3]Stern, *New York 1930*, page 343.

[4]*Architect* 15, April 1931, page 345.

[5]*New York Times*, April 21, 1931.

[6]Ibid., Section II, April 19, 1931, page 3.

Eight THE HOUSE OF TOMORROW: AMERICA'S FIRST GLASS HOUSE

[1]*Architectural Forum*, July 1933, page 51.

[2]Raley, *A Century of Progress: Homes and Furnishings*, page 71.

[3]Ibid.

[4]Joseph C. Folsom, "The House of Tomorrow," a chapter in a pamphlet on Chicago's Century of Progress International Exposition. Chicago: Cuneo Press, page 34.

[5]*Progressive Architecture*, February 1981, page 22.

[6]*AIA Journal*, January 1981, page 94.

Nine THE MOTOHOME: THE HOUSE THAT RUNS ITSELF

[1]*Architectural Forum*, April 1934, pages 277–82.

[2]*Architectural Forum*, December 1933, page 512.

[3]*American City*, September 1935, page 77.

[4]*Popular Mechanics*, June 1935, pages 805–06.

[5]*New York Times*, April 2, 1935, page 23.

[6]*Westchester Magazine*, January 1935, pages 9–10.

[7]*New York Times*, October 20, 1961, page 33.

Ten K₃H40: THE PROMISE OF PREFABRICATION

[1]*Architectural Record*, November 1929, page 401.

[2]Ibid., page 403.

[3]Ibid., pages 399–400.

[4]*Prefabricated Homes, Commercial Standard CS125-47*, 2nd ed., page 1.

[5]*Journal of the American Institute of Architects*, November 1948, page 220.

[6]Although the company announced its intention to erect a Q_2H4 model in the July 1932 issue of *Architectural Forum*, page 67, the actual model built appears to have been a reversed K_3H4DP, a more elaborate design, and was published in the January 1934 issue of *Architectural Record*, page 18.

Eleven THE POLYCHROME HOUSE: MOSAIC CONCRETE AND THE EARLEY PROCESS

[1]*Architectural Forum* (February 1935), page 187.

[2]*Journal of the American Concrete Institute* 31 (1935), pages 513–25.

Twelve LUSTRON: THE ALL-METAL DREAM HOUSE

[1]Koch, *At Home with Tomorrow*, page 111.

"Peek-a-Boo Domain," 112

Perkins, Lawrence, 167

Phelps-Dodge Research Laboratories, 88

Pierce, John B., Foundation, 16

Pierce-Arrow, 130

Pittsburgh Plate Glass, 158, 162, 165

Polychrome houses, 169–81

Pope, Loren, 122

Pope-Leighey House, *121*, 122, *123*, *124*, *125*, 181

Poplar Forest, *42*, 43

Popular Mechanics, 10, *102*

prefabrication, 12, 19, 160–65, *178*

Prince Albert Model Cottages, 10

Princeton University, 141, 154

Pullman Car and Manufacturing Corporation, 158, 162, 164

Quantico Naval Base, 199

Quinn, T. K., 91

Raley, Dorothy, 12

Ransome, William, 71

Rapson, Ralph, 204

Rebori, Andrew, 128

Reconstruction Finance Corporation, 187, 188, 193, 198, 199

Republic Steel Corporation, 16, *18*

Reynolds Metals, 130

Richards, John, house, 51, *53*, 130

Rickert, Howard, 122

Roosevelt, Sara Delano, 141

Rosa, Joe, 114

Ross, Frank P., 165

Rostone House, 128

Russell, Burdsall, and Ward, 56

St. John's College, 169

"Salon des Réfusés," 111

Sarah Pierce's Female Academy, 29

Saylor, Henry, 111

Schamberg, Mabel, 136

Schindler, Rudolf, 27

Scholer, Walter, 128

Schuette, Oswald F., 176–77

Science Illustrated, 96

Scientific American, 67, *70*, 71, 72–73, *73*, 74, 75

Sears, Roebuck & Company, 14, *14*, 15, 147, 166

Seattle World's Fair, 207

Skidmore, Owings and Merrill, 185

Sloan, Howard M., 201

Sloan, Samuel, 51

Small, George E., 76

Smart House, 209

Smith, A. O., Corporation, 158, 161

Smith, Lloyd R., 158

Smith, Robert, Jr., 128, 183

solar houses, 201–02, *202*

Spurzheim, Johann Kaspar, 41

Stanford University, 102

Stanorov and Morgan, 113

Stan-Steel House, 128, 183

Starr, Lewis E., 188

Sternfeld, Harry, 180

Stowe, Harriet Beecher, 30, 34, *37*

Strandlund, Carl, 183–98, *183*

Taliesin Fellowship, 117, 118

Taylor, Basil Gordon, 171, 173, 176, 181

Taylor, Frederick B., 143

Techbuilt House, 27, 204, *204*

Tennessee Valley Authority (TVA), 19, 20, *21*

Thermopane, 11, 83

Thomas and Son, 59

Thornton, William, 43

Time, 89, 112, 160, 198

Towards a New Architecture, 14, 107, 130

Transactions of the American Society of Mechanical Engineers, 57, *62*

A Treatise on Domestic Economy, 29, 30, 31, *31*, 33, 34

Tropical Home, 128

Truscon, 106

Tucker Motor Company, 187

Tuthill, William, 7

Union Screw Company, 56

U.S. Department of the Interior, 122

U.S. Forest Products Laboratory, 20, *20*

U.S. Steel, 16, 155, 161

Universal Atlas Cement Company, 180

University of Pittsburgh, 113

Usonian houses, 117–25; definition of, 120, 122

van der Rohe, Mies, 101, 167

Vaux, Calvert, 7

Veterans Administration, 22

Vicat, L. J., 57

Villa Savoie, 102, 104, *104*

Vitrolite, 11, 110

Wachsmann, Konrad, 26, 26

Wagner, Martin, *19*

Wallace, Henry A., 184

Wanamaker's Department Store, 141, 145, 148, 149, 153, 167

Wang, Dahong, *26*

Wank, Roland, 19

War Assets Administration, 187

Ward, William, 55–71

Ward's Castle, 55–71, 173

Warren, Waldo, 84

Wasserman, William S., 91

Webber, Elroy, 113

Weed, Robert Law, 128

Westchester Magazine, 146, 147

Western Female Institute, 30

Westinghouse, *15*, 16; House of Tomorrow, *39*

Wheeler, Todd, 167

Wherrett, Harry S., 158

Will, Philip, Jr., 167

Wolf, Herman, 90

Woman's Home Companion, 141, 148, 149

Wood, Richard, 113

Woodlawn Plantation, *121*, 122

Woodward and Lothrop, 10

World House, 210

World Housing, Inc., 208

Wright, Frank Lloyd, 8, 117–25, 137, 181, 202

Wright, Gwendolyn, 24–25

Wright, Henry, 23

Wyatt, Wilson, 184, 187, 188

Xanadu, 208, *208*

Young, Owen D., 145, 158

"Zipper House," 112

H. WARD JANDL is chief, Technical Preservation Services, for the National Park Service at the U.S. Department of the Interior. A graduate of Yale University, he has written and edited numerous publications, including *Houses by Mail: A Guide to Houses from Sears, Roebuck and Company* and *The Technology of Historic American Buildings*.

MICHAEL J. AUER holds a doctorate in American literature from the University of North Carolina at Chapel Hill. He is a preservation specialist with the National Park Service and is the author of *The Preservation of Historic Barns*.

JOHN A. BURNS, AIA, is deputy chief of the National Park Service's Historic American Buildings Survey/ Historic American Engineering Record. A graduate of Pennsylvania State University, he has lectured and written extensively on historic building and construction technologies and documentation as well as 19th- and early 20th-century architecture.